MOUNTAIN BIKING THE GREAT PLAINS STATES

Dennis Coello's America by
Mountain Bike Series

Iowa
Kansas
Nebraska
South Dakota
North Dakota

D1478427

Andy Knapp

Foreword, Introduction, and Afterword
by Dennis Coello, Series Editor

MENASHA
RIDGE
PRESS

FALCON™

Library of Congress Cataloging-in-Publication Data

Knapp, Andy, 1947-
   Mountain biking the Great Plains States : Iowa, Kansas, Nebraska,
South Dakota, North Dakota / Andy Knapp: foreword, introduction,and afterword
by Dennis Coello.—1st ed.
   p. cm. —(Dennis Coello's America by mountain bike series)
   ISBN 1-56044-327-8 (pbk.)
   1. All-terrain cycling—Great Plains—Guidebooks. 2. Great Plains—Guidebooks.
I. Title. II. Series: America by mountain bike series.
GV1045.5.G76K53 1996
796.6'4'0978—dc20   96-2662
                                                                 CIP

Photos by the author unless otherwise credited
Maps by Tim Krasnansky and Brian Taylor at RapiDesign
Cover photo by Dennis Coello

Menasha Ridge Press
3169 Cahaba Heights Road
Birmingham, Alabama 35243

Falcon Press
P.O. Box 1718
Helena, Montana 59624

 Text pages printed on recycled paper

CAUTION
   Outdoor recreation activities are by their very nature potentially hazardous. All par-
ticipants in such activities must assume the responsibility for their own actions and
safety. The information contained in this guidebook cannot replace sound judgement
and good decision-making skills, which help reduce risk exposure, nor does the scope of
this book allow for disclosure of all the potential hazards and risks involved in such
activities.
   Learn as much as possible about the outdoor recreation activities you participate in,
prepare for the unexpected, and be safe and cautious. The reward will be a safer and
more enjoyable experience.

Table of Contents

List of Maps

THE GREAT PLAINS *RIDE LOCATIONS*

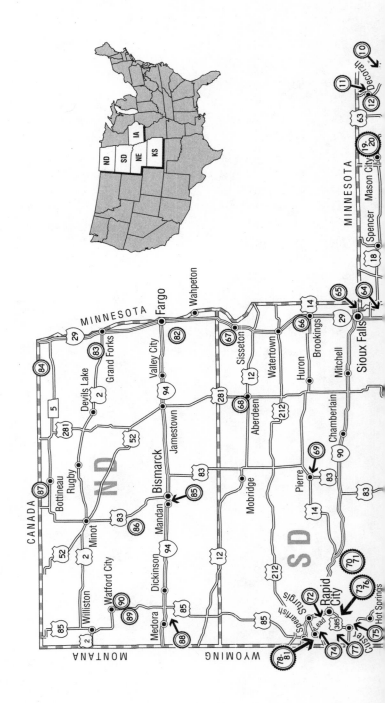

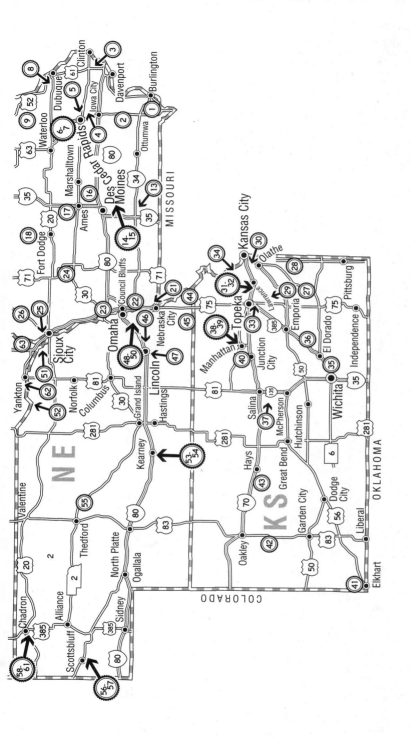

AMERICA BY MOUNTAIN BIKE *MAP LEGEND*

Ride trailhead

Primary bike trail | Direction of travel | Optional bike trail and trailhead | Other trail | Hiking Only trail

Interstate highways (with exit no.) | U.S. routes | State routes | Other paved roads | Unpaved, gravel or dirt roads (may be 4WD only)

U.S. Forest Service roads | Cities | Towns or settlements | Lake | Dam | Intermittent stream | Perennial stream

Lincoln | Elkhart | Norton

Approximate scale in miles | True North | Public Lands* | State Border

MILES

CIMARRON NATIONAL GRASSLANDS

✈ Airport

Fire tower or lookout

Observatory

♥ Archeological or historical site

Falls or rapids

Park office or ranger station

Boat ramp

Food

Picnic area

▲ Campground (CG)

Gate

Power line or pipeline

Cattle guard

House or cabin

Restrooms

Cemetery or gravesite

Lodging

Spring

Church

Mountain or butte

Stable, corral or ranch

Cliff, escarpment or outcropping

Mountain pass

Swimming Area

Drinking water

Mountain summit 3312 (elevation in feet)

Transmission towers

Mine or quarry

Tunnel or bridge

Remember, private property exists in and around our National Forests.

Acknowledgments

When I signed on to do the research for the Great Plains volume of *America by Mountain Bike,* it was difficult to imagine the many details that would go into the project. Now, many hundreds of bicycle miles and many thousands of automobile miles later, I can finally see these ideas and efforts in print and share them with others.

The enthusiastic cooperation of many bicyclists and park personnel in all of the five Great Plains states have made this effort possible. I would particularly like to thank the following persons for their ideas and for sharing their local knowledge: Gil Amis, Steve Bartels, John Bissell, Jr., Tom Bohm, Wayne Blaisdell, David Colburn, Bob Foster, John Gausman, Mike Hammer, Jim Hansen, Randy Harmon, Greg Harper, John L. Hobbs, Bob Honeywell, Dan Hughes, Kathy James, Craig Kirsch, Ken Lefler, Erik T. T. Lehner, Gary Lucas, Roger Lundquist, William Maasen, Doug Melby, Dick Messerly, Rick Knoke, Matthew Nowak, Pat Padden, Dan Streight, Rob Sturgis, Paul Talbert, and Rusty Wilder. There are many others whose names I don't know.

And thanks to my friend, Brad Johnson, who put up with my comings and goings in the Black Hills over the last two years. I also want to commend the patience of series editor Dennis Coello during the seemingly endless time that it took me to assemble all this information into the series format. I certainly want to thank my parents, who encouraged my early bike trips as a teenager around Lake Superior and to Alaska, where I came to appreciate the immense potential of the bicycle and the vastness of our continent and the delicacy of its natural state. And special thanks to my wife and daughter, who waited patiently through all the road trips and the late night hours at the computer.

Andy Knapp
Minneapolis

Foreword

Welcome to *America by Mountain Bike,* a 20-plus-book series designed to provide all-terrain bikers with the information they need to find and ride the very best trails everywhere in the mainland United States. Whether you're new to the sport and don't know where to pedal, or an experienced mountain biker who wants to learn the classic trails in another region, this series is for you. Drop a few bucks for the book, spend an hour with the detailed maps and route descriptions, and you're prepared for the finest in off-road cycling.

My role as editor of this series was simple: First, find a mountain biker who knows the area and loves to ride. Second, ask that person to spend a year researching the most popular and very best rides around. And third, have that rider describe each trail in terms of difficulty, scenery, condition, elevation change, and all other categories of information that are important to trail riders. "Pretend you've just completed a ride and met up with fellow mountain bikers at the trailhead," I told each author. "Imagine their questions, be clear in your answers."

As I said, the *editorial* process—that of sending out riders and reading the submitted chapters—is a snap. But the work involved in finding, riding, and writing about each trail is enormous. In some instances our authors' tasks are made easier by the information contributed by local bike shops or cycling clubs, or even by the writers of local "where-to" guides. Credit for these contributions is provided, when appropriate, in each chapter, and our sincere thanks goes to all who have helped.

But the overwhelming majority of trails are discovered and pedaled by our authors themselves, then compared with dozens of other routes to determine if they qualify as "classic"—that area's best in scenery and cycling fun. If you've ever had the experience of pioneering a route from outdated topographic maps, or entering a bike shop to request information from local riders who would much prefer to keep their favorite trails secret, or know how it is to double- and triple-check data to be positive your trail info is correct, then you have an idea of how each of our authors has labored to bring about these books. You and I, and all the mountain bikers of America, are the richer for their efforts.

You'll get more out of this book if you take a moment to read the Introduction explaining how to read the trail listings. The "Topographic Maps" section will help you understand how useful topos will be on a ride, and will also tell you where to get them. And though this is a "where-to," not a "how-to" guide, those of you who have not traveled the backcountry might find "Hitting the Trail" of particular value.

In addition to the material above, newcomers to mountain biking might want to spend a minute with the glossary, page 349, so that terms like *hard-pack, single-track,* and *water bars* won't throw you when you come across them in the text.

Finally, the tips in the Afterword on mountain biking etiquette and the land-use controversy might help us all enjoy the trails a little more.

All the best.

Dennis Coello
St. Louis

Preface

Mountain biking in the Great Plains? To many bicyclists this would seem to be an amusing contradiction in terms. Most people's experience with this region involves traveling across it, generally westbound or eastbound, to get somewhere else, noticing only how vast and flat and treeless it seems to be. For many decades in the nineteenth century, the history of the "Great American Desert" was the story of people enduring many hardships to get across this area. Still today, with our efficient network of interstate highways and jetways, most travelers scarcely take a second look.

Twenty-some years ago, I too joined this steady parade of traffic across the plains, making a series of trips to the western mountains and to Canada and Alaska. I was traveling by bicycle, however, and mile-by-mile, hill-by-hill, and headwind-after-headwind my various companions and I came to understand and even appreciate the vastness and yet the surprising diversity that the northern Great Plains has to offer. When I accepted the challenge to research this book, I felt confident that I'd find many interesting and unusual places to ride the "fat tires." In the two years that followed, I was never disappointed in what I discovered.

THE GREAT PLAINS REGION

Geographically, the Great Plains is a region of relatively treeless prairie stretching east to west from the forested Mississippi River valley to the foothills of the Rocky Mountains, and running south to north from Texas well into Saskatchewan and Alberta in Canada. The area has a semiarid, continental climate of hot summers and moderate to cold winters and ranges in elevation from several hundred feet in the southeast to 7,242 feet at Harney Peak in the Black Hills of South Dakota.

For the purposes of this book, five states are included in this territory: Iowa, Kansas, Nebraska, South Dakota, and North Dakota. Together, these states total 363,750 square miles, over one-tenth of the land area of the entire United States. With a combined population of approximately 8,170,000 people—only about 3 percent of the U.S. total—the Great Plains clearly has more open spaces than most parts of the country.

Iowa is actually on the eastern edge of the Great Plains proper, stretching from the Mississippi River lowlands, with its hardwood forests and commanding bluffs, to the beginnings of the open prairie region in the Missouri

A woodland trail leads to an overlook of the Platte River in Platte River State Park, Nebraska.

River drainage. Most of Iowa's important interior rivers drain southeastward to the Mississippi, and development of the state came from that direction.

The other four states, Kansas, Nebraska, and South and North Dakota, are stacked up neatly south to north, and they each have a somewhat similar geography consisting of eastern lowlands that were partially glaciated, rising gradually through rolling hill country to the semiarid high plains. Virtually all of these four were originally prairie lands, ranging from tall-grass prairie in the east to mixed- and short-grass prairie in the drier western areas. Nebraska and the two Dakotas contain areas in their far western sections of badlands—rugged, eroded, semidesert terrain that was seemingly useless in the eyes of the first European-American settlers. In addition, South Dakota contains a unique mountain uplift, the Black Hills, a precursor to the Rockies in Wyoming.

The Great Plains area is literally the heartland of the continent, for it contains both the geographical center of the United States, at Lebanon, Kansas, and of North America, at Rugby, North Dakota. The eastern portions of these four states, as well as virtually all of Iowa, make up some of the most productive agricultural lands in the world, and this region dominates U.S. production of crops such as corn, wheat, soybeans, and beef.

Common to all five states is the Missouri River, the original transportation corridor of the region. Exploration and development of the northern Great Plains as part of the United States closely followed this river and its tributaries. Evidence of human settlement in the region, however, goes back far earlier, perhaps as much as 15,000 years, to the waning millenniums of the Ice Age. Then, the prehistoric Missouri River, carrying vast quantities of meltwater, was the rough boundary between the glaciated and nonglaciated lands. When French-Canadian explorers from the north and Spaniards from the south reached this region in the 1600s and 1700s, there were well-developed Indian cultures in several areas based on primitive agriculture and protected town-sites. With the introduction of horses by the Spaniards, a more nomadic lifestyle revolving around buffalo hunting also appeared.

Political dealings in Europe resulted in the Louisiana Purchase by the newly founded United States in 1803. The purchase included virtually all of the lands in the five states being discussed here. Perhaps the defining historical event for much of this region was the Lewis and Clark Expedition, which was a result of President Jefferson's dreams of exploring the new western lands. This epic journey, lasting from 1804 to 1806, took the explorers by water-craft, by horseback, and by foot up the Missouri River to its headwaters in present-day Montana, across the northern Rockies, and down the Columbia River system to the Pacific.

Upon their return to St. Louis in 1806, Lewis and Clark brought back care-fully prepared maps and documents telling of the vast wilderness that made up the lands of the Louisiana Purchase. Thus, the process of the exploration and settlement of the American West was unleashed. The historical footnotes left by the Lewis and Clark Expedition are found all along the Missouri River valley. As you travel this region, these footnotes will appear in the many parks, museums, and historical markers along the route, which is designated a National Historic Trail.

Other explorations quickly followed that of Lewis and Clark, and soon there were many trails established across the plains for commerce and emi-gration to the west. The Platte River valley became the wagon train route of the Oregon Trail, the Mormon Trail, and later, the Pony Express route. In what is now Kansas, the Santa Fe Trail enabled development of trade with the Mexicans in the Southwest; the Smokey Hills Trail led to the Colorado gold rush; and the Chisholm Trail brought cattle north from Texas. In present-day North Dakota the Red River of the North acted as a trade route between Minnesota territory on the Mississippi and British Canada at Winnipeg.

Eventually, the plains themselves were opened up for settlement, and a period of warfare with the resident Native Americans followed. Unrestricted hunting of the vast herds of buffalo cut off the main livelihood of the Indians, reducing the countless millions of animals to a few hundred by the turn of the century. After the Civil War the advancing railroad system accelerated settlement of the plains region beyond the major river valleys, brought an end to the nomadic Indian cultures in the high plains, and ushered in the new agricultural states. The late 1800s and early 1900s were generally boom years on the prairie, bringing not only more population growth, but also resource and wildlife depletion.

Conservation efforts were gradually made to protect the plains environment. Local, state, and a few national parks were established to protect unique resources. Flood-control projects and wildlife refuges were set up to save water resources and migratory waterfowl. The Missouri River was tamed with a series of six dams built by the U.S. Army Corps of Engineers, creating huge lakes with thousands of miles of shoreline, and many other smaller reservoirs were created throughout all five states. The Black Hills, one of the earliest national forests, has been managed since 1905. After the dust bowl years of the Great Depression, many marginal croplands of the western plains were reclaimed and later consolidated into national grasslands, part of the national forest system. These public lands eventually were developed into many of the recreational facilities that are available in the plains states today.

MOUNTAIN BIKING IN THE GREAT PLAINS

After World War II, the improvements in the national highway system and the rising standard of living for most Americans resulted in a rapid growth of tourism and recreational opportunities. Previously remote areas, such as public lands in the plains states, became accessible, and an increasingly urban population began to enjoy the outdoors for its quiet, rejuvenating qualities. The environmental awareness movement combined with the interest in physical fitness fired up renewed interest in traditional outdoor activities, such as hiking, canoeing, bicycling, horseback riding, and cross-country skiing. Services and trails were gradually added to most public lands to cater to these groups.

With improvements in bicycle technology came the "mountain" or trail bicycle, and quickly, a new user group—you and I—appeared on the outdoor scene in the 1980s, looking for trails and suitable lands for riding. And of course, land managers found themselves with yet another user group asking for land access.

As in many other parts of the country, the sport of mountain biking in the Great Plains is growing steadily, and the opportunities for places to ride is changing regularly. Because of the relative lack of large urban areas and the falsely perceived monotony of the plains landscape, the sport has not developed as quickly as it has in the more popular eastern and western areas;

but now, from Dubuque to Dodge City and Grand Forks to Grand Island, mountain biking in the prairie lands is here to stay!

ORGANIZATION AND METHODOLOGY OF THIS BOOK

The search to find mountain bike riding areas in this vast part of the United States led me to try a number of "research" methods, including studying many maps, reviewing piles of tourist information, driving around to countless parks, preserves, and river bottoms, mailing questionnaires, and visiting with many park personnel and bike shop employees. It is these latter two groups who are the real local experts; they enabled me to focus on the places worth investigating further.

I found the folks working at the many specialty bicycle shops in the many cities and towns I visited were the best source of information on riding areas. Their willingness to take the time to share ideas with me is what made this book possible. The various sections of this guide contain listings of many of these bike shops where you can go for the latest trail information and last-minute parts and repairs. Many of these shops sponsor or know of local clubs that sponsor rides and other activities.

Park personnel in charge of trail areas were also helpful in my search for information. In general, park and agency managers are supportive of the multiple-use concept and are interested in learning about and providing biking access—when regulations, time, and tight budgets allow. Keep in mind that these people are often trying to balance competing demands for trail use, frequently by groups such as equestrians, who are firmly entrenched in some of these areas. Occasionally, you will still run into personnel at more remote locations who do not have a clear concept of just what a mountain bike is and who confuse them with motorized trail bikes or traditional skinny-tire bicycles.

In future years, more opportunities for mountain bikers will most certainly become available, but it will take some work by all trail users. Be courteous toward other trail users and be aware of the "rules of the road" discussed in Dennis Coello's Introduction. Be especially careful to obey any special rules unique to individual parks, since mountain biking may only be allowed in these places on a trial basis. If possible, let park management know that you appreciate the facilities they have established.

There are undoubtedly some good riding areas that I have overlooked or that will become available later in each of these states, and the local contacts in bike shops, clubs, and parks can help you find them.

Throughout the diverse plains region, there is a wide range of trails available for mountain biking, matching many different riding styles. They generally fit into the following categories:

Old railroad-corridor trails: These are mostly flat or gently graded routes built between rural towns on abandoned railroad rights-of-way. While these trails are not particularly exciting for serious mountain biking enthusiasts, they are great for beginners, family groups, and those interested in wildlife, photography, or history. These trails can also be an alternative to more delicate trails in other parks when they are too wet to ride, or when you just want to let 'er roll and cruise with the wind in your face. Keep in mind that these are all out-and-back trails; you will have to turn around somewhere and ride the same distance back to where you started. Iowa is one of the leading states in these "rails-to-trails" conversions, and many of these trails are available there.

Small regional or local parks with networks of single-track trails: Many of the larger cities, or towns with college populations, have park areas where local biking enthusiasts ride on official or unofficial trail systems. Some of these trails can be quite technical in nature and are often located in river bottom areas with sandy or muddy soil and scattered debris. Sometimes these parks also have less technical paths on levees or old roads. Since some of these trails are not officially sanctioned and are not listed in this guide, check locally on the status of biking there; mountain bikers have a responsibility to follow regulations and convey a positive image of their sport.

State parks and larger regional parks with more extensive single-track systems: All five of the plains states have at least a few state parks where the trail systems are open to mountain bikes, sometimes on a trial basis. The trails in these parks are generally existing hiking, cross-country ski, or horseback trail systems and may not be perfect for biking, but some of them provide the best all-around trail biking in the eastern half of the region. Most of these parks are heavily forested and have well-developed camping and picnic facilities on site. Some of the U.S. Army Corps of Engineers reservoir parks and the Black Hills National Forest recreation areas fit into this category. In general, park management people in these five states are just recently becoming aware of the growing interest in mountain biking and are looking at ways to accommodate this new phenomenon. Restricted budgets and competing user groups slow down this process. The extensive damage to many park areas in all five states during the 1993 floods has further limited funds but has created new opportunities for the time when trails are redesigned and rebuilt.

Federal land with extensive double-track or forest road networks: The national forests and the national grasslands of this region all have networks of four-wheel-drive access roads that can provide hundreds of miles of riding possibilities, some of which can be quite hilly and challenging. Good maps and advance preparation are essential for biking into the more remote parts of these areas. These federal lands generally allow wilderness camping, so there is the option of multi-day bike tours for those who are interested in serious exploration.

Federal lands with off-road-vehicle recreation areas: Selected federal areas, mostly the U.S. Corps of Engineers reservoir lands, have been set aside for motorized off-road use. These sites are usually crisscrossed with well-worn tracks that often climb and descend steep slopes. Caution must be used to avoid fast-moving vehicles, but these hard-surface areas can be alternatives to other parks where trail conditions are wet.

Difficulty ratings

Defining the difficulty level of these bike rides is somewhat subjective, since individual riding abilities and level of conditioning will make a difference between any two bikers, but here are some definitions as I have used them in the ride descriptions:

Easy: Flat, relatively smooth trails requiring only a steady, pleasant physical effort. Most "rails-to-trails" routes, dirt roads, and some four-wheel-drive tracks fit into this category. An eight- to fifteen-miles-per-hour pace should be possible for most riders on easy trails.

Moderate: Trails and roads with hills, sharp corners, uneven surfaces, and/or occasional obstructions requiring some exertion, maneuvering, and close attention much of the time. Five to ten miles per hour would be a likely pace on moderate trails.

Difficult: Trails requiring frequent technical skills, sustained aerobic effort, advance planning, delicate balance, and/or frequent dismounting to avoid obstacles. A pace of two to five miles per hour may be the best to hope for on this terrain.

These are only general guidelines, and most trails will include some or all of these levels.

For purposes of organization I have divided each of the five states into three sections: eastern, central, and western. These sections follow rough geographical areas when possible, and within each section, the rides are numbered from southeast to northwest. Each section also includes a general description of the area, contacts for further information, a bibliography, and a discussion of additional mountain biking possibilities in the area.

WEATHER, SEASONS, AND REGIONAL HAZARDS

Located far from the moderating effects of the oceans, the Great Plains region has a continental climate, one with hot summers and cold winters. There can be considerable variation in weather within the region at any given time, however, from both east to west and from north to south. The center of North America is a battleground between warm and cold air masses, often producing unpredictable weather and spectacular storms.

Large air masses can come from three general directions to influence the weather in the area. Cool or cold, dry air from the north and Canada generally produces fair weather and colder than average temperatures. Relatively moderate Pacific air masses can make it over the Rockies, bringing warmer air and some moisture, if the mountains haven't siphoned it all away. Warm, humid air from the Gulf of Mexico area will bring warmer than average weather, high humidity, and a potential for serious amounts of precipitation.

In the summer, temperatures can frequently reach the 80s and 90s in much of the five-state area, with 70s and 80s more common toward the northern end. Days in the 100s are possible anywhere on the plains. The boundaries between cool air masses and warmer, moist ones can produce heavy rains, thunderstorms, high winds, and tornadoes, so it is important to pay attention to changing weather patterns while you're involved in outdoor activities. Humidity during the summer months generally decreases in the region as you travel from east to west, and the semiarid high plains of western Nebraska and the Dakotas can offer a pleasant respite for "easterners" during the sticky months of July and August.

Autumn can also be a very pleasant time throughout the region as the humidity and the storms retreat to the south. Cool sunshine and changing colors along the woodland trails can be a very invigorating and inspiring experience for any bicyclist. Longer periods of damp and rainy weather can set in, however, making trail conditions too wet and slow to dry. Autumn riding conditions, with day temperatures in the 50s and nights just above freezing, can last into late October in North Dakota and well into December in southern Kansas.

Winter in the Great Plains will usually bring an end to the trail-riding season for all but the real diehards. In late September, the cold Canadian air masses and their northwest winds will begin to predominate in the Dakotas, eastern Nebraska, and Iowa, sometimes clashing with warmer air and Gulf moisture along fronts moving southwest to northeast, which can produce lots of snow. In the open plains, the incessant winds will blow most of the snow cover into protected, wooded areas, which is where most of the trails tend to be, so biking can become problematic. Periods of warm weather can produce cycles of freezing and thawing that make exposed trail surfaces, even the well-drained railroad-grade trails, too soft for bicycle tires. In southern areas, particularly Kansas, moderate winters may still allow for some nice off-season riding. Be sure to check locally for current conditions and respect the delicacy of certain trail surfaces.

The spring season reawakens the bicycling spirit, and once again the majority of us will be eager to hit the back roads and trails. But in the Midwest, the lingering winter will often throw late-season snow and ice storms our way, adding to the frustration of cabin fever. The freeze-thaw cycle and the dwindling snow cover in shaded portions of trails will keep many trails difficult to use for some weeks after nice weather has set in elsewhere. By midspring, when days are getting up into the 60s, most of the trail systems should be dry enough to use. This can mean mid- to late April in Kansas and Nebraska, and early to mid-May in Iowa and the Dakotas. Some trail systems in river valleys may be prone to flooding during the spring thaw period, pushing back the time when the trails will dry out. Seasonal and local variations can make a large difference, so again, be sure to check first before making an early-season trip.

Your most likely summertime concern will be protecting yourself from the sun, heat, and humidity. Use sunscreen when you're riding for long periods of time in the sun, particularly early in the season. Ultraviolet radiation can easily penetrate hazy and lightly cloudy skies. The combination of high temperatures and high humidity can make staying cool difficult when you are riding hard. It may be best in those conditions to plan rides for early morning or evening times, or plan a less ambitious route. Be sure to carry plenty of water and plan ahead for where you can get more. Serious riders in remote country may want to consider carrying one of the various lightweight water purifiers available for treating surface water supplies.

During the thunderstorm season, you should keep an eye on the southwestern horizon—the most likely direction for approaching bad weather. Allow plenty of time to work your way to shelter if the sky begins to look ominous. At the sound of thunder and/or the sight of lightning, stay away from elevated areas and away from isolated tall trees or structures. Many of the region's state parks have warning sirens or storm shelters. Be familiar with precautions for tornado warnings, and if you are using an area where there are stream beds or dry drainages, be aware of the possibility of flash flooding. The disastrous summer of 1993, when rain flooded rivers, towns, and parklands all across the plains states, is an extreme example of what unpredictable summer weather can bring.

Most likely, these summer storms will just drop some random showers as they pass by, possibly ushering in some cooler breezes as it clears. Be prepared with some good, lightweight raingear for that eventuality.

NON-WEATHER-RELATED HAZARDS

There are varieties of flora and fauna that can cause you trouble in many areas, but simple precautions can usually be made to avoid problems. Poison ivy is probably the most serious plant hazard; it is found in many hardwood forest areas throughout the eastern plains. If you know what it looks like and if you stay on the trails, it shouldn't present a problem. Most other plant problems involve thorns. Various cactus species, including the prickly pear, can be found in the western grasslands and badlands. Keep a close look ahead when riding overland in those areas. In the eastern woodlands, there is quite a variety of thistles and shrubs with sharp thorns and stickers that can cause grief to bare arms and legs if you ride headlong into the brush. As for these hazards affecting your bicycle, in two seasons of riding the plains region, the only flat tire I had to fix on the trail was from a large thorn picked up on the perimeter of an Iowa cornfield.

You are by far most likely to be inconvenienced by our insect friends. Anywhere there is standing water in the warm summer months, mosquitoes will almost certainly be present in the calm morning or evening hours. You can usually outride them, but if you are camping or exploring a river bottom area, a good insect repellent may be worth its weight in sanity. Biting flies can be a nuisance in some areas, especially around horse trails, and unfortunately they are often more persistent than mosquitoes, and repellents are less effective against them. Ticks are a common occurrence in wooded and brushy areas during the late spring and early summer. Certain types of wasps can get aggressive in late summer around picnic and campgrounds, where there is food. And finally, there are multitudes of harmless bugs that like to swarm on warm, still evenings above trails and other openings. If you like to ride at those times—and it's a great time to see wildlife—you may want to wear some sort of clear-lens eyewear to keep those swarms out of your eyes. And don't ride with your mouth open!

Larger critters pose a far smaller chance of giving you trouble, but it pays to watch out for several of them. Although the extreme fear many people have toward snakes is largely unfounded, the plains region is good habitat for several varieties of rattlesnakes. They are beneficial reptiles occupying an important niche in the food chain and help to control rodent populations. From the eastern river lowlands to the arid bluffs of the badlands, it is a good idea to watch where you are placing your feet and hands. Chances are, however, you will go for years and years without ever seeing a rattlesnake. The Great Plains was once the habitat for grizzly bears, wolves, elk, and buffalo (bison). Now, only the buffalo in a few areas pose a potential hazard. Once almost extinct, small buffalo herds have been re-established in several park areas. They are fast, ornery, and unpredictable. Bicyclists and anyone on foot should give them plenty of room should they be encountered. Range cattle, too, should be given as much leeway as possible. Although far less likely than buffalo to cause trouble, they are big and not entirely tame.

A final hazard for mountain bikers comes from other humans. Hunting on the open plains and in the woodlands is a time-honored tradition, and hunting seasons can span the times of some of the best bike riding in both the spring and autumn. Shotgun hunting for wild turkeys, pheasants, grouse, and waterfowl is popular in most areas. Of greater concern would be the rifle seasons for deer and antelope. Check with state natural resource or fish and game departments in advance for season dates in the various states, and if you plan to ride anyway, wear bright colors.

MAPS AND NAVIGATION

Many of the rides in this guidebook are found in relatively small parks not far from roads and towns. For these areas, the maps in this book or those available from park agencies should suffice for purposes of navigation. Basic skills of direction, judging distance and pace, and keeping track of your general location within an area are always valuable, of course. If you are planning longer rides in some of the more extensive lands of the western plains, maps with additional detail will be necessary. See the discussion of topographical maps in Dennis Coello's introduction. The topographical maps, and other alternative maps based on topographical information, for those particular rides are listed in the discussions of those rides.

BIKING ETIQUETTE

The introduction following this section has a complete discussion of mountain biking ethics that all riders should practice. Several points pertaining to mountain biking in the Great Plains are discussed below.

Many of the mountain biking opportunities in the agricultural plains states are found in state and county parks where the trails were originally designed for hikers and/or horseback riders. Always yield to these user groups and present a positive image of our sport for others who will follow. Respect the rules when trails are off-limits or closed for maintenance. Most park managers seem to have a positive attitude toward trail bicycling and toward the multi-use concept in general, but it is up to us in the mountain biking community to continue to earn the right to use the trails, and to show there is a growing demand for more trails.

To further the responsible image of mountain biking, it is important to be aware of the needs of additional user groups in that locale; for example, don't muddy up trout streams, obliterate cross-country ski tracks, or cause a commotion for wildlife observers. Fence gates in grazing lands should be left as you found them, or if there is an apparent problem, it should be reported to those in charge.

In this region, with its unpredictable weather and sometimes wet summers, there will be times when the trails are just too wet or fragile to allow responsible riding. It is very important to avoid contributing to trail erosion by riding on wet, muddy trail surfaces. Call ahead to avoid disappointment, and if you are traveling a long way to bike in a certain area, have in mind some alternate places to ride or alternate things to do. Some types of trails, such as railroad-grade trails or off-road-vehicle riding areas may be "hardened" to heavy use and may be rideable in poor weather.

Finally, if you have any question about the land status or the accepted rules in a particular location, remember that local bike shops and local park personnel will be able to get you pointed in the right direction.

For further information:

International Mountain Biking Association
P.O. Box 412043
Los Angeles, CA 90041
(818) 792-8830, (818) 796-2299 fax

IMBA promotes mountain biking through "environmentally and socially responsible use of the land," providing assistance to land managers, clubs, and the cycling industry.

National Off-Road Bicycle Association
1750 East Boulder Street
Colorado Springs, CO 80909
(719) 578-4717

NORBA serves as the primary governing organization for events and races and is also involved with teaching responsible mountain biking habits.

Bibliography:
The Academic American Encyclopedia, on-line edition, Grolier Electronic Publishing, Danbury, CT, 1993.

Andy Knapp

Introduction

Information on each trail in this book begins with a general description that includes length, configuration, scenery, highlights, trail conditions, and difficulty. Additional description is contained in eleven individual categories. The following will help you understand all of the information provided.

Trail name: Trail names are as designated on United States Geological Survey (USGS) or Forest Service or other maps, and/or by local custom.

Note: Information contained in the next six headings is included in the introductory paragraphs to each ride.

Length: The overall length of a trail is described in miles, unless stated otherwise.

Configuration: This is a description of the shape of each trail—whether the trail is a loop, out-and-back (that is, along the same route), figure eight, trapezoid, isosceles triangle, or if it connects with another trail described in the book.

Difficulty: This provides at a glance a description of the degree of physical exertion required to complete the ride, and the technical skill required to pedal it. Authors were asked to keep in mind the fact that all riders are not equal, and thus to gauge the trail in terms of how the middle-of-the-road rider—someone between the newcomer and Ned Overend—could handle the route. Comments about the trail's length, condition, and elevation change will also assist you in determining the difficulty of any trail relative to your own abilities.

Condition: Trails are described in terms of being paved, unpaved, sandy, hardpacked, washboarded, two- or four-wheel-drive, single-track or double-track. All terms that might be unfamiliar to the first-time mountain biker are defined in the Glossary.

Scenery: Here you will find a general description of the natural surroundings during the seasons most riders pedal the trail, and a suggestion of what is to be found at special times (like great fall foliage or cactus in bloom).

Highlights: Towns, major water crossings, historical sites, etc., are listed.

General location: This category describes where the trail is located in reference to a nearby town or other landmark.

Elevation change: Unless stated otherwise, the figure provided is the total gain and loss of elevation along the trail. In regions where the elevation variation is not extreme, the route is simply described as flat, rolling, or possessing short steep climbs or descents.

Season: This is the best time of year to pedal the route, taking into account trail condition (for example, when it will not be muddy), riding comfort (when the weather is too hot, cold, or wet), and local hunting seasons.

Note: Because the exact opening and closing dates of deer, elk, moose, and antelope seasons often change from year to year, riders should check with the local Fish and Game department, or call a sporting goods store (or any place that sells hunting licenses) in a nearby town before heading out. Wear bright clothes in fall, and don't wear suede jackets while in the saddle. Hunter's-orange tape on the helmet is also a good idea.

Services: This category is of primary importance in guides for paved-road tourers, but is far less crucial to most mountian bike trail descriptions because there are usually no services whatsoever to be found. Authors have noted when water is available on desert or long mountain routes, and have listed the availability of food, lodging, campgrounds, and bike shops. If all these services are present, you will find only the words "All services available in . . ."

Hazards: Special hazards like steep cliffs, great amounts of deadfall, or barbed-wire fences very close to the trail are noted here.

Rescue index: Determining how far one is from help on any particular trail can be difficult due to the backcountry nature of most mountain bike rides. Authors therefore state the proximity of homes or Forest Service outposts, nearby roads where one might hitch a ride, or the likelihood of other bikers being encountered on the trail. Phone numbers of local sheriff departments or hospitals have not been provided because phones are almost never available. If you are able to reach a phone, the local operator will connect you with emergency services.

Land status: This category provides information regarding whether the trail crosses land operated by the Forest Service, Bureau of Land Management, a city, state, or national park, whether it crosses private land whose owner (at the time the author did the research) has allowed mountain bikers right of passage, and so on.

Note: Authors have been extremely careful to offer only those routes that are open to bikers and are legal to ride. However, because land ownership changes over time, and because the land-use controversy created by mountain bikes still has not completely subsided, it is the duty of each cyclist to look for and to heed signs warning against trail use. Don't expect this book to get you off the hook when you're facing some small-town judge for pedaling past a "Biking Prohibited" sign erected the day before. Look for these signs, read them, and heed the advice. And remember there's always another trail.

Maps: The maps in this book have been produced with great care, and, in conjunction with the trail-following suggestions, will help you stay on course.

But as every experienced mountain biker knows, things can get tricky in the backcountry. It is therefore strongly suggested that you avail yourself of the detailed information found in the 7.5 minute series USGS (United States Geological Survey) topographic maps. In some cases, authors have found that specific Forest Service or other maps may be more useful than the USGS quads, and tell how to obtain them.

Finding the trail: Detailed information on how to reach the trailhead, and where to park your car is provided here.

Sources of additional information: Here you will find the address and/or phone number of a bike shop, governmental agency, or other source from which trail information can be obtained.

Notes on the trail: This is where you are guided carefully through any portions of the trail that are particularly difficult to follow. The author also may add information about the route that does not fit easily in the other categories. This category will not be present for those rides where the route is easy to follow.

ABBREVIATIONS

The following road-designation abbreviations are used in the *America by Mountain Bike* series:

CR	County Road
FR	Farm Route
FS	Forest Service road
I-	Interstate
IR	Indian Route
US	United States highway

State highways are designated with the appropriate two-letter state abbreviation, followed by the road number. *Example:* IA 14 = Iowa State Highway 14.

Postal Service two-letter state codes:

AL	Alabama	HI	Hawaii
AK	Alaska	ID	Idaho
AZ	Arizona	IL	Illinois
AR	Arkansas	IN	Indiana
CA	California	IA	Iowa
CO	Colorado	KS	Kansas
CT	Connecticut	KY	Kentucky
DE	Delaware	LA	Louisiana
DC	District of Columbia	ME	Maine
FL	Florida	MD	Maryland
GA	Georgia	MA	Massachusetts

MI	Michigan	OR	Oregon
MN	Minnesota	PA	Pennsylvania
MS	Mississippi	RI	Rhode Island
MO	Missouri	SC	South Carolina
MT	Montana	SD	South Dakota
NE	Nebraska	TN	Tennessee
NV	Nevada	TX	Texas
NH	New Hampshire	UT	Utah
NJ	New Jersey	VT	Vermont
NM	New Mexico	VA	Virginia
NY	New York	WA	Washington
NC	North Carolina	WV	West Virginia
ND	North Dakota	WI	Wisconsin
OH	Ohio	WY	Wyoming
OK	Oklahoma		

TOPOGRAPHIC MAPS

The maps in this book, when used in conjunction with the route directions present in each chapter, will in most instances be sufficient to get you to the trail and keep you on it. However, you will find superior detail and valuable information in the 7.5 minute series United States Geological Survey (USGS) topographic maps. Recognizing how indispensable these are to bikers and hikers alike, many bike shops and sporting goods stores now carry topos of the local area.

But if you're brand new to mountain biking you might be wondering, "What's a topographic map?" In short, these differ from standard "flat" maps in that they indicate not only linear distance, but elevation as well. One glance at a "topo" will show you the difference, for "contour lines" are spread across the map like dozens of intricate spider webs. Each contour line represents a particular elevation, and at the base of each topo a particular "contour interval" designation is given. Yes, it sounds confusing if you're new to the lingo, but it truly is a simple and wonderfully helpful system. Keep reading.

Let's assume that the 7.5 minute series topo before us says "Contour Interval 40 feet," that the short trail we'll be pedaling is two inches in length on the map, and that it crosses five contour lines from its beginning to end. What do we know? Well, because the linear scale of this series is 2,000 feet to the inch (roughly 2 3/4 inches representing 1 mile), we know our trail is approximately 4/5 of a mile long (2 inches × 2,000 feet). But we also know we'll be climbing or descending 200 vertical feet (5 contour lines × 40 feet each) over that distance. And the elevation designations written on occasional contour lines will tell us if we're heading up or down.

The authors of this series warn their readers of upcoming terrain, but only a detailed topo gives you the information you need to pinpoint your position exactly on a map, steer yourself toward optional trails and roads nearby, plus let you know at a glance if you'll be pedaling hard to take them. It's a lot of information for a very low cost. In fact, the only drawback with topos is their size—several feet square. I've tried rolling them into tubes, folding them carefully, even cutting them into blocks and photocopying the pieces. Any of these systems is a pain, but no matter how you pack the maps you'll be happy they're along. And you'll be even happier if you pack a compass as well.

In addition to local bike shops and sporting goods stores, you'll find topos at major universities and some public libraries, where you might try photocopying the ones you need to avoid the cost of buying them. But if you want your own and can't find them locally, write to:

USGS Map Sales
Box 25286
Denver, CO 80225

Ask for an index while you're at it, plus a price list and a copy of the booklet *Topographic Maps*. In minutes you'll be reading them like a pro.

A second excellent series of maps available to mountain bikers is that put out by the United States Forest Service. If your trail runs through an area designated as a national forest, look in the phone book (white pages) under the United States Government listings, find the Department of Agriculture heading, and then run your finger down that section until you find the Forest Service. Give them a call and they'll provide the address of the regional Forest Service office, from which you can obtain the appropriate map.

TRAIL ETIQUETTE

Pick up almost any mountain bike magazine these days and you'll find articles and letters to the editor about trail conflict. For example, you'll find hikers' tales of being blindsided by speeding mountain bikers, complaints from mountain bikers about being blamed for trail damage that was really caused by horse or cattle traffic, and cries from bikers about those "kamikaze" riders who through their antics threaten to close even more trails to all of us.

The authors of this series have been very careful to guide you to only those trails that are open to mountain biking (or at least were open at the time of their research), and without exception have warned of the damage done to our sport through injudicious riding. My personal views on this matter appear in the Afterword, but all of us can benefit from glancing over the following International Mountain Bicycling Association (IMBA) Rules of the Trail before saddling up.

1. *Ride on open trails only.* Respect trail and road closures (ask if not sure), avoid possible trespass on private land, obtain permits and authorization as may be required. Federal and State wilderness areas are closed to cycling.

2. *Leave no trace.* Be sensitive to the dirt beneath you. Even on open trails, you should not ride under conditions where you will leave evidence of your passing, such as on certain soils shortly after rain. Observe the different types of soils and trail construction; practice low-impact cycling. This also means staying on the trail and not creating any new ones. Be sure to pack out at least as much as you pack in.

3. *Control your bicycle!* Inattention for even a second can cause disaster. Excessive speed can maim and threaten people; there is no excuse for it!

4. *Always yield the trail.* Make known your approach well in advance. A friendly greeting (or a bell) is considerate and works well; startling someone may cause loss of trail access. Show your respect when passing others by slowing to a walk or even stopping. Anticipate that other trail users may be around corners or in blind spots.

5. *Never spook animals.* All animals are startled by an unannounced approach, a sudden movement, or a loud noise. This can be dangerous for you, for others, and for the animals. Give animals extra room and time to adjust to you. In passing, use special care and follow the directions of horseback riders (ask if uncertain). Running cattle and disturbing wild animals is a serious offense. Leave gates as you found them, or as marked.

6. *Plan ahead.* Know your equipment, your ability, and the area in which you are riding—and prepare accordingly. Be self-sufficient at all times. Wear a helmet, keep your machine in good condition, and carry necessary supplies for changes in weather or other conditions. A well-executed trip is a satisfaction to you and not a burden or offense to others.

For more information, contact IMBA, P.O. Box 412043, Los Angeles, CA 90041, (818) 792-8830.

HITTING THE TRAIL

Once again, because this is a "where-to," not a "how-to" guide, the following will be brief. If you're a veteran trail rider these suggestions might serve to remind you of something you've forgotten to pack. If you're a newcomer, they might convince you to think twice before hitting the backcountry unprepared.

Water: I've heard the questions dozens of times. "How much is enough? One bottle? Two? Three?! But think of all that extra weight!" Well, one simple physiological fact should convince you to err on the side of excess when it comes to deciding how much water to pack: a human working hard in 90-degree temperature needs approximately ten quarts of fluids every day. Ten quarts. That's two and a half gallons—12 large water bottles, or 16 small ones. And, with water weighing in at approximately 8 pounds per gallon, a one-day supply comes to a whopping 20 pounds.

In other words, pack along two or three bottles even for short rides. And make sure you can purify the water found along the trail on longer routes. When writing of those routes where this could be of critical importance, each author has provided information on where water can be found near the trail—if it can be found at all. But drink it untreated and you run the risk of disease. (See *Giardia* in the Glossary.)

One sure way to kill both the bacteria and viruses in water is to bring it to a "furious boil." Right. That's just how you want to spend your time on a bike ride. Besides, who wants to carry a stove, or denude the countryside stoking bonfires to boil water?

Luckily, there is a better way. Many riders pack along the effective, inexpensive, and only slightly distasteful tetraglycine hydroperiodide tablets (sold under the names Potable Aqua, Globaline, and Coughlan's, among others). Some invest in portable, lightweight purifiers that filter out the crud. Yes, purifying water with tablets or filters is a bother. But catch a case of Giardia sometime and you'll understand why it's worth the trouble.

Tools: Ever since my first cross-country tour in 1965 I've been kidded about the number of tools I pack on the trail. And so I will exit entirely from this discussion by providing a list compiled by two mechanic (and mountain biker) friends of mine. After all, since they make their livings fixing bikes, and get their kicks by riding them, who could be a better source?

These two suggest the following as an absolute minimum:

tire levers
spare tube and patch kit
air pump

allen wrenches (3, 4, 5, and 6 mm)
six-inch crescent (adjustable-end) wrench
small flat-blade screwdriver
chain rivet tool
spoke wrench

But, while they're on the trail, their personal tool pouches contain these additional items:

channel locks (small)
air gauge
tire valve cap (the metal kind, with a valve-stem remover)
baling wire (ten or so inches, for temporary repairs)
duct tape (small roll for temporary repairs or tire boot)
boot material (small piece of old tire or a large tube patch)
spare chain link
rear derailleur pulley
spare nuts and bolts
paper towel and tube of waterless hand cleaner

First-Aid Kit: My personal kit contains the following, sealed inside double Ziploc bags:

sunscreen
aspirin
butterfly-closure bandages
Band-Aids
gauze compress pads (a half-dozen 4'' × 4'')
gauze (one roll)
ace bandages or Spenco joint wraps
Benadryl (an antihistamine, in case of allergic reactions)
water purification tablets
Moleskin/Spenco "Second Skin"
hydrogen peroxide, iodine, or Mercurochrome (some kind of antiseptic)
snakebite kit

Final Considerations: The authors of this series have done a good job in suggesting that specific items be packed for certain trails—raingear in particular seasons, a hat and gloves for mountain passes, or shades for desert jaunts. Heed their warnings, and think ahead. Good luck.

Dennis Coello

IOWA

With over 2,777,000 residents, Iowa is the smallest and also the most populated of the five states included in this guidebook. Its 56,276 square miles stretch from the Mississippi River on the east to the Missouri River on the west. Iowa's geography is actually a transition from the heavily forested Mississippi River valley to the eastern edges of the open prairie lands of the vast Missouri River valley.

Much of the eastern quarter of the state consists of hardwood forests of hickory, elm, and oak with farmlands scattered amongst the hills and river valleys carved by the tributaries of the Mississippi. The central flatlands of Iowa, part of the former prairie transition area, are now almost entirely devoted to agriculture. In the western region bordering the Missouri River, the terrain gets more hilly; it is an area where loess—wind-blown silt—was deposited in extensive dunelike hills at the end of the last period of glaciation.

Human settlements appeared in what is now Iowa soon after the Ice Age ended, at least 10,000 years ago. The early Indians practiced primitive agriculture and established permanent villages along the rich river valleys. Burial mounds from some of these cultures are still visible on Mississippi River bluffs and other locations around the state. French explorers, including Jacques Marquette, reached the area in the 1670s. The Louisiana Purchase of 1803 added the territory to the United States, and by 1833, white settlers began to move in as the various Indian tribes were forced westward. Iowa became a state in 1846, with the first capital at Iowa City.

Towns grew up along most of the major rivers, and after the Civil War, competition for railroad access became common. With transportation systems in place and water power available on the rivers, agriculture developed into a major commercial activity, eventually centering on corn production. With the use of much of the corn as animal feed, the meat-processing industry also became one of the major industries. Manufacturing of heavy farm equipment brought Iowa into the industrialized economy of the twentieth-century Midwest. After a period of decline in the farming industry and the related manufacturing base, many high-technology industries are appearing in Iowa towns and cities, which has partially revitalized the state economy.

Iowa has a continental climate with cold winters and warm, humid summers. Rainfall, which supports the intensive agriculture, can vary greatly from drought conditions, to winter blizzards, to severe flooding, as in the 1993 disaster when most of Iowa's river valleys were inundated by torrential rains.

Mountain Biking in Iowa

Iowa has a higher percentage of its land under cultivation than any other state, and because of that, you might think that the state would be very limited in its bicycling opportunities. But the strong agricultural base supports a network of progressive towns and urban centers with a number of excellent colleges and universities. The citizens of these towns and cities, in turn, support an avid bicycling community of bike shops, clubs, organized rides, and bike trails.

The highway infrastructure in Iowa is well developed in the rural areas, so there are many opportunities for road biking. The famous RAGBRAI (Register's Annual Great Bicycle Ride Across Iowa) organized ride is nationally known as a major bicycling event. Iowa is one of the foremost states in the movement of creating recreational trails from abandoned railroad routes. This process involves gaining title to the rail corridor by authority of "banking" the land for possible future public transportation needs before it reverts to the adjacent landowners. This process has spread across the state, and now there are over 30 of these trails for bicyclists, hikers, and cross-country skiers. Because of their railroad heritage, these trails are often links to the past, running through old traditional communities and past various historic points. You can usually find the trailheads for these routes by looking along the old corridor of railroad facilities and grain elevators in each town.

Rail trails form the core of Iowa's trail system and have become a valuable resource for the recreational bicycling public. But with the national growth of mountain biking, demand for more challenging trails has appeared in Iowa as well. There is a well-developed recreational park system in Iowa, and several of the agencies involved are beginning to provide trail biking opportunities. In 1955 the state of Iowa enacted legislation allowing counties to set up County Conservation Boards, which acquire and maintain parks, wildlife areas, and preserves for public recreation and education. As a result, many of the state's counties have good quality parks that include trail networks, nature areas, and greenbelts. These trails, when open to mountain bikes, can provide technical riding in a more natural setting than the rail trails.

Iowa's state parks and state recreation areas also provide some trail systems open to mountain biking. These trails are usually more extensive and are often located in hilly river valleys and other prime scenic areas. Some of the trails have traditionally been equestrian trails, and some of these are open to bikers on a trial basis, so it is of prime importance to follow the rules of courteous riding toward horseback riders and other trail users. The U.S. Army Corps of Engineers, which has built several reservoirs on Iowa rivers, also manages parkland where there are bike trails available.

The many good bike shops located around the state can be your prime source of information on the local biking scene. They can provide ideas on where the newest places to ride are located, what events may be happening, and whether there are any clubs in the area. Around some of the larger cities and college towns, there are likely to be some unofficial trail areas, possibly with very technical trails, where clubs and other locals do some riding. These places can change periodically as local regulations are revised. One popular riding spot in a city park in the Des Moines–Ames area was voted off limits just a month before I wrote this. Check with local authorities if you are unsure of the legal status of a certain area.

A list of bike shops and clubs in each section of the state follows the introduction to that section. Each section also contains a discussion of additional mountain biking possibilities.

Iowa Bibliography

Enjoy Iowa's Recreation Trails, Iowa Natural Heritage Foundation, second edition, 1994. A spiral-bound booklet detailing 36 trails in the state, $7.50. See address below.

Iowa's Recreation Trails, Iowa Department of Transportation, Iowa Department of Natural Resources, July 1994. An 18-page listing of over 400 recreational trails. Contact: Department of Natural Resources (DNR), (515) 281-5145 or Department of Transportation, (515) 239-1621.

For Further Information

Division of Tourism
Department of Economic Development
200 East Grand Avenue
Des Moines, IA 50309
(515) 242-4705 or 1-800-345-IOWA

Geological Survey Bureau
109 Trollbridge Hall
Iowa City, IA 52242
(319) 335-1575
for Iowa DNR maps

Iowa Natural Heritage Foundation
505 Fifth Avenue, Suite 444
Des Moines, IA 50309-2321
(515) 288-1846

Iowa Trails Council
P.O. Box 131
Center Point, IA 52213-0131
(319) 849-1844

Rails-to-Trails Conservancy
1400 Sixteenth Street, NW
Washington, DC 20036
(202) 797-5400

Eastern Iowa

The Mississippi River and its tributaries dominate the geography of eastern Iowa, carving spectacular bluffs and picturesque river valleys that feature hardwood forests of hickory, elm, and oak. The landscape is scattered with "postcard" vistas of well-kept farms and quiet rural communities that are the defining image of life in Iowa. The northeastern corner of Iowa was not scraped smooth by the Pleistocene glaciation and is now the most hilly, most eroded part of the state, an area tourist brochures like to compare with the pastoral hills of Switzerland.

All the interior rivers of the region drain southeastward to the Mississippi. The major cities of the region date back to the days of river commerce and water power and are all found on these rivers. Burlington, Davenport, and Dubuque are old Mississippi River towns, and Iowa City, Cedar Rapids, and Waterloo are interior cities on the Iowa and Cedar Rivers. Despite a century and a half of development, these river corridors still provide many natural areas where deer, wild turkeys, and bald eagles may be spotted.

This terrain includes some of Iowa's most scenic parks and recreation areas and some of the most interesting mountain bike trails as well. As in all of Iowa, there are many railroad-conversion trails to choose from, including some of Iowa's most scenic ones. There are several state parks and recreation areas with good trail systems as well. The rides described in this section include five rail trails, four areas with hilly, moderate trails, and four with moderate to difficult, technical riding.

RIDE 1   GEODE STATE PARK

Geode State Park is one of the most popular recreation areas in the southeast corner of Iowa. The park is centered around a reservoir, created in 1950, that is now a popular fishing lake and swimming spot. A series of multi-use trails circumnavigate the lake, forming a six-mile loop that makes for an interesting variety of single-track biking in a rolling, oak hardwood forest area. Mostly easy to moderate, the trails have a few difficult spots with short, steep climbs and rocky spots. For bikers looking for an afternoon of fun riding with some reasonable challenges, this park is worth the trip. The forest cover means there is lots of shade during the hot summer months, and the beach offers another way to cool off after your ride. The park is also great during the maximum color season in mid-October.

RIDE 1 *GEODE STATE PARK*

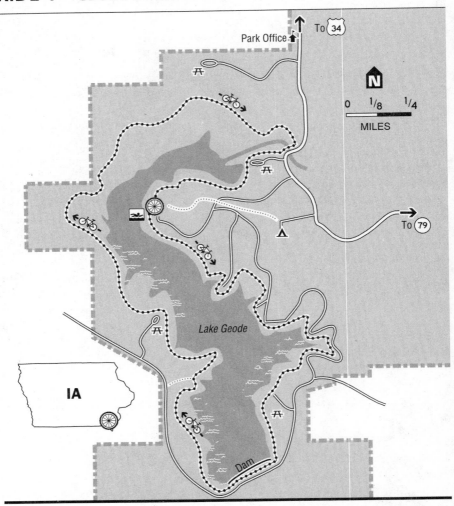

The Skunk River just to the south of the dam was once a busy riverboat route as settlers penetrated inland from the Mississippi. The nearby Mississippi River town of Burlington is one of the oldest cities in Iowa and has an extensive district of historic architecture; it also boasts Snake Alley, the "crookedest street in the world."

General location: Ten miles west of Burlington in Henry County.
Elevation change: This region is moderately hilly and the loop trail has lots of short ups and downs.

The trail system in Geode State Park offers many views of the lake.

Season: Midspring through late autumn. The spring thaw and periods of extensive rain may render the trail too soft and muddy for biking.

Services: The state park has picnic and camping facilities and a swimming beach. Other services are available in Burlington and New London.

Hazards: Watch for vehicles at the points where the trail system crosses the park roads. Watch for and yield to hikers.

Rescue index: There are almost always other people visiting the park. In season, there is a resident ranger.

Land status: Geode State Park is managed by the Iowa Department of Natural Resources.

Maps: A park brochure/map is available at the ranger station.

Finding the trail: Follow IA 79 west from Burlington to the east entrance of the park. The north entrance is 6 miles south of New London and US 34 on a county road. The loop trail can be reached at a number of points on the paved park road. One good place to start your trail ride is the beach area, where there is plenty of parking and in season, a concession stand.

Sources of additional information:

Geode State Park
Danville, IA 52623
(319) 392-4601

Bickels Bicycle Shop
305 East Agency Road
West Burlington, IA 52655
(319) 754-4410 or 1-800-354-4410

Clayton's Cyclery & Sports
110 North Main
Burlington, IA 52601
(319) 752-6251

Notes on the trail: Heading south from the beach area, the trail takes off from the southwest corner of the parking lot, crosses a bridge, and climbs up into the woodlands. Several times in the first mile there are lake-access roads to cross as the trail winds along the shoreline of the lake. There are flip signs at several of the trail entrances indicating whether the trails are open to bikes. At the south end of Lake Geode, the trail joins a park road to cross the dam that forms the lake. After meandering north through several picnic and day-use areas, the trail leaves the lake and runs through a more remote, heavily wooded section of the park. The final mile back to the beach area runs briefly on the north park road, across a stream, and through another picnic area.

RIDE 2 *KEWASH NATURE TRAIL*

Originally developed from an abandoned railroad grade between 1989 and 1991 by the Kewash Nature Trail Association, this 14-mile "linear park" consists of a crushed-limestone surface providing easy recreational bicycling. Several natural wooded areas add some scenic variety to a mostly rural setting along the trail corridor. Remnants of the natural prairie habitat can be found in places, where you might spot wild flowers and animal life. The Kewash Trail is typical of Iowa's many recreational rail trails, and bicyclists looking for some easy cruising or a good route for some family fun will enjoy this trail.

General location: The trail runs from the town of Washington, in Washington County, west to the county line at the town of Keota.
Elevation change: There are only very gradual elevation changes on the trail.
Season: Midspring to late autumn. Winter snow and thawing conditions may make the trail surface unusable for bikes during the off-season.
Services: Parking, water, and rest rooms can be found in the towns of Washington, West Chester, and Keota. Commercial services are available at the ends of the trail in Washington and Keota.
Hazards: Watch for vehicle traffic at highway and road crossings.

RIDE 2   *KEWASH NATURE TRAIL*

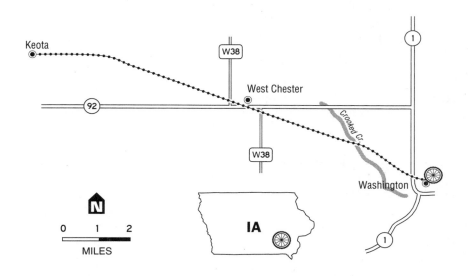

Rescue index: Help is available in the towns along the way.

Land status: Washington County Conservation Board.

Maps: A brochure with a diagram map is available from the Washington County Conservation Board. A map of the trail can also be found in the Iowa trail guide, *Enjoy Iowa's Recreation Trails,* published by the Iowa Natural Heritage Foundation. See the bibliography in the Iowa introduction for more information.

Finding the trail: There is parking in Washington on West Main Street at the north end of Sunset Park, and from there Sesquicentennial Way, a one-quarter mile paved link, runs to the Kewash Trail on the north side of town.

Sources of additional information:

Washington County Conservation Board
Box 889
Washington, IA 52353
(319) 653-7765

Rider Sales
102 East 3rd Street
Washington, IA 52353
(319) 653-5808

Notes on the trail: There are rest rooms and water at the Sunset Park starting point. After joining the Kewash grade and heading west, you will pass 14 Acre Prairie and Hayes Timber, 2 tracts of land with a few meandering walking trails. The Kewash then crosses IA 92 and follows a mostly wooded corridor across a creek, then northwest into a more open landscape to the small community of West Chester. This village, which is at the halfway point, is a nice spot for a break or a picnic lunch, or it can be a turn-around point for an out-and-back ride of 14 miles. Continuing west, the trail traverses more open prairie and rural vistas, terminating in Keota, on North County Line Road. Trail passes are required; daily passes costing $1 can be picked up at collection boxes at intersections along the trail. Trail hours are from 4:30 A.M. to 10:30 P.M.

RIDE 3   *SCOTT COUNTY PARK*

Scott County Park is a popular, well-developed recreation area just north of Davenport. A wide range of facilities are available here, including camping, picnicking, a petting zoo, nature center, swimming pool, and a golf course. The rolling, wooded terrain includes a formal and informal trail network that has become popular with local mountain bikers. Consisting of mowed-grass corridors and dirt single-track in a series of interconnected loops, these trails range from easy to difficult, allowing for either casual or aggressive riding. In general, the northern section of the area where biking is allowed contains the more challenging single-track riding, with some of the routes carved out of the woods by previous mountain bike use. The southern part of the area is made up of some trails designed for horseback riding and some for cross-country skiing and have wider, more gradual curves and hills. The area is mostly wooded, with well-established stands of hardwoods, but several open, grassy meadows add variety. Along the perimeter of the area, a mowed trail separates the woodlands from the fenced-off cornfields to the east. There are more than four miles of trail in the area, allowing for several hours to half a day's worth of enjoyable riding.

The nearby "Quad Cities" of Davenport and Bettendorf in Iowa, and Moline and Rock Island in Illinois have a variety of attractions including parks, museums, shopping, and riverboat gambling. Not too far from Scott County Park is the Buffalo Bill Cody Homestead, the boyhood home of the famous western figure.

General location: Near Long Grove, about 7 miles north of Davenport in Scott County.

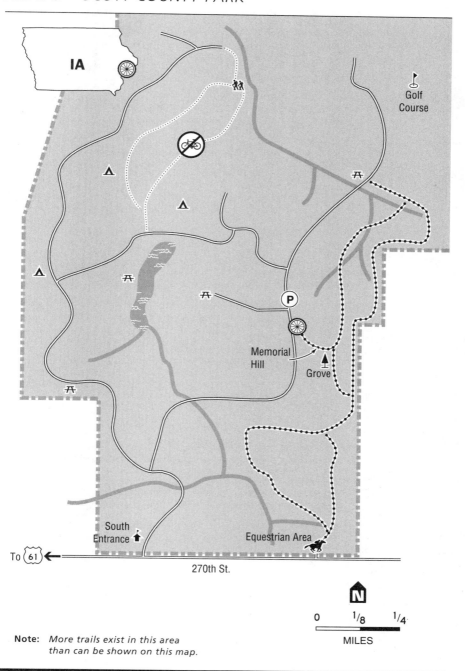

IA

Golf Course

Memorial Hill

Grove

P

South Entrance

Equestrian Area

To 61 ←

270th St.

N

0   1/8   1/4

MILES

Note: *More trails exist in this area than can be shown on this map.*

A sunny autumn morning is a great time to ride in Scott County Park near Davenport.

Elevation change: This is an area of gently rolling hills, but there are some short, steep climbs in and out of the creek bottoms.

Season: Midspring through late autumn. The area is frequently snow covered in winter, and the spring thaw period will render the trails too soft for riding in the early spring.

Services: The park has water, rest rooms, picnic and camping facilities, and a swimming pool. There is a convenience store near the highway exit. All other services are available in Eldridge and Davenport.

Hazards: Watch out for steep drops, rocks, and occasional logs on the trails. Yield the trail to hikers and horseback riders.

Rescue index: Park personnel are available during park hours.

Land status: Scott County Conservation Board.

Maps: A park map is available from the entrance station.

Finding the trail: Take US 61 to the Long Grove exit, then follow signs 1 mile east to Scott Park Road, north to 270th Street, and east to the south entrance. On the east park road, go to the parking lot just north of Memorial Hill, a Civil War memorial. The trails can be picked up in the grove of trees behind the memorial.

Sources of additional information:

Scott County Conservation Board
P.O. Box 213
Long Grove, IA 52756
(319) 285-9656 (park) or 381-1114 (headquarters)

Jerry and Sparky's Bicycle Shop
1819 East Locust
Davenport, IA 52803
(319) 324-0270

On Two Wheels
3616 Eastern Avenue
Davenport, IA 52807
(319) 386-5533

Notes on the trail: The trails are made up of a combination of technical single-track routes, equestrian trails, and mowed cross-country ski trails. From the grove of trees behind the Civil War memorial, turn north (left) to reach the technical area. The trails there wind around the slopes and drainage of a small stream, eventually reaching the park road and the edge of a golf course. There are many tracks in the area, some well established, some faint; it's a fun area just to mess around in and follow your whims of the moment. The trails to the south are wider and generally more open, with a few good hills and climbs.

Please confine your trail riding to the southeast corner of the park, where biking is allowed; other trails in the park are for hiking only. Park hours are from 6 A.M. to 10:30 P.M.

RIDE 4   *SUGAR BOTTOM RECREATION AREA*

The trails at Sugar Bottom Recreation Area have been designed specifically for mountain biking over a period of years by a cooperative effort between the Iowa City Off Road Riders (ICORR) and the Coralville Lake office of the U.S. Army Corps of Engineers. The result of this continuing project has been one of the finest trail systems for mountain bikers in eastern Iowa. It is a great example of what can be accomplished when biking groups work together with land management people. I was quite happy to discover this trail system after several days of checking out flat rail trail routes. The ICORR group deserves much praise for their work here.

Currently, there are about seven miles of mostly single-track, one-way trails, with several more miles planned, which will bring the system total to over ten miles. The trails are laid out as a series of loops and loops-within-loops on packed dirt with some grassy sections, providing a range of relatively easy to fairly technical options that should appeal to bikers of most abilities. The area is largely wooded, with some open meadowlands; you'll occasionally see deer, wild turkeys, and other animals. Plan on spending at least a couple of hours here to explore the whole system, and to reride some of the fun stuff.

RIDE 4 *SUGAR BOTTOM RECREATION AREA*

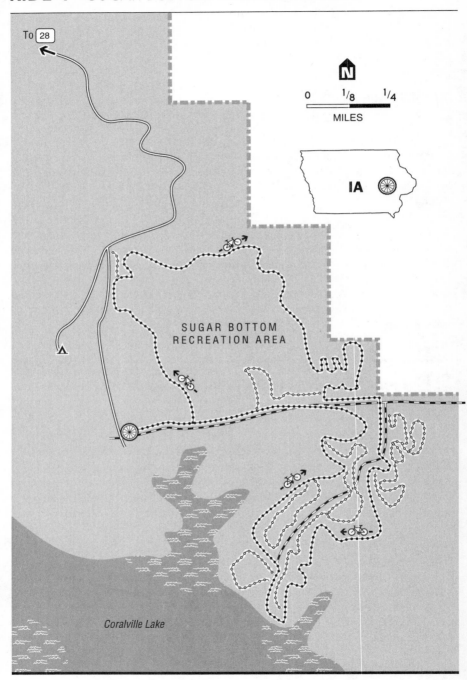

To 28

N

0   1/8   1/4
MILES

IA

SUGAR BOTTOM
RECREATION AREA

Coralville Lake

Nearby Iowa City, home of the University of Iowa and the original territorial and state capital, is a lively city worth a visit, and any mountain bikers traveling through the region on Interstate 80 will find this a nice place to take a break.

General location: On Coralville Lake near North Liberty, about 10 miles north of Iowa City in Johnson County.

Elevation change: This moderately hilly area has about 100´ of vertical relief.

Season: Midspring to late autumn. There is usually snow cover during the winter months, and springtime riding is prohibited until the ground is dried out.

Services: There is a campground, water, and rest rooms at the recreation area. Commercial services can be found in North Liberty or Iowa City.

Hazards: The trails here have been well designed, but the usual hazards of single-track riding may be encountered, such as sharp corners, steep descents, obstructions, and trees. Yield the trail to any hikers and horseback riders that may be encountered.

Rescue index: Help should usually be close by in this area.

Land status: U.S. Army Corps of Engineers, Rock Island District.

Maps: There is a trail map posted at the trailhead in the parking lot.

Finding the trail: Both Interstate 80/exit 240 and I-380/exit 4 lead to North Liberty. From there, take CR F28 northeast about 5 miles across the lake to the entrance to Sugar Bottom Recreation Area. Drive about 2 miles through the park to the beach parking lot. An information signpost at the trailhead gives current trail information.

Sources of additional information:

U.S. Army Corps of Engineers
Coralville Lake Office
(319) 338-3543

ICORR (Iowa City Off Road Riders)
15 Birch Court
North Liberty, IA 52317

Lefler's Schwinn
1705 First Avenue
Iowa City, IA 52240
(319) 351-7433

World of Bikes
723 South Gilbert Street
Iowa City, IA 52240
(319) 351-8337 or 1-800-794-8337

The mountain bike trails in Sugar Bottom Recreation Area near Iowa City are some of the best technical rides in Iowa.

Notes on the trail: Please note the specific rules for this area set by ICORR and the Corps of Engineers: All trails are one-way; follow the signs. Do not use the trails within 24 hours following a measurable rainfall. The trails are closed during the spring thawing season. These rules allow the trails to be maintained in excellent condition and make this area one of the top mountain biking areas in Iowa. Follow the dirt access road to the east to enter the various trail loops. The large loop on the north side of the access road makes a nice warm-up ride, and the newer, more technical loops are found on the south side of the area.

High water in the Coralville Lake reservoir may result in flooding of adjacent shoreline areas. In times of wet weather, there are a number of alternative places to ride in the Iowa City and Cedar Rapids areas, including an ATV area near Solon. Check out Ride 5 or the Additional Mountain Biking Opportunities in Eastern Iowa for more ideas.

RIDE 5

SAC AND FOX NATIONAL RECREATION TRAIL

This trail meanders for a little over seven miles along the wooded flood plain of the Cedar River and its local tributary, Indian Creek. In 1975 the Sac and Fox became the first National Recreation Trail established in Iowa. Extensive damage done to the trail during the floods of 1993 has been largely repaired; the trail now has a crushed-limestone and dirt surface. Mud stains from the flood can still be seen high on the tree trunks as you cruise through the lowlands. Out-and-back rides of up to 15 miles can be done, depending upon your starting point along the trail. The quiet environment of the thick, hardwood-forested creek valley provides a relaxing opportunity for local and visiting bicyclists to do some easy touring.

Adjacent to the trail is the Indian Creek Nature Center, which offers nature activities and a gift shop, and maintains about two miles of hiking-only nature trails close by. The city of Cedar Rapids is Iowa's second largest city and is an agricultural and meat-processing center, with many newer, high technology businesses growing in the area. Its many cultural attractions include the Czech and Slovak Museum, the largest of its kind outside the Slovak and Czech Republics. Linn County has many other opportunities for trail biking; look elsewhere in the Eastern Iowa section for more ideas.

General location: Immediately east of Cedar Rapids in Linn County.
Elevation change: This is a fairly level trail following the grade of the Cedar River and Indian Creek.
Season: Midspring to late autumn.
Services: Rest rooms and water are available at the nature center building. All other services are available in Cedar Rapids.
Hazards: Watch for walkers, hikers, and horseback riders, and take care on the bridge crossings.
Rescue index: The Indian Creek Nature Center is staffed during most daytime hours. Help is otherwise close by in the city.
Land status: Cedar Rapids Parks Department.
Maps: A trail map is available in the nature center or can be found in the Iowa trail guide, *Enjoy Iowa's Recreation Trails*, published by the Iowa Natural Heritage Foundation. See the bibliography in the Iowa introduction for more information.
Finding the trail: The parking lot and trailhead at the Indian Creek Nature Center can be reached by taking Mt. Vernon Road to Bertram Road, then south one mile to Otis Road. There are additional trailheads with parking lots at the southwest end of the trail on Cole Street off Otis Road and on Bertram

RIDE 5 *SAC AND FOX NATIONAL RECREATION TRAIL*

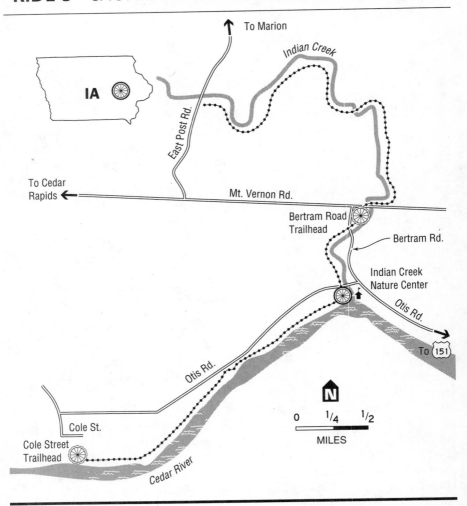

Road just south of Mt. Vernon Road. There is also foot and bicycle access on East Post Road at the northwest end of the trail.

Sources of additional information:

Cedar Rapids Parks Department
(319) 398-5080

Indian Creek Nature Center
(319) 362-0664

Notes on the trail: Starting at the centrally located Indian Creek Nature Center effectively divides the trail into 2 out-and-back rides of about 7 miles each. To do the trail as one long out-and-back, you must start at the Cole Street parking lot or at East Post Road. Biking is not allowed on the 2 hiking trails maintained by the Indian Creek Nature Center.

RIDE 6   *CEDAR VALLEY NATURE TRAIL*

The Cedar Valley Nature Trail is one of Iowa's premier rails-to-trails conversions and is a popular 52-mile link between Waterloo and Evansdale on the northwest end of the trail and Hiawatha and Cedar Rapids on the southeast end. The partially wooded corridor was a branch of the Illinois Central Gulf railroad, abandoned in 1977 and opened in 1984 as a recreational trail. Five towns along the route provide various services and points of interest. As with all the rail trails, the crushed-limestone surface is level and provides easy biking, making this route appealing to casual riders, families, or those who just want to get out and cruise along, with the trees and fields flying by.

The trail is a designated part of the American Discovery Trail, a coast-to-coast route coordinated by the American Hiking Society. In Iowa, this route will include the Raccoon River Valley Trail, the Heart of Iowa Nature Trail, the Cedar Valley Nature Trail, and the Hoover Nature Trail.

Because of its length, the Cedar Valley Trail traverses a good variety of eastern Iowa's scenic diversity. Several natural areas and parks on or near the route provide wooded preserves for further exploration or quiet escape. Trail users will cross the Cedar River, one of Iowa's major drainages, and observe both dynamic and fading examples of the state's rural heritage. Two restored rail stations located outside Gilbertville and in Center Point are historical reminders of the days when the trail corridor was an important intercity passenger link.

General location: Between Waterloo and Cedar Rapids, roughly paralleling Interstate 380.
Elevation change: This is a very level grade through gently rolling countryside.
Season: Spring through late autumn. The area is generally snow covered in the winter season.
Services: Restaurants, stores, and parking can be found in each of the major towns along the trail, including Evansdale, Gilbertville, LaPorte City, Brandon, Urbana, Center Point, and Hiawatha. Rest rooms can be found in at least a dozen points along the route. McFarlane County Park near La Porte City has camping and picnicking. All other services, including bike shops, are available in Waterloo or Cedar Rapids.

RIDE 6 *CEDAR VALLEY NATURE TRAIL*

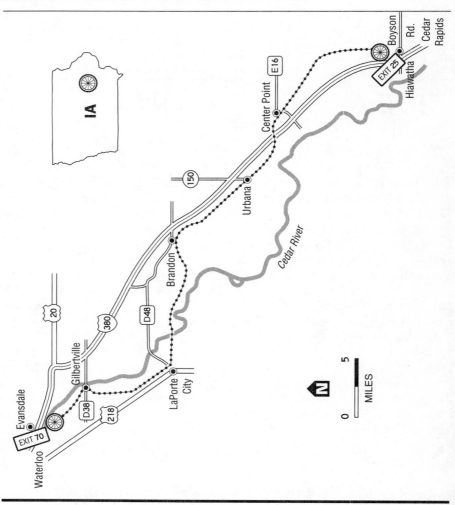

Hazards: Be aware of the weather conditions during thunderstorm season. On long rides, be sure to carry plenty of water and use sunscreen. Watch for vehicle traffic on crossroads.

Rescue index: Help is as close as the next town.

Land status: Owned and managed jointly by the Linn County Conservation Board and the Blackhawk County Conservation Board.

Maps: Trail maps can be picked up at most of the trailhead stations and can be found in the Iowa trail guide, *Enjoy Iowa's Recreation Trails,* published by

The 52-mile Cedar Valley Nature Trail crosses the Cedar River on an old railroad trestle.

the Iowa Natural Heritage Foundation. See the bibliography in the Iowa introduction for more information.

Finding the trail: The terminal trailheads are marked from I-380/exit 25 in Hiawatha and exit 70 in Evansdale. At the Evansdale exit, follow Gilbert Drive east from the north side of the freeway around and under the freeway to the south side, where there is a parking lot. At the well-marked Hiawatha trailhead, there is a large parking lot with water and rest rooms. Intermediate access points may be a little less clearly marked; consult the trail map or ask locally. Rail trail access points in small towns are usually located near the old town centers adjacent to commercial facilities that formerly depended upon the railroad, such as grain elevators.

Sources of additional information:

Linn County Conservation Board
1890 County Home Road
Marion, IA 52302
(319) 398-3505

Blackhawk County Conservation Board
2410 West Lone Tree Road
Cedar Falls, IA 50613
(319) 266-0328 or 266-6813

Notes on the trail: Efforts are currently being made to eliminate a 1-mile gap in the trail near Urbana. Trail passes of $2 are required and are available at various businesses or parks in the area.

RIDE 7 *PLEASANT CREEK STATE RECREATION AREA*

The trail system at Pleasant Creek State Recreation Area provides a potential single-track alternative to the various rail trails and wide, flat bike trails in the Cedar Rapids–Waterloo area. This multi-use trail forms a loop approximately ten miles long around the perimeter of the recreation area, providing many nice vistas of rolling meadows and woodlands as it encircles the dam-created lake. There are mostly gradual hills and curves, making for easy to moderate biking on the packed-dirt and grassy trails. Because the trail is also shared with horseback riders, sections can be somewhat bumpy and eroded. The south and southwestern sections of the trail generally have the most hilly, most wooded, and most remote portions of the loop.

The recreation area and its centerpiece lake were developed in the 1960s to answer a need for more outdoor recreation in this region. With the lake as the focal point, fishing, boating, and swimming are the most popular activities here, so the trails can offer an escape from the crowds on busy summer days. The spring and autumn seasons should offer even more solitude. The nearby Cedar Valley Nature Trail and the many attractions of the Waterloo and Cedar Rapids areas make this region a good one for visitors.

General location: Fifteen miles northwest of Cedar Rapids in Benton and Linn Counties.

Elevation change: Moderately rolling hills in the area provide some ups and downs within a range of about 100′ of elevation.

Season: Midspring to late autumn. Snow cover is likely from December to March, and the spring thaw period, usually in early April, renders the trails too soft for biking.

Services: Camping and swimming facilities are available at the park. Other services can be found in Center Point, Cedar Rapids, or Waterloo.

Hazards: The multi-use trail is popular with horseback riders; be prepared to yield the right-of-way. Watch for traffic when crossing the park roads. Hunting is allowed in portions of the recreation area.

Rescue index: Help can be obtained from the park staff in season or found in the nearby towns.

Land status: Pleasant Creek State Recreation Area is managed by the Iowa Department of Natural Resources.

Maps: A park map is available at the park entrance station.

RIDE 7 *PLEASANT CREEK STATE RECREATION AREA*

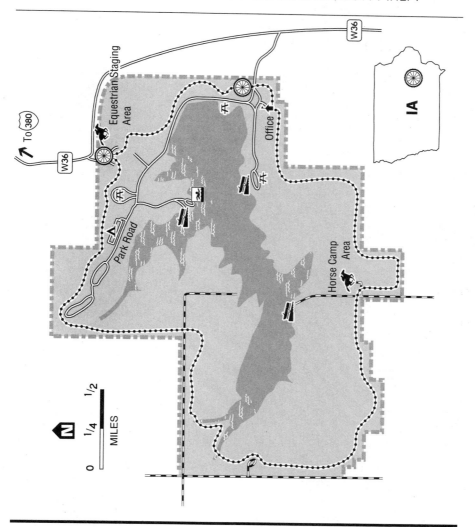

Finding the trail: The recreation area's east entrance is located 6 miles south of Center Point and I-380, or 4 miles north of Palo, on CR W36. The trail circles the perimeter of the park and can be reached from several points on the park road, including the east entrance road at the park boundary and the equestrian/snowmobile staging area off CR W36 on the north side of the recreation area.

Sources of additional information:

Pleasant Creek State Recreation Area
Box C
Palo, IA 52324
(319) 436-7716

Notes on the trail: The use of trails by mountain bikers is a relatively recent development here, so please be courteous and yield to other trail users. Avoid riding in times of wet weather, when the trail will be muddy.

RIDE 8 *HERITAGE TRAIL*

The Heritage Trail is another one of Iowa's first-rate rail trails, making its way through the rugged, forested bluff country of the Mississippi River valley from Dubuque on into the prairie ridges to the west. This 26-mile packed-dirt, gravel, and crushed-limestone trail is one of the most popular in Iowa, and a complete network of support services can be found in the towns along the route. These facilities, along with the camaraderie of other bikers on the trail, make this an ideal ride for novice groups, families with children, and others who enjoy the spectacular landscape of northeastern Iowa. This area is particularly nice during the autumn color season in October.

Future plans call for extending the trail several more miles into the city of Dubuque. There are a few informal mountain biking spots of a more technical nature around Dubuque; check with local bike shops for the latest information. Dubuque is one of the great classic Mississippi River towns with a rich historical and cultural tradition, making it one of the most interesting destinations in Iowa. Dyersville calls itself the "Farm Toy Capital of the World" and is the location of the Basilica of St. Francis Xavier, one of the most striking rural churches in Iowa.

General location: The trail runs from Dubuque to Dyersville in Dubuque County.
Elevation change: The trail steadily climbs over 450′ at a very easy grade as it rises out of the Mississippi valley toward the west.
Season: Midspring to late autumn. The area is generally snow covered in the winter, when parts of the trail are used for cross-country skiing or snowmobiling.
Services: All services are available in Dubuque and Dyersville. Facilities in the intermediate towns consist of rest rooms, stores, restaurants, and camping.
Hazards: Watch for vehicle traffic on the road crossings. On long rides, be sure to carry plenty of water and use sunscreen in the summer months.

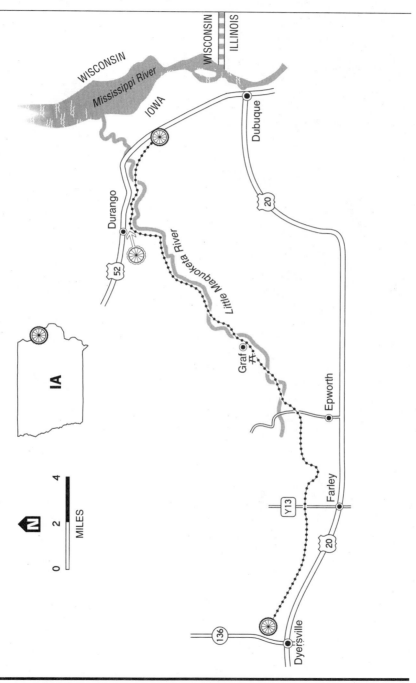

The Heritage Trail west of Dubuque is one of the most scenic in Iowa.

Rescue index: Help can be reached at any of the trailside towns.

Land status: Dubuque County Conservation Board.

Maps: A Heritage Trail map and fact brochure is available from local businesses. A map of the trail can also be found in the Iowa trail guide, *Enjoy Iowa's Recreation Trails,* published by the Iowa Natural Heritage Foundation. See the bibliography in the Iowa introduction for more information. A detailed 48-page trail guide, *Guide to Heritage Trail,* is available for $2 from the Dubuque County Conservation Board (see the address listed below).

Finding the trail: The eastern trailhead is 2 miles north of Dubuque on US 52. The western end is in Dyersville, on IA 136. Trailheads are also located in the towns of Durango, Graf, Epworth, and Farley.

Sources of additional information:

Dubuque County Conservation Board
13768 Swiss Valley Road
Peosta, IA 52068
(319) 556-6745

Dubuque Chamber of Commerce
770 Main Street
Dubuque, IA 52001
(319) 557-9200 or 1-800-255-2255 ext. 9200

Dyersville Area Chamber of Commerce
1424 9th Street, SE
Dyersville, IA 52040
(319) 875-2311

Bike Shack
2600 Dodge Street (Plaza 20)
Dubuque, IA 52003
(319) 582-4381

Bicycle World
1072 Central Avenue
Dubuque, IA 52001
(319) 556-6122

Notes on the trail: Perhaps the most scenic section of this trail is the climb out of the valley from Durango to Farley, where the grade follows the Little Maquoketa River and leaves the major highways behind. Here you will pedal below steep limestone cliffs, under several bridges, and past quiet farmsteads patched into the river valley. The small village of Graf has several services catering to trail users and makes a good halfway or turn-around point. Benches and tables are located along the route at regular intervals. There is a daily trail fee of $1.10, payable at local businesses or at self-registration stations at the trailheads. Trail use is not allowed after 10:30 P.M.

RIDE 9   *VOLGA RIVER STATE RECREATION AREA*

Volga River State Recreation Area, located only an hour or so from Waterloo, Cedar Rapids, or Dubuque, has the most extensive system of serious trails for mountain biking in northeastern Iowa. There are almost 20 miles of single- and double-track trails that form a variety of loops throughout the recreation area. Most of them climb up onto the series of bluffs overlooking the Volga River and Frog Hollow Creek, making for some good ups and downs and nice views of the wooded river valley. The mixed trail surfaces of mowed grass, packed dirt, rocks, and sandy spots, coupled with a few challenging climbs, make for an interesting variety of mostly moderate to some difficult riding. The trails here have been used for mountain bike races on occasion but are equally suited for more leisurely exploration. Plan on spending at least several hours to a full day riding this pleasant area.

The hills are forested with oak, elm, and cedar, with aspen and cottonwood common in the lower areas. Open meadowlands and a few active farm fields are also present. Waterfowl, upland bird life, beaver, raccoon, fox, and deer

RIDE 9 *VOLGA RIVER STATE RECREATION AREA*

IA

Frog Hollow Lake

Lima Tr.

Dam

Frog Hollow Tr.

Frog Hollow Creek

Park Road

Office

West Entrance

To 150

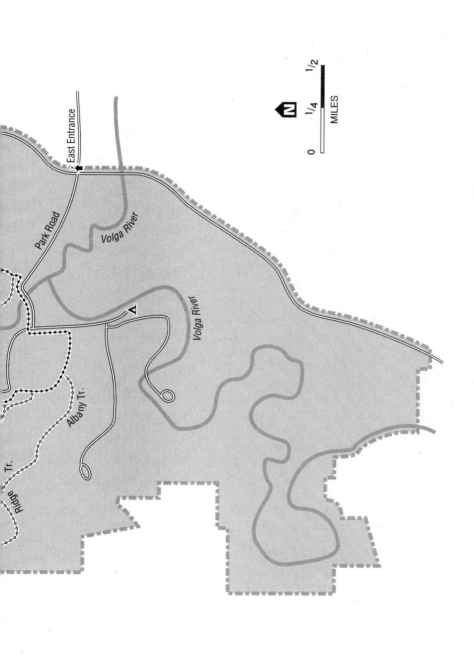

East Entrance

Park Road

Volga River

Volga River

Albany Tr.

Ridge Tr.

N

0 1/4 1/2
MILES

The Frog Hollow Trail is part of a 20-mile trail system in Volga River State Recreation Area.

are likely to be seen in the recreation area. The wooded hills and valleys of northeastern Iowa have a number of other mountain biking opportunities that make this region perhaps the best in the state for its variety.

General location: Five miles south of West Union in Fayette County.
Elevation change: The Volga River cuts through the recreation area, creating some bluffs with a total elevation range of 250′.
Season: Midspring to late autumn. The area will generally have snow cover from December to March. Spring thaw will make the trails too soft or muddy for biking well into April.
Services: There is a "nonmodern" campground by the Volga River, with pit toilets and running water available. Rest rooms can be found at Frog Hollow Lake. Other services are available in Fayette or West Union.
Hazards: There are several steep, rocky descents around the trail system. Watch for vehicle traffic when crossing the paved park roads. Hunting is allowed here in season.
Rescue index: There is a ranger station at the west entrance, and there are generally other park users in the area.
Land status: Volga State Recreation Area is managed by the Iowa Department of Natural Resources.
Maps: A park map is available at the ranger station.

Finding the trail: Follow IA 150 south from West Union or north from Fayette to the west park entrance. The trail system crosses the park roads in a number of places. A good starting place is the parking lot by the rest rooms just before the Frog Hollow Lake access point. An alternate starting point is the Albany primitive campground, which is popular with horseback riders.

Sources of additional information:

Volga River State Recreation Area
Fayette, IA 52142
(319) 425-4161

Notes on the trail: The various trail sections are named and are marked with signs. If you start at the Frog Hollow Lake parking lot mentioned above, the trailheads for the Lima Trail and the Frog Hollow Trail are just to the south. For an 8-mile loop typical of this area, follow one of the Lima Trail loops uphill to the east and south around to the east entrance road. You will be traversing some rolling hills and a variety of woodlands on a corridor kept wide by snowmobile use in the winter. On the park road, head west across the river, then south a bit to the Albany Trail, which provides access to the Frog Hollow Trail or the more hilly Ridge Trail. On the north side of the west entrance road, the Frog Hollow Trail makes a steep climb onto another bluff with good views, then drops down to the creek and back to the trailhead.

These trails are designed for multiple use; please yield to hikers and horseback riders.

RIDE 10 *YELLOW RIVER STATE FOREST*

The northeast corner of Iowa, missed by the last glaciers of the Pleistocene and carved by many Mississippi River tributaries, is the most hilly part of the state. Yellow River State Forest is situated among some of the most scenic parts of this bluff country and is perhaps the most extensively forested area left in Iowa. The system of forest roads here, including some low maintenance roads and an abandoned railroad grade, combine to provide almost 20 miles of back-road riding in a hardwood-forested, almost mountainous semi-wilderness.

Several interesting loop tours of up to 12 miles can be put together by connecting two of the longest low maintenance roads or the old railroad grade with a short section of IA 364. Several additional roads provide some out-and-back rides on the ridges or in the valleys of the state forest. Some of the roads are nontechnical, easy riding, but others offer some challenging climbs, rough spots, and fast descents of moderate difficulty.

RIDE 10 *YELLOW RIVER STATE FOREST*

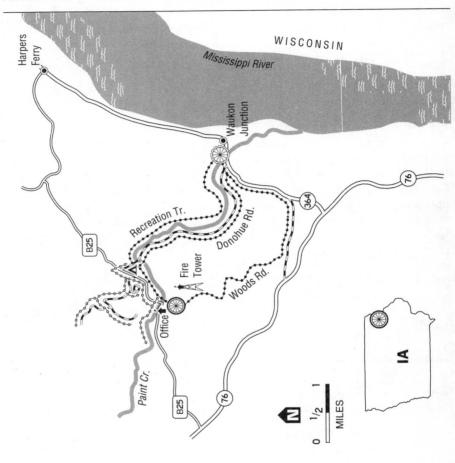

Each of the various forest roads and trails here has some distinct characteristics that make it possible to satisfy most bikers' interests. Woods Road, which runs from the park headquarters area to the south end of the forest, climbs almost 400′ to a fire tower—the only fire tower in Iowa—before descending and climbing again through some rugged ravines. The Donohue Road, a dirt four-wheel-drive track, is much more level, following the course of Big Paint Creek toward the Mississippi. The abandoned railroad grade, once part of the Chicago, Minneapolis, Saint Paul & Pacific system, is now a recreational trail also following the course of Big Paint Creek. On the north side of County Road B25 is a three-plus-mile, out-and-back dirt road system that climbs steeply onto a high ridge with several scenic viewpoints overlooking the Paint Creek valley.

This area is worth at least a full day for those who like to explore, although a fast workout could cover most everything in a morning or afternoon. The "green-up" period in midspring or the autumn color season of October are particularly nice times to visit the Mississippi River bluff country. Because of the extensive forest cover, this area is a great spot to see animal life and migratory birds of all sorts.

Allamakee County offers area visitors many options. Many of the county back roads are great for both road bicycling and automobile touring. A number of the towns are good for antiques hunters and have buildings on the National Register of Historic Places. Effigy Mounds National Monument, about five miles south of Yellow River State Forest, has one of the finest collections of prehistoric burial mounds in North America. Just outside of Waukon Junction to the north on IA 364 is Paint Rock Bluff, a prominent limestone cliff that was a sacred Indian site and, later, a landmark for riverboat travel.

General location: Near the Mississippi River between IA 76 and IA 364 in southwestern Allamakee County.

Elevation change: There is over 400′ of vertical relief in this area, ranging from 620′ near the Mississippi to over 1,050′ on the ridge crests.

Season: Midspring to late autumn. The area is generally snow covered from December to March. Spring thaw will make trails and roads muddy into April.

Services: Several campgrounds and sources of water are located near the park headquarters building. Limited services can be obtained in Harpers Ferry. Most other commercial services can be found in the towns of Waukon or Marquette.

Hazards: Motor vehicle traffic may be encountered on the roads. Be especially alert for vehicles on fast blind-curve descents. Hunting is a popular activity here; check locally for seasons.

Rescue index: There are usually other people using established forest facilities, but the dirt roads get only intermittent traffic.

Land status: Yellow River State Forest is managed by the Iowa Department of Natural Resources.

Maps: There is a topographical map showing most of the trails and roads on display at an information shelter just west of the park visitor center on CR B25. A basic diagram map of the forest can be obtained from the park office. The Paint Creek Unit Winter Trails Map, if available, does a better job of showing the topographical features and roads of the state forest. Contact the

Yellow River State Forest is protected by snow cover in this winter view of the Big Paint Creek valley.

Geological Survey Bureau, 109 Trollbridge Hall, Iowa City, IA 52242, (319) 335-1575, for Iowa DNR maps. The USGS 7.5 minute topographical maps of this section of the forest are Waterville and Harpers Ferry.

Finding the trail: The most central location to start biking is the park office and visitor center, 2 miles east of IA 76 on CR B25. There is parking adjacent to the office building in the area marked for hiking trail parking. An alternate trailhead is at the southeast end of the railroad grade recreation trail at the east end of the bridge on IA 364 in Waukon Junction.

Sources of additional information:

Yellow River State Forest
729 State Forest Road
Harpers Ferry, IA 52146
(319) 586-2254 or 586-2548

Allamakee County Tourism
101 Allamakee Street
Waukon, IA 52172
(319) 568-2624

Decorah Bicycles
110 Winnebago Street
Decorah, IA 52101
(319) 382-8209

Notes on the trail: The Woods Road or Fire Tower Road starts at a sawmill and maintenance area just east of the park office and visitor center. After about 3 miles of climbing up and down the ridges, the road will pass some open fields and end at a wider gravel road. Turn left (east) for a 1.5-mile descent to IA 364 and another one-and-one-half-mile cruise into Waukon Junction. You can return to the forest headquarters area via either Donohue Road or the railroad-grade trail.

The Donohue Road takes off up a hill about a third of a mile west of the bridge at the west edge of the village. The road passes a subdivision, then turns into a rougher four-wheel-drive track. The recreation trail starts at the bridge, where there is parking for a few vehicles. After about 4 miles Donohue Road fords the creek, crosses the recreation trail, and continues past an equestrian campground to meet CR B25. In times of high water, the creek crossing may not be possible. The recreation trail continues along the creek and crosses the highway at a picnic site just east of the park headquarters area. If you are doing this loop, you may prefer to reverse the direction and do the easier, level sections first.

Roads and trails in the state forest may be closed at various times due to fire danger, logging, or other reasons. Call in advance for current information. Carry plenty of water, especially in hot, humid weather; the long ascents on some of the roads can provide a pretty good workout. There are other trails in the Yellow River State Forest that are dedicated to hiking and horseback riding. Please avoid biking on these trails, or check with the local forest officials to get updated trail information.

RIDE 11 *DECORAH CITY PARKS*

The city of Decorah is comfortably nestled into the hilly Upper Iowa River valley with the ambiance of a classic New England village. In the steep river bluffs surrounding the town, a series of forested city parks contains a uniquely rugged trail system available for mountain bike use. With the presence of Luther College, this dynamic little town has an avid biking population, so the trails get a lot of use. There are a total of eight to nine miles of interconnected trails in these parks, and some of them are as technical as any trails you will find in Iowa, and will challenge even the best of riders. At the very least, novice riders should practice their skills elsewhere before tackling the hardest trails here.

The Lower Ice Cave Trail is a relatively easy one-mile single-track following the banks of the river. This is a nice out-and-back warm-up ride for the steep climbs you'll encounter on the Ice Cave Hill trails across the road. You may have to push your bike up parts of the ridge, but once on top, there are

RIDE 11 *DECORAH CITY PARKS*

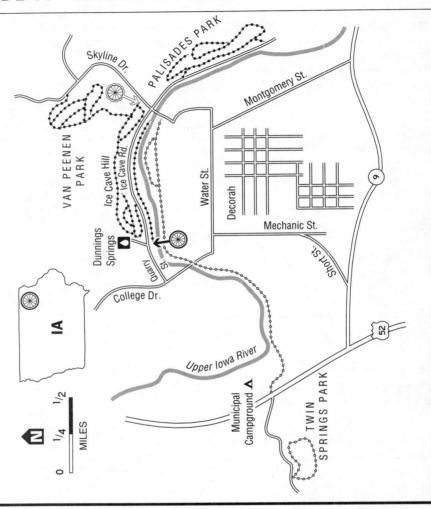

great views of the town below and some challenging single-track ridge-top riding through the thick pine woods. A connecting trail leads from the ridge out to the Van Peenen Park trail system. Largely used for cross-country skiing in the winter, these generally moderate double-track trails provide a series of tightly connected loops on some wooded slopes and an open ridge. South of Skyline Drive, Palisade Park offers more moderate riding on another ridge overlooking the town. All these trails can be reached from a parking spot across from Dunnings Springs, site of a grist mill built in 1860. The "Ice

Cave" formation after which the ridge is named is a cavelike crevasse in the limestone cliff that you can visit farther east on Ice Cave Road.

On the south side of the river the Oneota Drive Trail makes a flat, one-mile connection to Twin Springs Park and the municipal campground. Twin Springs Park, off US 52 on the west side of town, has a short loop of trail that provides some technical riding. The surrounding rural areas of Winneshiek County adjacent to the Upper Iowa River have many miles of hilly back roads offering various loop possibilities for those who have more time to explore this area. Check with Decorah Bicycles for some suggestions.

General location: In the city of Decorah, in Winneshiek County.
Elevation change: Steep river bluffs along the Upper Iowa River provide about 250′ of vertical relief.
Services: All services are available in Decorah.
Season: Midspring to late autumn. The area is generally snow covered from December to March. Spring thaw will generally make the trails muddy into April.
Hazards: Rocks and other obstructions, steep descents, and exposed cliffs may be encountered on some of the trails.
Rescue index: Help is close at hand in town.
Land status: City of Decorah Parks and Recreation.
Maps: Maps showing hiking, biking, and ski trails are available from the Decorah Parks and Recreation Department.
Finding the trail: There are trail systems at various places around the town. The best place to start for the most technical trails is off College Drive on the north side of the upper Iowa River. Just past a supermarket turn east on Quarry Street and go one-quarter mile to a parking area near the river just across from the road into Dunnings Springs. The Lower Ice Cave Trail along the river starts here. Access to the Ice Cave Hill trails can be made one-quarter mile east on Ice Cave Road, an extension of Quarry Street. Watch closely for the trail that goes right up the hill. The Van Peenen Park trails can be reached via a connecting trail from Ice Cave Hill or from a road access on Skyline Road at a point just beyond a quarry at White Tail Road. There is no off-road parking at that access point. The Palisade Park trails can be reached by continuing on Ice Cave Road, past the Skyline Drive bridge, one-quarter mile to the turnoff. There is an additional trail access point and small parking area at the east end of the Ice Cave Hill trail on Skyline Drive across from a maintenance building near the river bridge.

Sources of additional information:

Decorah Parks and Recreation
P.O. Box 513
Decorah, IA 52101
(319) 382-4158

Trails on Ice Cave Hill overlook the picturesque city of Decorah.

Decorah Bicycles
110 Winnebago Street
Decorah, IA 52101
(319) 382-8209

Notes on the trail: Try to keep track of your general location as you bike around; directions and unmarked trail junctions can get confusing in the wooded areas. Avoid using the trails after periods of rain or when trails are muddy.

RIDE 12   *PRAIRIE FARMER RECREATIONAL TRAIL*

This 18-mile trail is one of Iowa's typical railroad-conversion trails, connecting several small towns in a setting of rural scenery mixed with periodic woodlands and remnants of the natural tall-grass prairie. The original railroad bed dates back to 1866, when the route was part of a line running from McGregor on the Mississippi River to Cresco. It eventually became part of the Milwaukee and St. Paul Railroad, forming a busy rail link during the heyday of railroading in the first half of the 1900s. Passenger service was

RIDE 12 *PRAIRIE FARMER RECREATIONAL TRAIL*

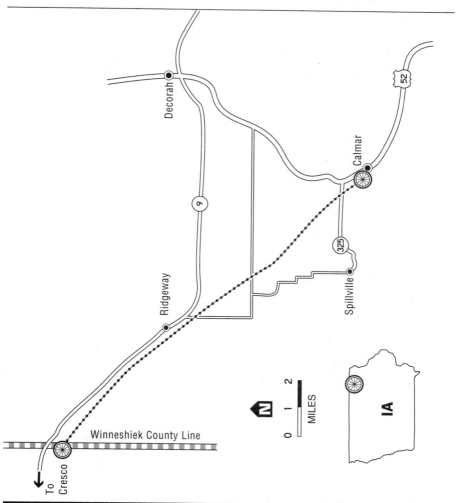

discontinued in 1960, and the Calmar to Cresco section of the grade was converted to recreational use by the Iowa Department of Transportation and the Winneshiek County Conservation Board. Today, the smooth, well-maintained crushed-limestone trail carries hiking, biking, and skiing traffic in a more relaxed atmosphere than it did during the age of iron rails and steam power.

A bit west of the trail on IA 325, the nearby village of Spillville, which has Czech heritage, offers several interesting inns and shops, and is good for an off-the-beaten-track side trip. Southwest of Calmar, the Fort Atkinson State Preserve features a re-created fort from the 1840s and an interpretive museum. More technical mountain biking can be found nearby in Decorah or in Yellow River State Forest (see Rides 10 and 11).

General location: The trail runs from Calmar in Winneshiek County northwest to the Howard County line near Cresco.

Elevation change: There are only very slight elevation changes on this old railroad grade.

Season: Midspring to late autumn. The area is usually snow covered from December to March.

Services: All commercial services can be found in Calmar, Decorah, and Cresco. Food can be found in Ridgeway.

Hazards: Watch for vehicle traffic at road crossings and on city streets in Ridgeway.

Rescue index: Help can be found in the various towns along the way.

Land status: Winneshiek County Conservation Board.

Maps: A basic map and brochure can be obtained from the Winneshiek County Conservation Board. A map of the trail can also be found in the Iowa trail guide, *Enjoy Iowa's Recreation Trails,* published by the Iowa Natural Heritage Foundation. See the bibliography in the Iowa introduction for more information.

Finding the trail: The most popular starting point is located in Calmar, on US 52, 9 miles south of Decorah. There is parking at the trailhead by the restored train station in downtown Calmar. There is also parking along the trail at Ridgeway Park at the east end of the town of Ridgeway, on IA 9. At the west end of the trail there is a small parking lot just south of IA 9, on 345th Street, one-quarter mile east of IA 139.

Sources of additional information:

Winneshiek County Conservation Board
2546 Lake Meyer Road
Fort Atkinson, IA 52144
(319) 534-7145

Decorah Bicycles
110 Winnebago Street
Decorah, IA 52101
(319) 382-8209

Notes on the trail: The trail makes a detour through city streets in Ridgeway starting at Ridgeway Park. Follow the signs to resume the ride west. There is a group of trail volunteers who assist the Conservation Board with maintenance and patrol duties. They can provide assistance if needed. Trail hours are from 6 A.M. to 10:30 P.M.

ADDITIONAL MOUNTAIN BIKING OPPORTUNITIES IN EASTERN IOWA

Unpaved Trails

The Hoover Nature Trail is the most extensive rail trail project being developed in Iowa. This 115-mile network is being built on the roadbed of the Chicago, Rock Island and Pacific Railroad between Cedar Rapids (and the 52-mile Cedar Valley Nature Trail) and Burlington on the Mississippi River. Links to Muscatine, Iowa City, and the existing Kewash Trail are projected in this ambitious plan. A link proposed in 1992, the Cedar Lake Connector Trail, will connect the Hoover Trail with the 52-mile Cedar Valley Nature Trail, creating a network of almost 200 miles. Approximately 27 miles of trail are open for use, with 13 miles in several short segments surfaced with crushed limestone for bicycling. Finished segments include one near West Branch and the Hoover Presidential Library and another from Nichols to Conesville in Muscatine County. The Hoover Trail is designated as part of the American Discovery Trail, a coast-to-coast route coordinated by the American Hiking Society. For additional information: Hoover Nature Trail, P.O. Box 123, West Liberty, IA 52776, (319) 627-2626.

The Jackson County Recreation Trail is a four-mile rail trail in a quiet rural river valley setting. This easy trail runs northeast from Spragueville on Deer Creek, along the Maquoketa River, past limestone cliffs, to a trailhead four miles north of Preston. For further information: County Conservation Board, Courthouse, Maquoketa, IA 52060, (319) 652-3783.

The town of Solon, north of Iowa City in Johnson County, has two biking areas. Four miles west on IA 382 and north on CR W6E is an all-terrain-vehicle area. Use caution when motorized traffic is in the area. Also near Solon is the Solon-MacBride Trail, a five-mile connection between the town and Lake MacBride State Park.

The Matsell Bridge Natural Area, in Linn County near Springville, has a six-mile trail. This area is managed by the Linn County Conservation Board.

Squaw Creek Park, in Linn County east of Cedar Rapids, has a seven-mile dirt trail through the park. This area is also managed by the Linn County Conservation Board.

Many areas of the Mississippi River bluff country have scenic, unpaved back roads in classic rural settings. Some of the best are in Allamakee County. See the discussion of Yellow River State Forest (Ride 10). For a descriptive brochure and map, contact Allamakee County Tourism at the address listed in that ride.

Paved Trails

The Cedar Valley Lakes Trail Network is a collection of four trails connecting several parks in the Cedar Falls/Waterloo vicinity. Over ten miles of the network are paved.

The Great River Road Trail is a 16-mile, concrete-surfaced shoulder of a hilly county road running along the Mississippi valley from Guttenburg to McGregor.

The Duck Creek Parkway Trail in Davenport, one of the Quad Cities, is a 12-mile urban greenbelt trail.

For Further Information

Blackhawk County Conservation Board
2410 West Lone Tree Road
Cedar Falls, IA 50613
(319) 266-0328 or 266-6813

Linn County Conservation Board
1890 County Home Road
Marion, IA 52302
(319) 398-3505

Linn County Trails Association
P.O. Box 2681
Cedar Rapids, IA 52406

Bike Shops and Clubs

ICORR (Iowa City Off Road Riders)
15 Birch Court
North Liberty, IA 52317

Melon City Bike Club, Inc.
P.O. Box 431
Muscatine, IA 52761

The shops mentioned below provided me with useful information. There are a number of other good bicycle shops throughout eastern Iowa; check the area yellow pages for more information.

Europa Cycle & Ski
4302 University Avenue
Cedar Falls, IA 50613
(319) 277-0734

Harper's Cycling & Fitness
1106 Grandview Avenue
Muscatine, IA 52761
(319) 263-4043 or 263-9073 fax

Lefler's Schwinn
1705 First Avenue
Iowa City, IA 52240
(319) 351-7433

On Two Wheels
3616 Eastern Avenue
Davenport, IA 52807
(319) 386-5533

Racquet Master Bike & Ski
345 Edgewood Road NW
Cedar Rapids, IA 52405
(319) 396-5474 or 396-4591 fax

or

321 South Gilbert Street
Iowa City, IA 52240
(319) 338-9401

Central Iowa

Most of central Iowa is a flat-to-rolling plain consisting of some of the richest agricultural lands in the world. Traveling on Interstates 35 or 80, you will see miles and miles of neatly organized, productive farms. Farther south, toward the state of Missouri, there are more hills and woodlands. Parts of the area were once busy with coal mining activity, which gradually became unprofitable because of the coal's high sulfur content. The major rivers of the central region flow southeastward toward the Mississippi River, and several have large reservoirs on them, providing flood control and recreational areas. In 1993 extensive flooding occurred on many of these rivers anyway, causing much damage to towns and parks throughout Iowa.

Iowa's capital city of Des Moines is the hub of this region, positioned at the center of the state's transportation systems. Other regional centers include Ottumwa, Marshalltown, Ames, Fort Dodge, and Mason City. The rural highway system throughout this region is very conducive to road bicycling, but finding places for mountain biking here in the heartland requires a bit of a search. The rides listed in this section include five rail trails and four parks with somewhat more challenging terrain.

RIDE 13   CINDER PATH

The 9.5-mile Cinder Path is Iowa's oldest rails-to-trails conversion trail, having been established by the Lucas County Conservation Board after the route was abandoned by Burlington Northern in 1972. Most of the trail follows the valley of the Chariton River, which provides a densely wooded corridor and lots of shade for bicycling in southern Iowa's hot summers. Near the Chariton end of the trail is Barber Woods, a county nature preserve in the Chariton River lowlands that contains a stand of hickory trees, otherwise rare in the area. There are several observation stands and rest stops built along this stretch that make nice spots for wildlife observation or a picnic. About two-thirds of the way to Derby you will encounter a covered wooden bridge, which was built after the railroad abandonment.

As an older trail, the Cinder Path shows its age a bit, with overhanging tree branches and some overgrown, eroded spots on the gravel, cinder, and packed-dirt trail surface, but this just adds to the trail's charm as an out-of-the-way destination. Remnants of the railroad days can still be seen here and there. This is a great trail for those looking for a quieter, more natural setting and a bit more of a riding challenge than the usual rail trail provides.

RIDE 13 *CINDER PATH*

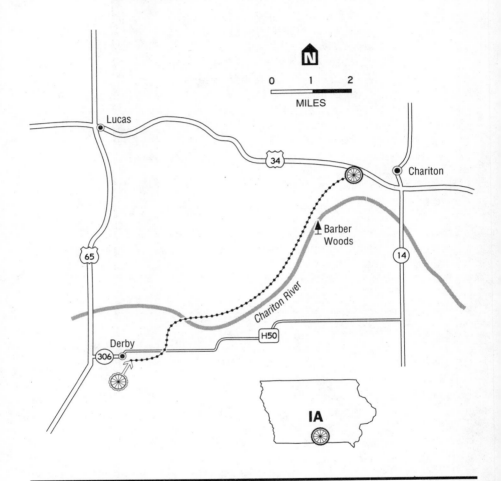

The Lucas County Historical Museum in Chariton includes exhibits of over 5,000 items from the community life and mining history of the region (open Wednesdays and Sundays). The town of Albia, 25 miles east, is a historic old mining and railroad town featuring good turn-of-the-century architecture.

General location: The trail runs between Chariton and Derby in Lucas County.
Elevation change: There is a very gradual uphill grade from Chariton to Derby.

Deep shadows predominate inside a covered bridge on
the Cinder Path.

Season: Midspring to late autumn.

Services: All services available in Chariton. Limited services in Derby.
Camping can be found at Red Haw Lake State Park, east of Chariton.

Hazards: You may encounter branches and rocks on the trail surface here and
there. One mile east of Derby is a high-speed county highway crossing.
Hunting is allowed in season.

Rescue index: Help is available in either town at the ends of the trail.

Land status: Lucas County Conservation Board.

Maps: An information brochure with a county map is available in the area.
A basic map of the trail can be found in the Iowa trail guide, *Enjoy Iowa's
Recreation Trails,* published by the Iowa Natural Heritage Foundation. See
the bibliography in the Iowa introduction for more information.

Finding the trail: The Chariton trailhead and parking lot are located on
US 34 on the western outskirts of Chariton. The Derby trailhead is hidden

behind some grain storage bins on the east side of town, 1 block south of the main city street. Parking is available at a nearby city park.

Sources of additional information:

> Lucas County Conservation Board
> Box 78
> Chariton, IA 50049
> (515) 774-4749; park ranger (515) 774-2314

> Chariton Chamber and Development Corp.
> (515) 774-4059

Notes on the trail: Across the highway from the Chariton trailhead is a 1.5-mile exercise trail. A 3.5-mile extension of the trail west of Derby is scheduled to be developed in the future.

RIDE 14 *LAKE AHQUABI STATE PARK*

Ahquabi State Park has a four- to five-mile loop trail around a reservoir lake in a hilly, heavily wooded setting. This wide single- to double-track trail presents several short climbs and curves and a lot of nice woodland touring at a moderate level of difficulty on a graveled, packed-dirt, and mowed surface. The park is a haven for wildlife, and there is a good chance you will see deer in the morning or evening hours. Ahquabi is a well-established state park where a number of 1930s Civilian Conservation Corps buildings are still providing service after sixty years. In 1994 and 1995, major renovation work was done in the park. The trails are open, but the causeway across the northeast arm of the lake remains to be completed.

Nearby Indianola is the location of Simpson College and the National Balloon Museum, where the history of ballooning is on display. Annual hot-air balloon contests are held here as well. Twenty miles to the north, the urban Des Moines area offers many services and attractions.

General location: Five miles south of Indianola in Warren County.
Elevation change: This moderately hilly region produces numerous short ups and downs around the perimeter of the lake.
Season: Midspring to late autumn.
Services: The state park has picnic, camping, and beach facilities. Other services can be found in Indianola or Des Moines.
Hazards: There are rocky spots and occasional branches and logs on some of the trail sections. Watch for vehicle traffic when crossing parking lots and park roads.

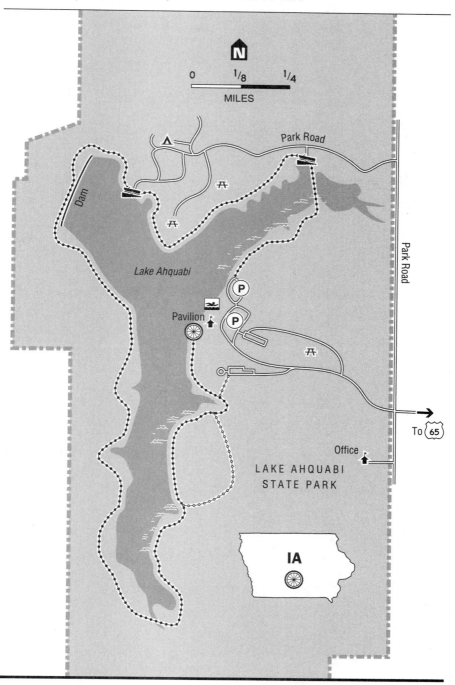

A quiet November day allows a late-season ride in Lake Ahquabi State Park.

Rescue index: There are almost always staff personnel and visitors in the park.

Land status: Lake Ahquabi State Park is managed by the Iowa Department of Natural Resources.

Maps: A park brochure with a trail map is available at the entrance station.

Finding the trail: The park is 5 miles south of Indianola on US 65, then 1 mile west on IA 349. The lake loop trail can be picked up from several points on the park road system. From the main parking lot at the beach and concession stand, the trail starts at the south edge of the beach area.

Sources of additional information:

> Lake Ahquabi State Park
> Indianola, IA 50125
> (515) 961-7101
>
> Bicycle Shop
> 106 East 2nd Avenue
> Indianola, IA 50125
> (515) 961-5341

Notes on the trail: Heading around the lake clockwise (south) from the beach area, the trail winds along the lakeshore and through the woods, crossing several small ravines and a bridge at the south end of the lake. The forested west side of the lake is the most remote section of the ride. After crossing the lake outlet, the trail corridor winds in and out of the picnic and boat ramp areas on the north side. The trail crosses a small causeway back to the east side and the final stretch back to the beach area.

There are other trails in the park designated for hikers only; please avoid biking on them. For the latest information on the trail system, check at the park office.

RIDE 15 *GREAT WESTERN TRAIL*

The Great Western Trail is a popular rail trail route that runs 17 miles from a suburban setting in Des Moines into some of Iowa's classic rural landscape of rolling hills, small fields and farms, and wooded river valleys. The smooth, crushed-limestone surface with periodic rest shelters and numerous access points allows for some easy out-and-back rides of various lengths. The original railroad bed dates back almost 100 years to the Chicago, St. Paul and Kansas City Railroad. A bit of the history of the area can be seen at a rest stop along the trail where you can read about the life of the now defunct town of Lida. The northern end of the trail shows the growth of modern Des Moines as it meanders past suburban homes and through a golf course. At the North River crossing, the trail passes through a heavily wooded corridor that is a haven for wildlife.

General location: The trail runs from southwest Des Moines in Polk County to Martensdale in Warren County.
Elevation change: This old railroad grade has very gradual elevation changes within a 150′ range.
Season: Midspring to late autumn. The area is often snow covered in the winter months.
Services: Rest rooms and some services are located at the trailheads in Des Moines and Martensdale and along the trail in the towns of Orilla and Cumming. There are 3 rest stops with water along the route. Other services can be found in Des Moines, Martensdale, and Indianola.
Hazards: Watch for vehicle traffic at the various road and highway crossings.
Rescue index: Help is as far as the next town along the trail.
Land status: The Polk and Warren County Conservation Boards have jurisdiction over their respective sections.
Maps: Trail map billboards are posted at the various access points. Printed maps can be obtained from the county conservation boards or from some local businesses. A map of the trail can also be found in the Iowa trail guide, *Enjoy*

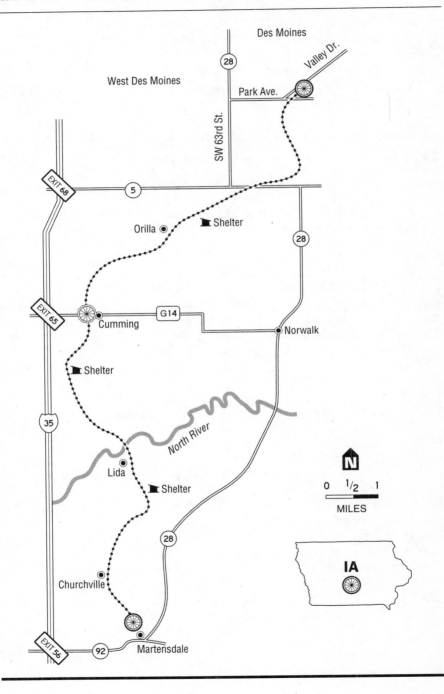

Iowa's Recreation Trails, published by the Iowa Natural Heritage Foundation. See the bibliography in the Iowa introduction for more information.

Finding the trail: The northern trailhead and parking area are located at Park Avenue and Valley Drive in Des Moines. There is parking and an access point in Cumming on CR G14. The southern trailhead and parking lot are on the western edge of Martensdale on Inwood Street.

Sources of additional information:

> Polk County Conservation Board
> Jester Park
> Granger, IA 50109
> (515) 999-2557

> Warren County Conservation Board
> 1565 118th Avenue
> Indianola, IA 50125
> (515) 961-6169

Notes on the trail: The last three-quarters of a mile at the Martensdale end of the trail is paved. Trail hours are from sunrise to sunset.

RIDE 16   *CHICHAQUA VALLEY RECREATION TRAIL*

This classic 20-mile railroad-grade trail crosses through a forested river valley and some open farm country in central Iowa's rich agricultural setting. The trail opened in 1987 and was built with a finely crushed limestone surface on the abandoned roadbed of the Chicago and Northwestern Railway. Originally the Wisconsin, Iowa, and Nebraska Railway, this section was built in 1883, bypassing the then-existing towns in the area. The present towns along the route appeared quickly at that time to provide water and wood for the steam-driven trains. Today, these railroad whistle-stop towns, Valeria, Mingo, Ira, and Baxter, provide trailside services for hikers and bikers.

The proximity to Des Moines and the presence of good trail facilities make this a popular bicycling route in the summer months, good for family outings and easy touring. Attractions in the area include the Jasper County Historical Museum in Newton; the Trainland USA toy train museum in Colfax; and in Des Moines, a zoo, numerous museums, historical sites, and the state capitol building.

General location: The trail runs from near Bondurant, about 5 miles outside of Des Moines, to Baxter, in Jasper County.

Elevation change: Gradual elevation changes within a range of about 200′ are noticeable at times on this old railroad grade.

RIDE 16 *CHICHAQUA VALLEY RECREATION TRAIL*

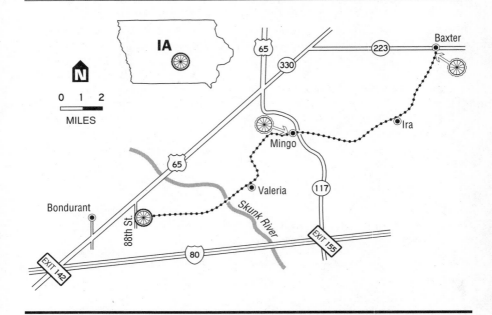

Season: Midspring to late autumn. The area is often snow covered in the winter months.

Services: There are rest rooms and picnic shelters at the west end trailhead and in Mingo, Ira, and Baxter. Basic services are available in the towns along the trail. Nearby camping facilities include Chichaqua Wildlife Area on the Skunk River northeast of Bondurant. All other services can be found in Newton and Des Moines.

Hazards: Watch for vehicle traffic at the various road and highway crossings. Use caution passing walkers and casual bicyclers.

Rescue index: Help is as far as the next town along the trail.

Land status: The Polk and Jasper County Conservation Boards have jurisdiction over their respective sections.

Maps: Printed maps can be obtained from the county conservation boards or from some local businesses. A map of the trail can also be found in the Iowa trail guide, *Enjoy Iowa's Recreation Trails,* published by the Iowa Natural Heritage Foundation. See the bibliography in the Iowa introduction for more information.

Finding the trail: The trailhead on the west end is one-half mile south of US 65 on 88th Street, one mile east of Bondurant. The trailhead at the east end is located in downtown Baxter off IA 223. Additional parking can be found in Valeria, Mingo, and Ira.

The Chichaqua Valley Trail runs through a typical mix of Iowa's woodlands and farmlands.

Sources of additional information:

Polk County Conservation Board
Jester Park
Granger, IA 50109
(515) 999-2557

Jasper County Conservation Board
115 North 2nd Avenue East
Newton, IA 50208
(515) 792-9780

Notes on the trail: "Chichaqua" was the Fox Indian name for the Skunk River. The trail is officially closed during the hours of 10:30 P.M. to 5 A.M. No trail fee is required.

RIDE 17

MCFARLAND AND PETERSON COUNTY PARKS

These two parks, only a few hundred yards apart on the Skunk River, contain an interconnected trail system totaling over eight miles that winds through forested river bottoms and along the edges of prairie and farm fields. There is a connection to an additional six miles of double-track trails and gravel roads north along the Skunk River Greenbelt, an adjacent collection of county land. The mostly single-track trails in the county parks are made up of packed dirt and mowed grass, with some sandy and soft areas and small hills, resulting in some easy to moderate riding conditions. You will be riding through a wide variety of vegetation in this area, from large hardwood stands in the river bottoms to open, brushy areas along fields and river banks. The trail configuration allows for a series of loops and out-and-back side trips that can total anywhere from one to ten miles as you desire. The better part of a day can easily be spent exploring here.

Remnants of the history of the Skunk River region show up along the trail as you pass an old nineteenth-century cabin, cross a stagecoach trail, and visit a pioneer cemetery. A small lake and beach in the Peterson Park section make a good destination for a picnic or afternoon break. The Conservation Center at the McFarland trailhead is the location of the county environmental education program, and information on local natural history and the parks can be picked up here. Nearby Ames is the home of Iowa State University and of a number of excellent museums.

General location: About 4 miles north of Ames in Story County.
Elevation change: Moderate hills in the Skunk River Valley provide a few good climbs and descents in this otherwise flat region.
Season: Midspring to late autumn. In times of high water, various sections of the trails here may be impassable. The area is usually snow covered during the winter months.
Services: McFarland Park has water, rest rooms, picnic areas, and a primitive camping site. All other facilities can be found in Ames.
Hazards: There are a variety of trail surface conditions here, including some sandy spots and a few log stairways, so watch your speed. Be aware of traffic while you're riding between the two parks on the county road.
Rescue index: There are generally staff people at McFarland Park during the daytime.
Land status: Story County Conservation Board.
Maps: Trail maps can be picked up at the conservation center at the trailhead in McFarland Park.

The Skunk River is a focal point of the trail system in Peterson and McFarland parks.

Finding the trail: You can reach the parks from Ames on CR R63 (Dayton Avenue). Go right at a **T** intersection one-half mile to the McFarland entrance, or take Interstate 35/exit 116. Travel west one mile on CR E29, and north on CR R63. The trail into McFarland Park runs north from the west end of the parking lot at the Conservation Center. A trail connects McFarland Park with Peterson Park and the trails there. There is also parking in the Peterson unit at the entrance on the east side of the Skunk River, as well as near the beach at the west end of the park. You can reach the north end of the Skunk River Greenbelt from I-35/exit 123, then traveling west a short distance to a parking lot on the south side of CR E18.

Sources of additional information:

Story County Conservation Board
McFarland Park
RR 2, Box 272E
Ames, IA 50010-9651
(515) 232-2516

Michael's Cyclery
320 Main Street
Ames, IA 50010
(515) 232-9125 or (800) 246-9125

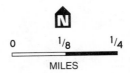

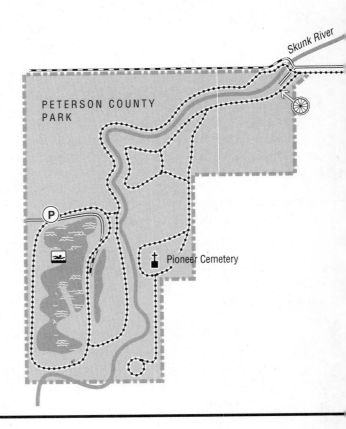

PETERSON COUNTY
PARK

Skunk River

P

Pioneer Cemetery

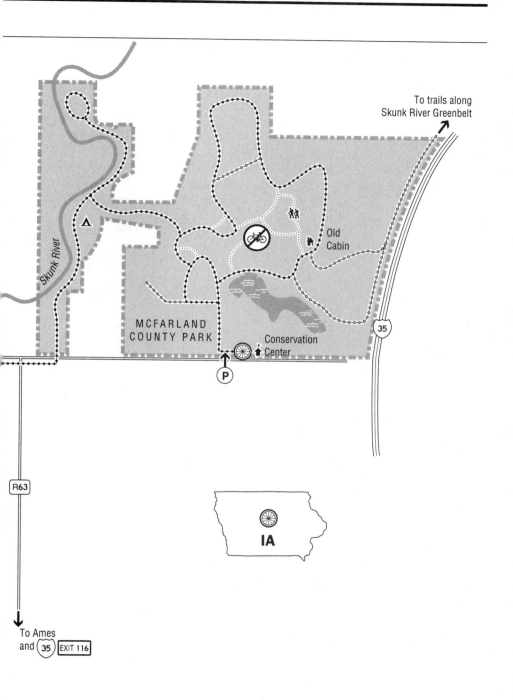

To trails along
Skunk River Greenbelt

Skunk River

Old
Cabin

MCFARLAND
COUNTY PARK

Conservation
Center

35

P

R63

IA

To Ames
and (35) EXIT 116

Two Wheel Travel
300 Main Street
Ames, IA 50010
(515) 232-3669 or 232-7448 fax

Notes on the trail: A few of the trails in the center of the McFarland unit have been designated for hikers only. Watch for signs and avoid riding bike trails when conditions are muddy or wet. One suggested route that encompasses much of the area begins at the parking lot and takes you out to the historic cabin. After reaching the cabin, turn north and follow the outer perimeter of the McFarland trails, keeping to the right, around to the Skunk River flood-plain. You will be passing through the edge of a restored prairie, then entering the thick hardwood forest typical of Iowa's river valleys. After passing a hikers-only stairway and crossing a bridge, you will end up in the primitive camping area. Here you can turn north and ride a loop along the old stage trail, or head south (left) along the river to the park boundary and the road over to Peterson Park.

In Peterson, you can do out-and-back loops on either side of the river. The trail on the west side follows closely along the river through floodplain wood-lands and along the edge of a farm field to a loop around the small lake with a swimming beach. Beware, one of only two flat tires I had in all the miles of researching this book came from a large thorn at the edge of a cornfield on this loop. On the east-side trail at the parking lot, a double-track trail leads to some more small wooded loops, to the pioneer cemetery, which dates back to the mid-1800s, and to an old sandy excavation area. You can retrace your route or take the county road directly back to the McFarland parking lot. Park hours are 5 A.M. to 10:30 P.M.

RIDE 18 *THREE RIVERS TRAIL*

Since 1991 Humboldt County in north central Iowa has developed about 35 miles of two old railroad grades into a scenic, rural recreational trail system that largely parallels the eastern and western branches of the Des Moines River. With quiet forested river lowlands on the western end, small towns, numerous bridges, and the open farmlands of the eastern end, this trail offers a lot of variety. There are access points with parking in Bradgate, Rutland, Dakota City, and Thor, so easy out-and-back rides of almost any length can be done. Most of the original railroad trestles are still in use on the trail, and the longest ones, over IA 3 and over the East Fork of the Des Moines, provide great views. A spur trail extending from Humboldt to Gotch State Park along another old rail line is being completed with only one section in litigation. The eastern extension of the trail into Eagle Grove is currently being developed by

RIDE 18   *THREE RIVERS TRAIL*

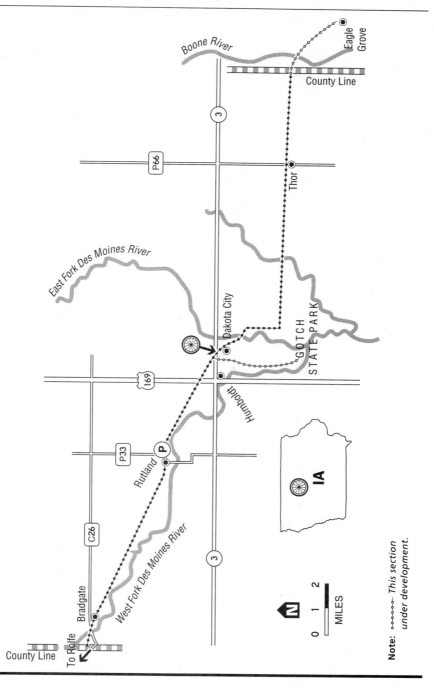

Note: ○○○○○ *This section under development.*

The present end of the Three Rivers Trail meets the old railroad tracks west of Bradgate.

Wright County. At the west end, the limestone trail surface ends at the old rails, several miles short of Rolfe in a thickly wooded wildlife area.

The Dakota County Farm Museum in Dakota City features a restored and furnished one-room school, a log cabin, a barn, and a mansion dating back to 1879. West of Bradgate is the site of the last Indian battle in Iowa.

General location: The completed trail will run from Rolfe in Pocahontas County across Humboldt County to Eagle Grove in Wright County. The Humboldt County section is essentially finished.
Elevation change: There are only slight elevation changes on this trail.
Season: Midspring to late autumn. Cross-country skiing is possible in winter.
Services: Trailside rest rooms are available in Rutland and Dakota City. A picnic shelter and campground are located in Gotch Park, 4 miles south of Humboldt on the spur trail. All other facilities are available in Humboldt, Dakota City, or Fort Dodge.
Hazards: Watch for traffic at road crossings. Golf carts are allowed on the trail to enable handicapped access.
Rescue index: Help is available in the towns along the trail.
Land status: Humboldt County Conservation Board.
Maps: A visitor's guide with a map can be obtained from the Humboldt County Conservation Board, listed below. A map of the trail can be found in the Iowa trail guide, *Enjoy Iowa's Recreation Trails,* published by the Iowa

Natural Heritage Foundation. See the bibliography in the Iowa introduction for more information.

Finding the trail: Access with parking is available in Bradgate, Rutland, Dakota City (on 5th Street North), and Thor.

Sources of additional information:

Humboldt County Conservation Board
Courthouse
Dakota City, IA 50529
(515) 332-4087
or Humboldt Chamber of Commerce, (515) 332-1481

Notes on the trail: Trail hours run from sunrise to sunset. No user fee required.

RIDE 19   *LIME CREEK NATURE CENTER*

The Lime Creek Nature Center is located on land donated by two cement companies, and it is returning to its natural state as a forested flood plain of the Winnebago River on the north side of Mason City. Wildlife diversity and the occasional remnants of nineteenth-century life are highlights you'll encounter here. There are about seven miles of trails in or adjacent to the nature center area that form a network of several loops and side trails suitable for an hour or so of pleasant riding in a quiet wooded setting and around the perimeter of a small prairie area. The terrain is mostly easy, but the mixed trail surface of grass, clay, rocks, and a few short hills add some challenge to the riding. A connecting trail leading south into Mason City crosses a creek at a scenic little limestone canyon, then passes the foundation of Russell's Mill which, established in 1855, was the first enterprise in the city.

The nature center facility has a nice display of mounted animals, a collection of live animals, a resource library, and periodic programs. Mason City has several good museums, an interesting downtown area, and the country's last electric trolley system, which runs out to the popular lake town of Clear Lake.

General location: Two miles north of Mason City in Cerro Gordo County.
Elevation change: This area is relatively flat, with only a few little hills along the Winnebago River banks.
Season: Midspring to late autumn. The region is usually snow covered during the winter months. The spring thaw period in April may render the trails too soft and muddy for riding.

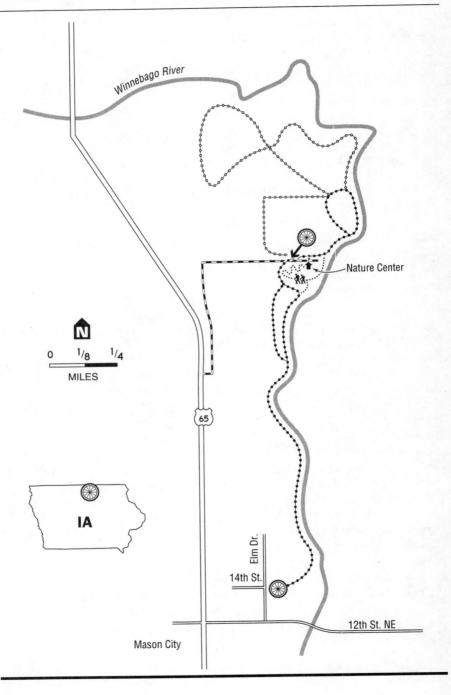

Winnebago River

Nature Center

N

0   1/8   1/4
MILES

65

IA

Elm Dr.

14th St.

12th St. NE

Mason City

A creek crossing provides views of a small canyon on the trail from Mason City into Lime Creek Nature Area.

Services: The nature center visitor's building has water and rest rooms, as well as a nature exhibit. All other services are available in Mason City.

Hazards: The rich soil of the riverbanks can be slippery when wet, and there are occasional rocky spots. Be prepared to yield to walkers.

Rescue index: Help is usually close by.

Land status: Cerro Gordo County Conservation Board.

Maps: A map billboard is on display outside the visitor center. A handout brochure/map is also available inside the center.

Finding the trail: Take US 65 north two miles from downtown, then three-quarters of a mile east on a well-marked access road. Trails depart from the visitor center parking lot or the end of the access road near the maintenance buildings. A trailhead at 14th and Elm Drive in Mason City leads to the nature area, which is 1 mile north.

Sources of additional information:

Lime Creek Nature Center
3501 Lime Creek Road
Mason City, IA 50401
(515) 423-5309

Wayne's Ski & Sports
12 South Federal Avenue
Mason City, IA 50401
(515) 423-2851 or 423-3825 fax

Notes on the trail: Two one-mile-long loops at the north end of the trail system are currently closed until the spring of 1996 while the area is "reconditioned" by the cement company that formerly occupied the site. You can still bike on a couple of miles of trail that travel around the edge of an old field, along the banks of the Winnebago River, and past the ruins of an old brewery. Avoid using the concrete "Easy Access Trail," which is just to the south of the visitor center. This was designed with handicapped individuals, casual walkers, and families in mind. An alternate trail across from the west end of the parking lot provides access to the south end trails. Nature Center hours run from 6 A.M. to 10:30 P.M.

RIDE 20   *SHELL ROCK RIVER GREENBELT AND PRESERVE*

The Shellrock Greenbelt is a one-lane dirt road running five miles through a wooded corridor spread out along the Shell Rock River. Although vehicle traffic is allowed at most times, it is nonetheless a pleasant place to do a relaxed ride. Along the route is the Shellrock Preserve, a wildlife refuge with a few additional trails; at the north end is Wilkinson Pioneer Park, with a picnic area and a scenic covered bridge. This mostly easy route can be done as an out-and-back ride or combined with some of the local back roads to create a loop. Like many trails in Iowa, this one is particularly nice on a sunny day in October, when autumn colors are at a peak and the limestone cliffs along the river are more visible.

General location: Along the Shell Rock River between Rock Falls and Nora Springs in northwestern Cerro Gordo County.
Elevation change: Occasional low hills along the river provide some ups and downs in this otherwise flat area.
Season: Midspring until the first snows in late autumn.
Services: Commercial services are available in Nora Springs and Mason City.
Hazards: Slow vehicle traffic may be using the corridor road. Watch for fast-moving vehicles on the crossroads. Hunting is allowed along the greenbelt corridor. Use caution during hunting season.
Rescue index: Help can be found in the two towns on either end of the greenbelt.
Land status: Cerro Gordo County Conservation Board.
Maps: A county park information brochure and location map (showing the location of the trails) is available from the Lime Creek Nature Center.
Finding the trail: Access to the trail on the north end of the greenbelt is located on 295th Street across the river and east of the south end of Wilkinson Pioneer Park near Rock Falls. The main entrance to Wilkinson Park is at the

RIDE 20 *SHELL ROCK RIVER GREENBELT AND PRESERVE*

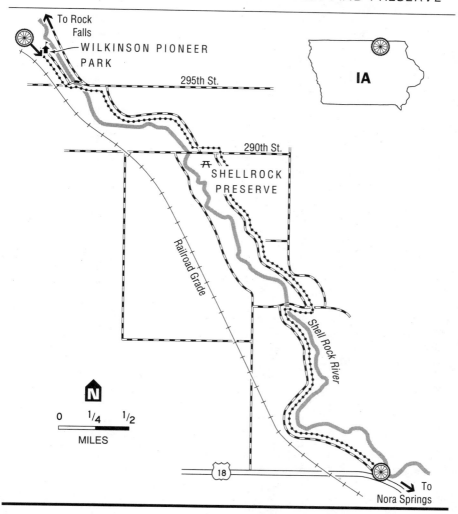

end of CR B20 in Rock Falls. There is an access point on the south end of the greenbelt road on US 18 on the western outskirts of Nora Springs.

Sources of additional information:

Lime Creek Nature Center
3501 Lime Creek Road
Mason City, IA 50401
(515) 423-5309

Wayne's Ski & Sports
12 South Federal Avenue
Mason City, IA 50401
(515) 423-2851 or 423-3825 fax

Notes on the trail: Wilkinson Park is a good place to start a ride in this area. The greenbelt road heads southeast from 295th Street along the east side of the river and meanders past low limestone cliffs overlooking the river and over some low hills. You will cross a bridge before you reach 290th Street, where the greenbelt route continues just to the east as it enters the Shellrock Preserve. There are more picnic facilities here and a few side trails. The route continues south for two miles and on a local road crosses to the west side of the river, where it continues south through a mixture of woodlands and meadows. The route ends at US 18. Cerro Gordo County parks are open from 6 A.M. to 10:30 P.M.

ADDITIONAL MOUNTAIN BIKING OPPORTUNITIES IN CENTRAL IOWA

Unpaved Trails

Cedar River Greenbelt/Harry Cook Nature Trail. These two trails form a six-mile link between Mitchell and Osage in Mitchell County, mostly following the Cedar River. There are good facilities in both towns and along the trails. Contact Mitchell County Conservation Board, 415 Lime Kiln Road, Osage, IA 50461, (515) 732-5204.

Fort Dodge Nature Trail is a three-mile-long rail trail following a wooded creek on the outskirts of Fort Dodge. The trailhead is on Williams Drive north of downtown.

The Heart of Iowa Nature Trail, still under development, provides some pleasant rural riding on the finished portions, and some opportunities for the more adventurous to explore some undeveloped sections of the corridor. The trail is being built on a 32-mile section of abandoned railroad grade that runs through a variety of open farmland and forested river and creek valleys between Slater in Story County and Melbourne in Marshall County. A seven-mile section on the west end is almost complete, and a four-mile section in Marshall County is open and features the Hoy Bridge, a 200-foot concrete arch bridge over a deep creek gorge.

Plans for the future of the Heart of Iowa Nature Trail are ambitious. It is designated as part of the American Discovery Trail, a coast-to-coast route coordinated by the American Hiking Society. A 100-mile loop trail is also envisioned, connecting the Heart of Iowa Trail with the Chichaqua Valley Trail and the Saylorville–Des Moines Trail. East from Cambridge, the trail

Biking through a covered bridge is a highlight in Wilkinson Park near the north end of the Shell Rock River Greenbelt.

corridor is in an undeveloped state, but parts of it are mountain bikeable. Maintenance and drainage work are being planned for the rough sections around the Skunk River, where damage from the 1993 floods remains. There is a county bridge over the river south of the trail route that is now open. The undeveloped trail continues to the east county line. The best bet for exploring these unfinished sections may be to do them in the late spring, after the spring thaw, but before the grasses and weeds get too tall. Contact Story County Conservation Board, McFarland Park, RR2 Box 272E, Ames, IA 50010-9651, (515) 232-2516, or Marshall County Conservation Board, 1302 East Olive Street, Marshalltown, IA 50158, (515) 754-6303.

Pioneer Trail and Comet Trail near Grundy Center. These two rail trails are under development in Grundy County, north of Marshalltown. Half of the planned 12-mile Pioneer Trail is completed; eventually it will connect four towns with local parks and natural areas. The Comet Trail has four completed miles of trail connecting two towns with the Wolf Creek Recreation Area. Contact the Grundy County Conservation Board, P.O. Box 36, Morrison, IA 50657, (319) 345-2688.

The Polk County Conservation Board (in the Des Moines area) is currently evaluating various alternatives for bike trails in their park system, including some areas where informal mountain biking activity is now going on. Contact them for the latest information on biking opportunities: Polk County Conservation Board, Jester Park, Granger, IA 50109, (515) 999-2557.

Prairie Rail Trail is a 12-mile route being developed from Roland to Zearing along a flat, grassy corridor paralleling CR E18 in Story County. The Roland trailhead is on the northeast edge of town adjacent to the city ballpark.

Wapsi–Great Western Line, near Riceville in Howard and Mitchell Counties. This four-mile trail, starting on the east side of Riceville, follows a river corridor and an old railroad grade, crossing an 1887 wrought-iron truss bridge. A loop extension will increase the length to ten miles.

Paved Trails

Clive Greenbelt Trail follows the wooded corridor of Walnut Creek for six miles through the western suburbs of Des Moines.

Dickenson County Spine Trail is a ten-mile link between the town of Spirit Lake and Milford in the popular lakes district of Iowa.

Linn Creek Greenbelt Parkway in Marshalltown connects a series of city parks over a six-mile course along Linn Creek and the Iowa River.

The 34-mile *Raccoon River Valley Trail* is the longest paved trail in Iowa, roughly following the Raccoon River through a wooded and rural setting from Waukee to Yale, mostly in Dallas County west of Des Moines. Many trailheads and services are available on this popular route. Contact Dallas County Conservation Board, 1477 K Avenue, Perry, IA 50220, (515) 465-3577.

Saylorville–Des Moines River Trail runs 24 miles from the Saylorville Lake Recreation Area along the Des Moines River into the capital city, where it becomes the East River Bike Trail. The north end of the trail continues past Polk City to Big Creek State Park, where it winds along a reservoir lake. Numerous recreational facilities surround the Saylorville Reservoir, and some have been used as sites for more technical biking, but check on current rules in these areas. Contact U.S. Army Corps of Engineers, 5600 NW 78th Avenue, Johnston, IA 50131, (515) 276-4656.

Volksweg Trail is a seven-mile trail running from the town of Pella to the Red Rock Reservoir area. Other state and local recreation areas surround the reservoir and have additional trails. Check locally for the status of mountain biking on these trails. Contact U.S. Army Corps of Engineers, Park Manager, Lake Red Rock, 1105 Highway T15, Knoxville, IA 50138, (515) 828-7522, or Mike Visser's Cycle Works, 745 210th Avenue, Pella, IA 50219, (515) 628-3481.

Bike Shops and Clubs

The shops mentioned below provided me with useful information. There are a number of other good bicycle shops throughout central Iowa; check the area yellow pages for more information.

Bill's Cyclery
3719 SW 9th Street
Des Moines, IA 50315
(515) 282-7161

Bike World
2929 Merle Hay Road
Des Moines, IA 50311
(515) 255-7047 or 255-2025 fax
Club: Iowa Off Road Cyclists (IORC)

Michael's Cyclery
320 Main Street
Ames, IA 50010
(515) 232-9125
or 1-800-246-9125

Modern Bike
1515 East Euclid Avenue
Des Moines, IA 50313
(515) 263-2000

North Iowa Touring Club
P.O. Box 1281
Mason City, IA 50401

Rasmussen's Bike Shop
840 1st Street, Suite A
West Des Moines, IA 50265
(515) 277-2636

Wayne's Ski & Sports
12 South Federal Avenue
Mason City, IA 50401
(515) 423-2851 or 423-3825 fax

Western Iowa

The western quarter of Iowa is part of the Missouri drainage, where numerous small rivers flow to the southwest. Much of the western edge of the region is made up of low undulating hills that were formed by deposits of wind-blown loess at the end of the Ice Age. This is the most hilly part of western Iowa, and it contains the best terrain for mountain biking. The northwestern corner of the state, which borders the Big Sioux River, a major tributary of the Missouri, is an extension of the flat, fertile plain of central Iowa. Near the Minnesota border and the town of Spencer is a district of glacially carved lakes, which is a popular vacation area.

Major cities of the region are Council Bluffs and Sioux City, both on the Missouri River. Council Bluffs, across from Omaha, Nebraska, is the approximate location of Lewis and Clark's first meeting with Indians as they journeyed up the river in 1804. In Sioux City, the monument to Sergeant Floyd, the only person to die on the Lewis and Clark Expedition, was the first registered National Historic Landmark.

Two state parks with challenging trails, a recreation area with easy trails, and three rail trails are described in this section.

RIDE 21   *WAUBONSIE STATE PARK*

Almost eight miles of hilly, forested, multiple-use trails are available for mountain biking here in one of Iowa's classic state parks. The oak, hickory, ash, and elm hardwood forest is situated in an area of steep, eroded bluffs formed from loess, a wind-driven sediment deposited in the Missouri River valley in the waning centuries of the Ice Age. Originally an equestrian area, the trails here are generally wide single-track, with rough and eroded spots possible and lots of good climbs and descents. The trail surface is mostly graded and packed dirt, so sections can be quite muddy in the spring and when it rains. Laid out as a series of loops, the trails can provide rides of various lengths, providing a morning or afternoon of moderate to aggressive biking. Combined with a trip to Indian Hills State Park (Ride 44), which is 30 miles south in Nebraska, you can put in a busy day of riding the hilly Missouri River bluffs, probably the most challenging terrain in the Omaha–Council Bluffs region.

The Sunset Ridge Interpretive Trail, a hiking trail near the park office, runs one mile to an overlook where—on a clear day—you can see four states: Iowa, Nebraska, Missouri, and Kansas.

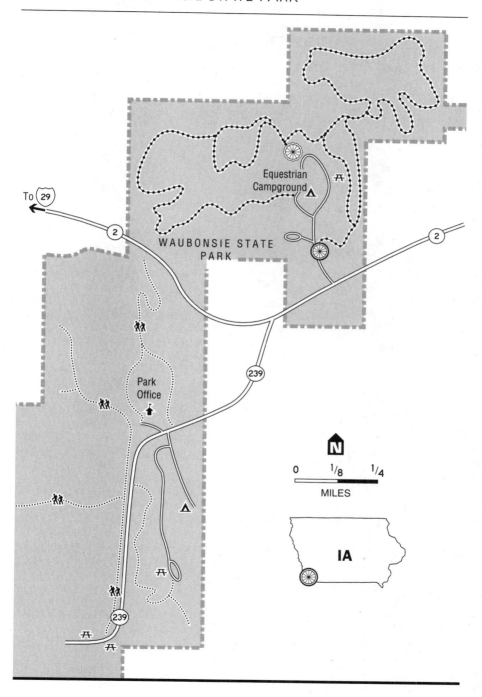

To 29

2

2

WAUBONSIE STATE PARK

Equestrian Campground

239

Park Office

239

N

0   1/8   1/4
MILES

IA

The multi-use trails in Waubonsie State Park climb up and down through many thickly wooded ravines.

General location: Six miles south of Sidney in Fremont County.

Elevation change: There is a range of about 200′ in the trail area.

Season: Midspring to late autumn. The loess soil can be very muddy after a rainfall and during the spring thaw.

Services: The park has water, rest rooms, and picnic and camping facilities. The nearby towns of Hamburg, Sidney, and Nebraska City have most other services.

Hazards: Watch your speed on blind corners and steep descents, and stay alert for horseback riders.

Rescue index: Help can be reached at the park office on IA 239.

Land status: Waubonsie State Park is managed by the Iowa Department of Natural Resources.

Maps: A brochure with a diagram map is available at the park office.

Finding the trail: From Interstate 29/exit 10, follow IA 2 for 5 miles east to the Equestrian Campground, one-quarter mile east of the junction with IA 239. There are 3 trailheads in that immediate campground area.

Sources of additional information:

Waubonsie State Park
RR2, Box 66
Hamburg, IA 51640
(712) 382-2786

Notes on the trail: There are a few directional signs along the trails, but not all junctions are marked, so pay attention to your route and be prepared to explore a bit. These trails get considerable horseback use, and you should be prepared to yield to pedestrian and horse traffic. Sections of the trail system have been graded, exposing the soil, so it is perhaps best to plan riding here in times of relatively dry weather. Avoid skidding descents and corners to minimize mountain bikers' share of trail erosion. The wooded, north-facing slopes in this area may take some time to dry out in the spring and after significant rainfall. Please do not bike on the park trails intended for hiking.

RIDE 22   *WABASH TRACE NATURE TRAIL*

The 63-mile Wabash Trace runs southeast from the outskirts of the Omaha–Council Bluffs metropolitan area through scenic low-lying hills, farmland, and small communities to the Missouri state line. About 52 miles are complete, and an additional 11 miles are expected to be completed soon, making the trail Iowa's longest rail trail corridor to date. The finely crushed limestone surface provides for easy biking, and the many towns and trailheads in the area have good support facilities, which enable you to choose from out-and-back rides of many different lengths. Along the trail there is an interesting contrast of towns ranging from busy county centers to quiet villages left over from the railroad era that time is slowly passing by. Open rural vistas alternate with heavily wooded sections, where the trail forms a shady tunnel through the trees. Wildlife is common along the trail corridor.

The original Wabash Depot in Shenandoah, which is on the National Register of Historic Places, has been restored and moved to a park adjacent to the trail route. Today, one can stand on that quiet platform and imagine those glory days of the steam railroads when the whistle blew and the station became the center of town life. A growing urban recreational trail system in Omaha and Council Bluffs will complement the Wabash Trace Nature Trail, providing residents and visitors to this area with a variety of bicycling opportunities.

RIDE 22 *WABASH TRACE NATURE TRAIL*

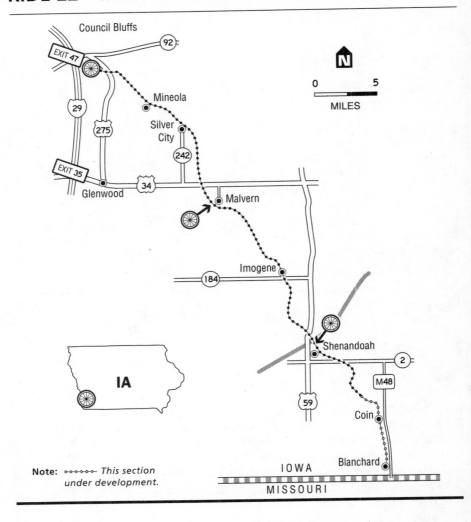

Note: ◦-◦-◦-◦-◦ *This section under development.*

General location: The trail runs from Council Bluffs to Blanchard, on the Missouri border, crossing through Pottawattamie, Mills, Fremont, and Page Counties.

Elevation change: As a former railroad grade, this trail has very gradual elevation changes, ranging from 980′ at the northern trailhead to 1,250′ in the hills farther south. In the area around Shenandoah, the trail is more level, ranging from 1,000′ to 1,100′.

Season: Midspring to late autumn. There will often be snow cover in the winter months.

The Wabash Trace Nature Trail meanders south from Shenandoah toward the Missouri border.

Services: Parking, water, rest rooms, and a map sign are available at the Council Bluffs trailhead. Some services are available in the various trailside towns listed below in "Finding the trail." All other services are available in Council Bluffs, Malvern, and Shenandoah.

Hazards: Use caution when passing pedestrians and crossing roads with motor vehicle traffic. Keep an eye on the weather conditions during the thunderstorm season. On long rides, be sure to carry plenty of water and use sunscreen.

Rescue index: There is generally help nearby in the towns along the trail. The northern end of the trail, from Council Bluffs to Malvern, receives the most frequent use.

Land status: Southwest Iowa Nature Trails Project is currently managing the land for the Iowa Natural Heritage Foundation.

Maps: A brochure with trail information and a general location map is available at some businesses and tourist information offices in the area. A basic map of the trail can be found in the Iowa trail guide, *Enjoy Iowa's Recreation Trails,* published by the Iowa Natural Heritage Foundation. See the bibliography in the Iowa introduction for more information.

Finding the trail: The northern trailhead can be reached from US 275, just southeast of the junction with IA 92 in southeast Council Bluffs. In Malvern, there is some parking at the trail 2 blocks west of Main Street on West 5th Street.

Shenandoah has parking in Sportsmans Park at the Wabash Depot on IA 48, three-quarters of a mile east of US 59. The trail heads east out of Shenandoah at another park on CR J32, just east of where IA 48 turns north. More parking, water, and picnic facilities are located there. Trailheads in Mineola, Silver City, Imogene, Coin, and Blanchard all have parking.

Sources of additional information:

Southwest Iowa Nature Trails Project, Inc.
P.O. Box 69
Malvern, IA 51551
(712) 246-4444

Notes on the trail: The trail now is virtually complete from Council Bluffs to Shenandoah. Construction is currently under way on a major bridge for the trail across the Nishnabotna River just north of Shenandoah. The finished trail continues through Shenandoah and ends 5 miles south. Surfacing is currently progressing on the final 11 miles of the corridor near the small town of Coin. The section is passable by mountain bike. Trail passes of $1 per day are required.

RIDE 23   *WILSON ISLAND RECREATION AREA*

There are about five miles of trails here—a mixture of mowed double-track and packed-dirt single-track—forming a series of loops out from the campground area. It is generally easy riding, but you will encounter some bumpy spots and maybe some downed branches and logs. The inner loops wind through the woodlands and along some fields and meadows. The banks of an oxbow lake, a remnant channel of the Missouri, are the highlight of the outer loop. The thick cottonwood forest supports much wildlife, and if you watch and listen, you most likely will observe birds, small animals, and possibly deer. The campground, picnic facilities, and playground make this a nice spot for a family outing, and the trails are suitable for younger riders and novices.

Just to the north of Wilson Island is the DeSoto National Wildlife Refuge, a major stopping point for migrating ducks and geese and a wintering spot for

RIDE 23 *WILSON ISLAND RECREATION AREA*

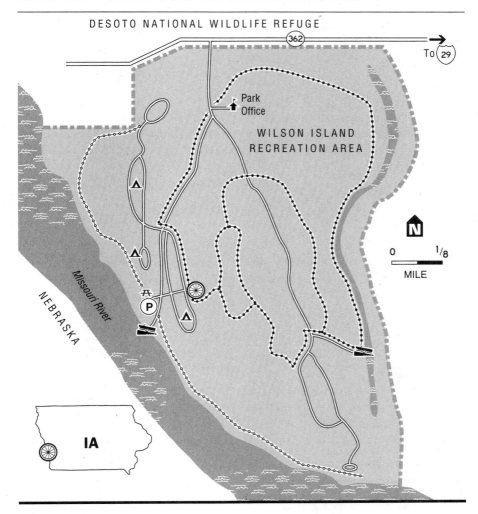

DESOTO NATIONAL WILDLIFE REFUGE

362

To 29

Park
Office

WILSON ISLAND
RECREATION AREA

N

0   1/8
MILE

Missouri River

NEBRASKA

IA

bald eagles. The visitor center here has two nature trails and some historical
and wildlife conservation displays.

General location: On the Missouri River, about 20 miles north of the Omaha–
Council Bluffs area.
Elevation change: This area is located on a very level floodplain of the
Missouri River.
Season: Midspring to late autumn. Snow cover is likely in the winter months.

Services: The recreation area has rest rooms, water, and picnic and camping facilities. Other services are available in the town of Missouri Valley or Council Bluffs.

Hazards: These are multi-use trails, so keep an eye out for hikers. Watch for traffic when you cross the paved park roads. Hunting is allowed here in season.

Rescue index: There are generally staff personnel or visitors present in the park.

Land status: Wilson Island State Recreation Area is managed by the Iowa Department of Natural Resources.

Maps: A brochure with a diagram map is available at the entrance station.

Finding the trail: The entrance to the recreation area is on IA 362, 4 miles west of Interstate 29/exit 72. Parking is available at the picnic area near the boat ramp on the river. The trails depart from the east side of the campground circle, just south of the central crossroad.

Sources of additional information:

Wilson Island State Recreation Area
RR2, Box 203
Missouri Valley, IA 51555
(712) 642-2069

Notes on the trail: Trail junctions are not all marked, so keep track of your general location. Be prepared for mosquitoes in the warm evenings of summertime.

RIDE 24   *SAUK RAIL TRAIL*

A 13-mile segment of an old Chicago Northwestern Railroad line has been converted into a recreational trail in the quiet, rural setting of Carroll and Sac Counties. Much of the trail traverses open farmland, where the sun and the wind and wide-open vistas will give you a feeling for the scope of western Iowa; but there are also small stretches of woodlands and valleys that provide some shade and refuge for wildlife. Friendly small towns unhurried by the pace of life elsewhere offer places to rest and look around. Like Iowa's other rail trails, the smooth, level, limestone surface presents little technical challenge other than distance.

Future plans for the Sauk Rail Trail include extending it to more than double its length and connecting it with existing state parks on each end of the trail. A 3.8-mile, paved hiking and biking trail in Swan Lake State Park south of Carroll is open for use and will eventually be connected to the rest of the Sauk Trail via city streets and parks. On the north end, in Sac County, the trail

RIDE 24 *SAUK RAIL TRAIL*

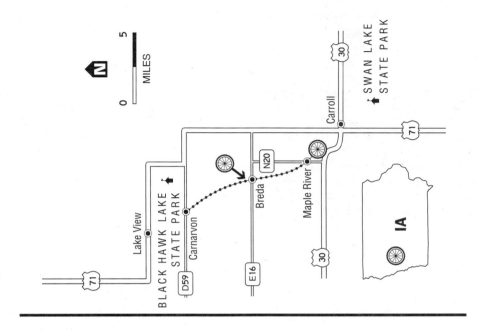

will loop around Black Hawk Lake and provide access to Black Hawk Lake State Park, for a total trail system of 33 miles.

General location: The trail currently runs from Maple River in Carroll County to Carnarvon in Sac County.

Elevation change: This is a very level trail in an area of gently rolling hills.

Season: Midspring to late autumn. There often will be snow cover during the winter months.

Services: There is camping at Swan Lake State Park south of Carroll and Black Hawk Lake near Lake View. Other services can be found in Carroll, Lake View, and Sac City.

Hazards: Watch for vehicle traffic at the various road and highway crossings.

Rescue index: Help is as far as the next town along the trail.

Land status: The Carroll and Sac County Conservation Boards have jurisdiction over their respective sections.

Maps: A basic map of the trail can be found in the Iowa trail guide, *Enjoy Iowa's Recreation Trails,* published by the Iowa Natural Heritage Foundation. See the bibliography in the Iowa introduction for more information.

The restored railroad station in Breda on the Sauk Rail Trail provides a spot for a shady break.

Finding the trail: The Maple River Trailhead, 3 miles west of Carroll on US 30 and 1 mile north on CR N20, has parking. There are rest rooms, water, and parking at the old train station on CR E16 in Breda. The Carnarvon trailhead on CR D59 also has parking.

Sources of additional information:

Carroll County Conservation Board
Route 1, Box 240A
Carroll, IA 51401
(712) 792-4614

Sac County Conservation Board
2970 280th Street
Sac City, IA 50583
(712) 662-4530

Steve's Bicycle Sales & Repair
225 East 5th Street
Carroll, IA 51401
(712) 792-6397

Notes on the trail: Trail hours are from 5 A.M. to 10:30 P.M. There is a user fee of $1 per person per day to help with upkeep of the trail.

RIDE 25   *STONE STATE PARK*

Stone State Park is located in the hilly bluffs east of the Big Sioux River and its confluence with the Missouri. These rugged hills are part of the wind-blown soil or loess hills formed after the Ice Age, typical of western Iowa along the Missouri River. There are about six miles of hilly multi-use trails available for mountain bike use in the southern section of the park. These challenging trails provide some moderate to difficult riding on a mostly wide, packed-dirt single-track corridor through a thick hardwood forest. Spectacular views of the Big Sioux and Missouri River valleys to the west are the reward for climbing to the top of the highest ridge. Several loops are possible, all of which have some interesting ups and downs. This is one of the nicest places to ride in western Iowa.

The park dates back to the 1880s, when it was a private preserve and zoo. In the 1930s the Civilian Conservation Corps program built many of the classic park buildings that are in the park today. Many attractions can be found in nearby Sioux City, including several good museums, a casino river-boat, and a 100-foot-tall monument marking the grave of Sergeant Floyd, the only member of the Lewis and Clark Expedition to die during the epic journey.

General location: In the northwest corner of Sioux City adjacent to the Big Sioux River in Woodbury County.

Elevation change: The hilly trails range in elevation from 1,150´ to almost 1,400´ at the top of the ridge.

Season: Midspring through late autumn. The park will generally have snow cover during the winter months. Spring thaw and wet weather may make the trails too muddy for biking.

Services: Picnic areas, water, rest rooms, and camping are available in the park. All other facilities can be found in Sioux City.

Hazards: Steep descents, eroded areas, and loose rocks may be encountered on the trails. Be alert for traffic if you bike on the narrow, hilly park roads.

Rescue index: Help is usually not far away in this park.

Land status: Stone State Park is managed by the Iowa Department of Natural Resources.

Maps: A park brochure with a map is available at the park office.

Finding the trail: The main park entrance can be reached on IA 12 on the west side of the city. The best trailhead and a parking lot are located just inside the east entrance of the park on Talbot Road.

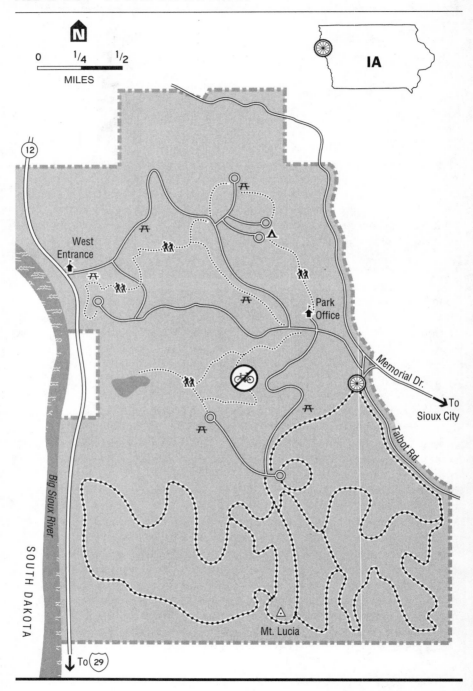

N

0   1/4   1/2

MILES

IA

12

West
Entrance

Park
Office

Memorial Dr.

To
Sioux City

Talbot Rd.

Big Sioux River

SOUTH DAKOTA

Mt. Lucia

To 29

Three states can be seen from Mt. Lucia on the Stone State Park trails.

Sources of additional information:

Stone State Park
Sioux City, IA 51103
(712) 255-4698

Albrecht Cycle Shop
200 5th Street
Sioux City, IA 51101
(712) 258-6050

Notes on the trail: The trailhead on Talbot Road has a sign post with a trail map, and the trails are marked as well. The trails alternately climb and descend through thickly wooded ravines, where they eventually reach Mt. Lucia, the highest point at 1,391′. Here you'll have a great view of the surrounding landscape. Follow the outside of the loop system and you'll see the best of what's here, but don't hesitate to check out other paths.

Two miles of the trail system on the west side are currently closed for rehabilitation because of erosion damage. There are other hiking and nature trails in the central and northern parts of the park that are not designated for bicycle use. Please avoid using those routes and stay on the park road system if you want to explore other sections of the park. The Iowa Department of Natural Resources is monitoring mountain bike use of the trails in the state parks where biking is allowed, so all riders should cooperate by presenting a good image of the sport. If you are uncertain of current trail conditions, check at the park office before riding here.

RIDE 26 *PUDDLE JUMPER TRAIL*

This is an easy two-mile railroad-conversion trail connecting the towns of Orange City and Alton in a heavily farmed area with few other nearby trails. Despite its short length, there are a number of trailside facilities that make this ride a good family outing. Alongside the crushed-stone surface of this trail you'll notice a marked exercise fitness course and a number of prairie plant identification signs. At the center access point, halfway along the trail, is a wooden picnic shelter with rest rooms and water. There are several observation platforms built at intervals for viewing a small herd of buffalo in the field just beyond the right-of-way.

The trail runs through mostly open rural countryside, with a wooded corridor providing shade at the west end. The busy college town of Orange City has a distinct Dutch flavor, complete with windmills and tulips, and the quieter town of Alton, nestled in the Floyd River valley, presents a postcard image.

General location: The trail runs between Orange City and Alton in Sioux County.
Elevation change: There is a very gradual rise in elevation from east to west here.
Season: Midspring to late autumn. Cross-country skiing is possible in winter.
Services: Rest rooms, a picnic shelter, and water can be found at the central trailhead at the midpoint of the trail. All commercial services can be found in the two towns.
Hazards: Watch for hikers and children at the various trail stops.
Rescue index: Help is as close as Alton and Orange City.
Land status: City of Orange City.
Maps: A basic map of the trail can be found in the Iowa trail guide, *Enjoy Iowa's Recreation Trails,* published by the Iowa Natural Heritage Foundation. See the bibliography in the Iowa introduction for more information.
Finding the trail: The Orange City trailhead is located one-quarter mile south of IA 10 on CR K64. The central trailhead and the Alton trailhead are reached by gravel roads heading south from IA 10. Parking is available at all 3 points.

Sources of additional information:

City Hall
125 Central Avenue SE
Orange City, IA 51041
(712) 737-4885

RIDE 26 *PUDDLE JUMPER TRAIL*

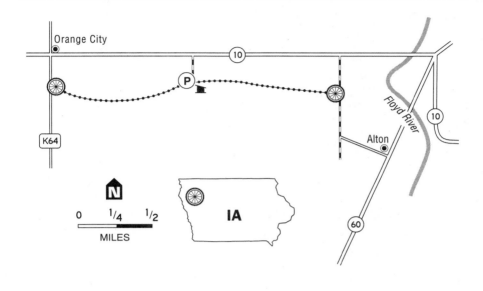

The Bike Store
118 2nd Street NW
Orange City, IA 51041
(712) 737-3180 or 737-2910

Notes on the trail: No trail user fee is required. To bike into the town of Alton from the Alton trailhead, ride south on the gravel road up a hill to one of the city cross streets. Look for the church steeple. Near the center of town is a city park that has water.

ADDITIONAL MOUNTAIN BIKING OPPORTUNITIES IN WESTERN IOWA

There are a number of trails in Council Bluffs along the Missouri River. Riverside Park south of I-80 and Dodge Park near I-480 provide parking and access to the levee system and various trails along the river bottoms. Check local bike shops for further information.

The Dickinson County Spine Trail is a ten-mile paved recreation trail that connects the towns of Spirit Lake, Okoboji, and Milford in the Iowa lakes district. This area is a popular vacation destination, and there are many family attractions available. Contact: Dickinson County Conservation Board, 1013 Okoboji Avenue, Milford, IA 51351, (712) 338-4786.

Bike Shops and Clubs

The shops mentioned below provided me with useful information. There are a number of other good bicycle shops throughout western Iowa; check the area yellow pages for more information.

Albrecht Cycle Shop
200 5th Street
Sioux City, IA 51101
(712) 258-6050

Sioux City Scheels
2829 Hamilton Boulevard (Market Place)
Sioux City, IA 51104
(712) 252-1551 or 252-4577 fax

Sioux County Bicycle Club
(712) 737-8055

True Wheel Cycling & Fitness
120 West Broadway
Council Bluffs, IA 51501
(712) 328-0767
An additional location is at
5480 North 90th Street, Omaha, NE 68134.

Bibliography

Streight, Dan, *Eastern Nebraska & Western Iowa Trail Guide,* third edition, Bike Rack, Omaha, NE, 1994.

KANSAS

Kansas is at the center of the contiguous 48 states and as a result is a historical and geographical transition point from north to south and from east to west. Northeastern Kansas is an extension of the forested lowland river valleys of the vast Mississippi basin. It is an area of rich farmland and dynamic Midwestern cities. In the southeast, the hilly terrain reflects the character of the rugged Ozark region in Missouri and Arkansas. The central and north-western prairies of Kansas rise steadily to meet the high plains and Rocky Mountain front range in Colorado. And in the far southwest, the arid plains are similar to the hot semideserts of the Southwest, being less than 60 miles from Texas and New Mexico at the corner point.

With an area of 82,275 square miles, Kansas is the largest of the five states covered in this guidebook. The variation in topography of the Kansas plains can be grouped conveniently into three sections. Eastern Kansas is a region of lowlands below 1,000 feet in elevation consisting of grasslands and farmlands interspersed with wooded areas of oak, hickory, and elm. A small edge of the Ozark upland appears in the southeast corner near Missouri and Oklahoma. And along the Missouri River, an extension of the wind-formed loess hills found in Nebraska and Iowa has left rich soil.

The central section of Kansas is a series of distinct groups of hills divided by many small stream valleys; the Flint Hills, the Red Hills, and the Smokey Hills all have areas of unusual rock formations, cliffs, and buttes. The western third of Kansas, in contrast to the other plains states to the north, is generally the flattest part of the state, sloping gradually up to about 3,500 feet at the Colorado border.

Kansas has a continental climate of hot summers and moderate to cold win-ters. Rainfall is heaviest in the spring and summer months, and humidity decreases as you travel from east to west. Contrasts in weather systems between north and south often produce violent storms, especially in summer, when thunderstorms and tornadoes can be a hazard.

This region of the Great Plains has been the subject of European-American exploration for almost 500 years. Francisco Vasquez de Coronado, traveling down the course of the Cimarron River, reached present-day Kansas in about 1540. After the Louisiana Purchase was made by the United States in 1803, a series of expeditions passed through the area, including Lewis and Clark in 1804, Zebulon Pike in 1806, and Stephen H. Long, who described the region as the "Great American Desert," in 1819.

The Santa Fe Trail, which ran from northeast to southwest across present-day Kansas, was the first major European-American development in the area. It was mainly a trade route, whereas other trails to the north were emigration routes for settlers seeking new land. Trade with the Spanish in Mexico had gone on for years, but when Mexican independence was established in 1821, traffic on the route picked up considerably and received steady use until the advancing railroads rendered the trail obsolete in the 1880s.

Kansas was opened to settlement in 1854 by the Kansas-Nebraska Act, and the Native American population was forced south into what is now Oklahoma. Violence broke out in areas of Kansas over the slavery issue, and the struggle continued until Kansas became a state in 1861 at the start of the Civil War. The railroad boom of the 1870s brought large numbers of settlers, pushing the borders of agriculture westward, until drought created the dust bowl from the prairie lands that had been largely plowed under.

The present economy of Kansas is a balance between manufacturing, services, and agriculture. There are declining oil reserves in the south-central region, and coal is found in the southeast. Tourism consists to a great degree of providing transportation services for east-to-west travel across the state. Today, Kansas and its population of 2,478,000 face the future relatively free of the urban problems found on the east and west coasts.

Mountain Biking in Kansas

Communities of avid road bicyclists have long been established in the larger population centers of Kansas, particularly in the Kansas City–Lawrence–Topeka area and in Wichita. However, state, regional, and local authorities are just becoming aware of the need for off-road trail facilities. In some places, park personnel and local bike shops or clubs have joined forces to develop trail systems. As a result, a network of places to mountain bike is emerging throughout the state.

Many of the bikeable trail systems in Kansas are found in recreation areas centered around reservoir lakes that were developed originally for flood-control and irrigation purposes. Some of these areas are managed by the U.S. Army Corps of Engineers, and others are now under the control of the state park system or county park departments. These recreation areas generally have the most challenging single-track biking opportunities.

Kansas has a considerable network of unpaved back roads, and there are mountain bike enthusiasts who prefer the adventure of riding the wide-open expanses of the prairie, particularly in the rolling Flint Hills region. The rails-to-trails movement is also being introduced to Kansas. For example, the 50-mile-long Prairie Spirit Rail Trail, south of Ottawa, offers families and riders of all abilities a pleasant place to ride and see the sights. And finally, the Cimarron National Grassland, one of the few extensive pieces of federal land in Kansas, offers some trails and back roads where you'll enjoy mountain biking with a western flavor along the route of the old Santa Fe Trail. As I describe some of these areas in more detail, I'm sure you will be as pleasantly surprised as I was at the variety of ways to see Kansas by mountain bike.

For Further Information

Travel and Tourism Division
Kansas Department of Commerce
700 SW Harrison, Suite 1300
Topeka, KS 66603-3712
(800) 2 KANSAS

Kansas Department of Wildlife and Parks
Office of the Secretary
900 SW Jackson, Suite 502
Topeka, KS 66612-1233
(913) 296-2281

Kansas Trails Council
1737 Rural Street
Emporia, KS 66801
(316) 342-5508

Eastern Kansas

Much of eastern Kansas is a transition region between the oak and hickory forest lands prevalent in Missouri to the east, and the open, tall-grass prairie common in areas to the west. Prairie fires, once a natural occurrence, acted to renew prairie habitat and inhibit the spread of the forest cover. Changing climate patterns, as well as the intervention of human activity, bring continual shifts in the balance between these open grasslands and the woodlands.

The chaotic history of this region is today only visible in the museums and monuments as one travels through this pastoral land. Settlement of the vicinity began steadily after the Santa Fe Trail opened in 1821, eventually forcing the resident Native American tribes out of the area. There was considerable warfare in eastern Kansas before the Civil War between pro- and antislavery groups, and noted abolitionist John Brown was active in the area in 1855. "Bleeding Kansas" was the name attached to the state during this violent period. Today, the region is predominately agricultural, with a service sector based in the strong urban areas of the northeast. Coal mining was undertaken in various areas, eventually centering in the Pittsburg area, and oil and natural gas reserves are being extracted in the southern portion of the state.

The cities of northeastern Kansas have developed an avid mountain biking population that has helped to encourage the establishment of some good trail systems in the region. Many of the mountain bike trails in the parks of eastern Kansas are available because of cooperation between park officials and local bike shops and clubs. These people are to be commended for their efforts. In this section, I will describe three reservoir parks with some fairly technical trails, some city and county parks with small but good trail systems, a rail trail route, and a unique set of trails in the Fort Leavenworth Military Reservation.

RIDE 27   *PRAIRIE SPIRIT RAIL TRAIL*

The only major railroad-conversion trail in Kansas is now being developed in the rolling farmlands of the east-central part of the state south of Interstate 35. Eighteen miles of the planned 50-mile route are completed with a crushed-limestone surface, and two more development phases have been scheduled to finish the project. Some undeveloped sections of the trail corridor are rideable, grassy double-track. The trail surface and adjacent corridor are wider than many other rail trails, and it has an open, spacious feel.

RIDE 27   *PRAIRIE SPIRIT RAIL TRAIL*

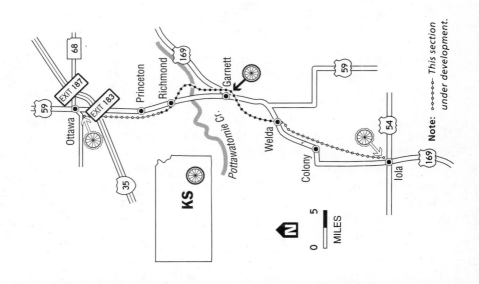

Scenery along the trail is a mixture of rural farmlands and hardwood forest with stands of hickory and oak. Remnants of the original tall-grass prairie habitat common in the eastern Great Plains can be found in places. Towns along the line provide interesting destinations for the trail user, as they did for railroad passengers a century ago. Ottawa has several blocks of restored, colorful, classic Main Street architecture, and in Garnett, an ornate county courthouse dominates the town square.

The railroad right-of-way was originally built by the Leavenworth, Lawrence and Galveston Railroad Company in the 1860s, acquired by the Atchison, Topeka & Santa Fe line in 1899, and abandoned in 1990 by the KCT Railway Corp. The Kansas Department of Wildlife and Parks began to implement the trail project in 1992, and Friends of the Prairie Spirit Rail Trail, a volunteer group, is coordinating a fund-raising effort.

Since the trail is within one hour of driving from the Topeka, Lawrence, and Kansas City urban areas, this trail should prove to be popular with recreational bicyclists looking for a pleasant rural tour.

General location: The trail corridor runs from Ottawa in Franklin County to Iola in Allen County. The currently completed 18-mile section is centered around Garnett in Anderson County.

Elevation change: This is essentially flat terrain with only gradual variations in elevation.

Season: The trail should be bikeable year-round, except during times of winter snowfall and spring thawing.

Services: All services can be found in Ottawa, Garnett, and Iola.

Hazards: Watch for vehicle traffic at road crossings. Be courteous when passing hikers and other trail users.

Rescue index: Help is available in the various towns along the way.

Land status: Kansas Department of Wildlife and Parks.

Maps: A pamphlet with a very basic location map is available from regional bike shops and the Kansas Department of Wildlife and Parks.

Finding the trail: The trail generally parallels US 59. Access can be made from the various towns along the route.

Sources of additional information:

> Friends of the Prairie Spirit Rail Trail
> P.O. Box 71
> Garnett, KS 66032-0071
>
> Kansas Department of Wildlife and Parks
> See address and phone listed under the Kansas introduction, above.

Notes on the trail: The finished 18-mile section of the trail runs from Richmand to Welda. North of Garnett, Pottawatomie Creek is one of the most natural woodland environments found along the trail, and there is a good chance you will see some wildlife in the area. Deer, raccoon, wild turkey, herons, beaver, and many other creatures may be seen, particularly if you are riding in the early morning or evening hours.

RIDE 28   HILLSDALE STATE PARK

Hillsdale Lake is a newcomer to the system of reservoirs in Kansas. Little more than a decade old, this Corps of Engineers project doesn't yet show up on the topographical maps, and recreational facilities around the lake are still being developed by the Kansas Department of Wildlife and Parks. There are up to about 20 miles of lightly developed trails looping around the bluffs and woods along the east side of the lake. The area has been used as a horseback riding area for a number of years, and now mountain bike use is becoming more common.

Most of the sections of trail are dirt single-track, but there are some areas of grassy double-track where the route follows old roads and fence lines. Biking on these trails varies from moderately easy to moderately difficult, with

RIDE 28 *HILLSDALE STATE PARK*

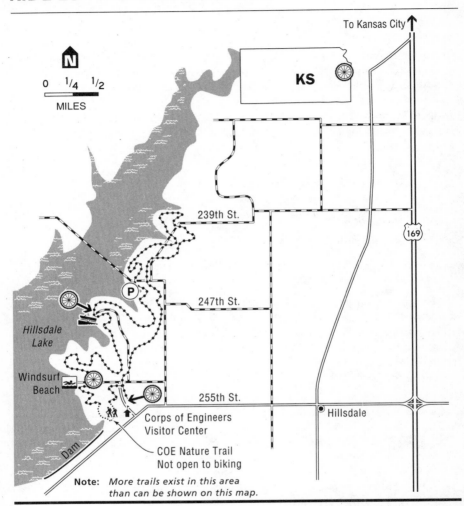

To Kansas City

KS

0   1/4   1/2
MILES

239th St.

247th St.

*Hillsdale
Lake*

Windsurf
Beach

255th St.

169

Hillsdale

**Corps of Engineers
Visitor Center**

COE Nature Trail
Not open to biking

Dam

Note: *More trails exist in this area
than can be shown on this map.*

narrow, brushy sections, occasional steep spots with scattered limestone rocks and downed branches and logs. The areas of public land are mostly wooded, with some older stands of oak and hickory and second-growth, brushy forest cover advancing into old farm fields. Some open meadowlands and a few limestone cliffs add some variety to the setting. This is a pleasant area, great for a quick escape from the city to do some leisurely exploration or some fast-paced riding.

The Hillsdale reservoir is part of an extensive flood-control project implemented by the U.S. Army Corps of Engineers in the vast Missouri River drainage, which was authorized in 1954. The dam was completed in 1982 on Big Bull Creek, a tributary of the Marais de Cygnes River, eventually creating the 7400-acre lake and its 51 miles of shoreline. Wildlife is fairly abundant in the park, where you'll see deer, raccoon, coyotes, occasional rattlesnakes, and lots of waterfowl. The submerged trees in the lake provide good fish habitat, so fishing is popular here. Spring and autumn can be nice times of the year to use the trails here, when the days are cooler than in the summer and the lack of leaves provides a more open feel to the terrain.

General location: In Miami County, about 15 miles south of Olathe (metropolitan Kansas City).

Elevation change: Moderately hilly terrain along the bluffs of the reservoir provide up to 100′ of vertical relief.

Season: The trails should be rideable most of the year except during times of winter snow, spring thawing, or significant rains.

Services: Water, rest rooms, a beach, and a campground are part of the Hillsdale State Park facilities. Hillsdale has several small stores. All commercial services can be found in the town of Paola or in metropolitan Kansas City.

Hazards: Uneven terrain, rocks, and occasional steep hills require your attention. Some sections of the trail close to the lakeshore may be flooded in times of high water. Hunting is a popular activity in the reservoir area. Check locally for seasons.

Rescue index: Help should be available at the visitor center or other recreational facilities.

Land status: U.S. Army Corps of Engineers, Kansas City District. The Kansas Department of Wildlife and Parks has management authority over recreational use of the Hillsdale lands.

Maps: No complete map of the trail system is available at this time.

Finding the trail: From US 169, take 255th Street west through Hillsdale about 2 miles to the state park area. Three good places to park and start your ride are the Corps of Engineers visitor center, the windsurfing beach, or the Marysville boat ramp, 1.5 miles north of the visitor center. The latter two sites require a Kansas state park entry permit.

Sources of additional information:

Hillsdale State Park
26001 West 255th Street
Paola, KS 66071
(913) 783-4507

Project Manager, Hillsdale Lake Office
U.S. Army Corps of Engineers
Route 3, Box 205
Paola, KS 66071
(913) 783-4366

Notes on the trail: The various dirt roads that cross the park lands provide access to different points along the trail system and allow for many possible combinations of routes to ride. Some trails get much more use than others, with the northern end getting the least. The western half of the trail system roughly parallels the contours of the lakeshore, winding north in and out of little bays. The eastern half of the system zigzags through woods and fields, crossing the various local roads to return to the start. Periodic sections of the trail system have been marked with red ribbons, but don't count on them being everywhere. Yield to equestrians using the trails, and respect private property that adjoins the park lands. Do not bike on the Hidden Spring Nature Trail near the Corps of Engineers visitor center. The state park has recently instituted a fee system for vehicle entrance.

RIDE 29   *BLACK HAWK HORSE, BIKE, AND HIKING TRAIL*

The Black Hawk Trail is one of the many recreational facilities at Pomona Lake, another of the flood-control reservoirs in Kansas managed by the U.S. Army Corps of Engineers. This route is actually a parallel set of two trails, mostly single-track, that run along the narrow corridor between the normal shoreline of the reservoir and the public land boundary. Most of the area is wooded, with oak and other hardwoods, and there is much brushy second-growth around old fields and meadows. You are never far from views of the water, with old stone fences, overgrown roads, and other remnants of the past appearing here and there.

There are almost 25 miles of trails in the system as it stretches around both sides of a bay. The parallel trails run along the east side for a distance of over seven miles, in effect creating a narrow loop of fifteen miles. A single trail continues around the north and west sides of the bay, adding another ten miles to the total. These sections can be done as an out-and-back ride, or combined with local dirt roads to form short loops. Most of the trails are relatively level, mostly dirt, with some rocky areas and narrow spots, creating a moderately challenging course. The section along the west side of 110-Mile Creek northwest of Forbes Road is the most hilly part of the trail system.

Pomona Lake was created by a 110-foot dam in 1963 as part of the project to limit flooding in the Kansas and Missouri River watersheds. Other recreational facilities around the lake include eight developed parks and the Pine Ridge Interpretive Center, which provides environmental education on the local area. 110-Mile Creek got its name from being that distance west of Independence, Missouri, on the old Santa Fe Trail. After the Native Americans were moved out of the area in 1859, settlement proceeded rapidly; and with the coming of the railroads, coal mining became the dominant industry for a few years in the 1880s. Today, the region is mostly agricultural.

RIDE 29 *BLACK HAWK HORSE, BIKE, AND HIKING TRAIL*

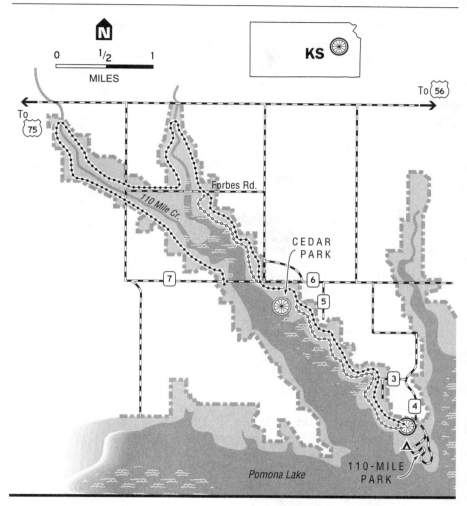

General location: About 25 miles south of Topeka on Pomona Lake in Osage County.

Elevation change: The trails parallel the shoreline of the reservoir and stay within a 50′ range of the normal lake elevation of 975′.

Season: Trails should be accessible most of the year except during times of winter snow or significant rains. There may be periods of high water, when portions of the trail near the shore are impassable.

Services: Water, rest rooms, and picnic and camping facilities can be found at various points around Pomona Lake, including 110-Mile Park at the trailhead. All commercial services are available in Lyndon, the county seat, or Topeka.

The Black Hawk Trail system winds through the wooded slopes adjacent to Pomona Lake.

Hazards: High water may make crossing some low areas on the trail hazardous. Hunting is allowed on much of the project land.

Rescue index: There are generally visitors present in the established park facilities. Access to a road can usually be made every few miles.

Land status: U.S. Army Corps of Engineers, Kansas City District.

Maps: A trail map can be obtained from the Information Center at the dam or by calling in advance.

Finding the trail: The trailhead is located at the entrance to 110-Mile Park on the north side of the lake. Take US 75 south 4 miles from the US 56 junction, then go east on Anderson Turnpike (a local road) for 5 miles, and then 4 miles south to the park. There are some signs giving directions. Other access points to the trail system include Cedar Park, on Interior Road 6, and various points on Forbes Road.

Sources of additional information:

Pomona Project Office
U.S. Army Corps of Engineers
Route 1, Box 139
Vassar, KS 66543
(913) 453-2201

Notes on the trail: Two blaze systems define the route of the trails. Orange blazes mark the route along the lakeshore. Blue blazes mark the higher route roughly following the project area boundary. The single trail on the north side is marked with blue blazes, and the section along the west side of the creek and bay is marked with orange blazes. Additional trails are planned for the west side of the bay that will almost double the length of the system.

Charlie's Checkpoint is a primitive group campsite about 1 mile from the trailhead that may be reserved in advance. Although local rules state that bicycles have the right-of-way over horses, you should be prepared to yield if necessary, as a matter of courtesy and good will. Please stay on the trails and leave any gates you may encounter as you find them.

RIDE 30   *SHAWNEE MISSION PARK*

Shawnee Mission Park, the largest in the Johnson County park system, allows off-road mountain biking along a one-mile section of nature trail on a low, forested ridge overlooking the park lake. With the additional interconnected side trails meandering through the area, there are perhaps three to four miles of mostly moderate single-track riding with a variety of technical features that keep anyone looking for a moderate challenge interested. The dirt track is generally smooth, but there are sections of limestone rocks, occasional logs, tight corners, and overhanging branches to watch out for.

This is the sort of small technical area where it is most fun just to head in for an hour or two and follow your impulses as to which way to turn. One trail trends northeastward to Ogg Road, and various alternate branches take off here and there. When you are ready to call it quits, you can work your way back to the start or exit to the park roads. Without leaves in the spring and fall the ridge is relatively open and airy. In summer, the trees and brush produce thick tunnels of greenery for a more enclosed feeling.

Immediately to the west of the park is Mill Creek Streamway Park, another Johnson County park, where there is an eight-mile paved walking and bicycling trail comprised of a loop at the south end below a dam and a meandering extension to the north along the Mill Creek lowlands. This system can be reached from the same trailheads used for the mountain bike trails in Shawnee Mission Park. This combination of the two trail systems offers something for all levels of recreational riders, making this park one of the most popular riding areas in the Kansas City area.

General location: In the city of Shawnee in Johnson County.
Elevation change: Rolling hills in the park produce some short climbs and descents.
Season: The park is open all year. Trails should be rideable most of the year except during periods of winter snow, spring thawing, or significant rainfall.

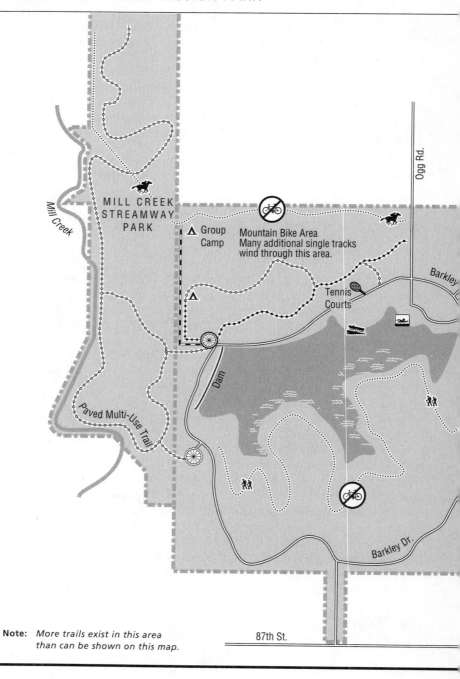

Note: *More trails exist in this area
than can be shown on this map.*

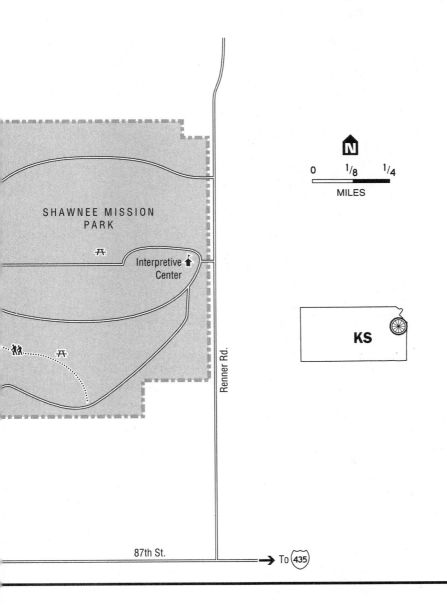

SHAWNEE MISSION
PARK

Interpretive
Center

Renner Rd.

N

0   1/8   1/4
MILES

KS

87th St.   To 435

The small mountain bike trail network in Shawnee
Mission Park can provide a few hours of enjoyable riding.

Services: The park has water, picnic areas, and other recreational facilities. All other services are available in the Kansas City area.

Hazards: Watch for traffic on the park roads. Be alert for the usual hazards of technical trails—rocks, logs, water bars, sharp corners, and overhanging branches.

Rescue index: Help is readily available in the park.

Land status: Johnson County Park and Recreation District.

Maps: An information pamphlet and park map are available from the park interpretive center at the entrance road.

Finding the trail: From Interstate 435, take Exit 3/87th Street west, then take the first right (north) onto Renner Road and go 1 mile to the park entrance. Take Barkley Drive through the park to the trailhead parking lot at the north end of the dam. The adjacent paved bike trail in Mill Creek Streamway Park can be reached from this trailhead or from a larger parking lot just up the hill from the south end of the dam.

Sources of additional information:

Shawnee Mission Park
7900 Renner Road
Shawnee, KS 66219
(913) 888-4713

Bike Source
11912 West 119th Street
Overland Park, KS 66213
(913) 451-1515 or (800) 728-8792

Notes on the trail: Toward the east end of the trail system, there are spur trails exiting to the tennis courts on Barkley Road and out to Ogg Road. On the west end, some of the trails exit near a group campsite on a dirt north-south access road; follow this access road south, then east a short way, and return to the trailhead at the dam. The trail system can be fairly busy at times, so watch out and listen for other bikers, and control your speed. Please do not ride on the horseback trails that run along the north side of the bike trail area from Ogg Road to the Mill Creek Streamway Park. Other hiking and horseback trails in the park should be avoided as well. Summer park hours are 5 A.M. to 11 P.M. Hours vary in other seasons.

RIDE 31 *LAWRENCE RIVERFRONT PARK TRAILS*

The north side of the Kansas River in Lawrence has two types of trails that should appeal to mountain bikers of most abilities. The Lawrence Riverfront Park Trail is a ten-mile system of recreational bike paths on the top of the levees along the river. The bike paths provide easy, nontechnical riding for casual and family riders. Adjacent to the east end of this system is a series of trails on the river floodplain with more challenging single-track riding through the wooded lowlands. This approximately four-mile out-and-back course (8 miles total) is mostly packed dirt with some sandy spots and can be fairly fast riding. It is moderately difficult, with a few challenging sections of dips, short climbs, tight corners, and good-sized logs. For an alternative to returning on the single-track trail, there are a number of points where you can cut through to the levee trail for a quick cruise back to town.

Lawrence is a great city for bike enthusiasts. These trails can be a warm-up for a trip to the nearby Clinton State Park, which features probably the best technical biking area in Kansas (see the next ride). Lawrence itself is an interesting city, with a strong cultural background dating back to 1854, when New Englanders began to settle here. The city has an avid bicycling community and a good network of urban bike routes.

RIDE 31 *LAWRENCE RIVERFRONT PARK TRAILS*

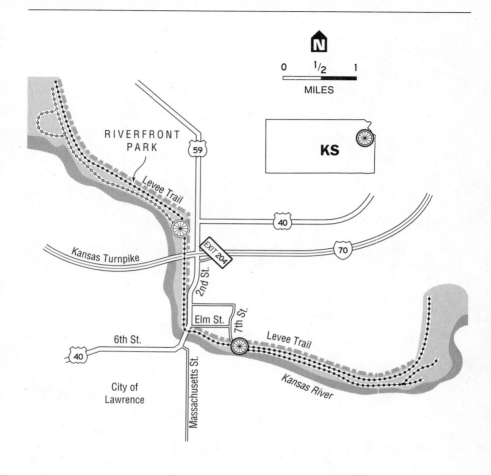

General location: On the north side of the Kansas River in the city of Lawrence.

Elevation change: The trails are located on a flat river floodplain.

Season: The trail system should be accessible most of the year except during times of winter snow, spring thawing, or significant rains. There may be periods of high water, when the trails on the river side of the levee are impassable.

Services: All services can be found in the city of Lawrence.

Hazards: On the floodplain trails there are some sharp corners, steep dips, and occasional logs. Watch for oncoming bicyclists and pedestrians.

Miles of trails on the Kansas River floodplain are a quick jaunt from downtown Lawrence.

Rescue index: Help is available in town.
Land status: City of Lawrence.
Maps: Park information and maps are available from Lawrence Parks and Recreation Department.
Finding the trail: The Riverfront Trail can be accessed at the north end of the bridge at 2nd Street (US 40/24 or Massachusetts Street, downtown). For the floodplain trails, go east on Elm to 8th and Oak Streets, near the boat ramp. The trail goes east from there. Another access to the levee trail system is located near the junction of US 59, 40, and 24, north of the Interstate 70 interchange.

Sources of additional information:

Lawrence Parks and Recreation Department
P.O. Box 708
Lawrence, KS 66044
(913) 832-3450

Sunflower Bike Shop
804 Massachusetts Street
Lawrence, KS 66044
(913) 843-5000 or 843-6884 fax

Notes on the trail: During the 1993 floods, the river bottoms of the Kansas River were under water for a good part of the summer, but a cooperative effort restored the trails to good condition. Mountain bike races are held here periodically. Lawrence park hours are 6 A.M. to 11:30 P.M.

RIDE 32 *CLINTON STATE PARK*

The 12 to 15 miles of trails in Clinton State Park comprise probably the best technical mountain biking area in Kansas. Inquiries I made into places to bike in my early trips to Kansas repeatedly yielded the name of Clinton State Park, and I certainly wasn't disappointed when the morning came to ride the trails here. Two interconnected, marked single-track trails along the hardwood-forested bluffs stretch out over the length of the state park and offer a number of loop and out-and-back ride possibilities. Short, steep climbs and drops, tight corners, roots, rocks, and more rocks will greet you as you maneuver your way around here. Much of the system is a moderate to difficult, technical challenge that will keep most riders busy for the better part of a day or an enjoyable weekend.

The Clinton Lake reservoir is one in a series of Corps of Engineers flood-control projects in Kansas. Construction on the dam was started in 1972, and the reservoir reached its functioning water level in 1980. Recreation was planned into the development process from the start, and today, Clinton Lake offers one of the widest arrays of outdoor activities of any of the reservoir recreation areas. Much of the oak-wooded shoreline has been left in a semi-natural state, with service facilities built into the background. The Woodridge Park area on the west end of the lake has been set aside in an undeveloped state for hikers and backpackers looking for a natural setting.

The Clinton State Park, managed by the Kansas Department of Wildlife and Parks, has the most modern park facilities and the most extensive trail system as well. The original trail was designed for hiking by the Kansas Trails Council in the 1980s. Mountain bikers were allowed to use the trails beginning in 1989, and since then, additional trails have been added and trail maintenance has improved. The trail network generally follows the wooded corridor between the lakeshore and the park road system, winding in and out of small valleys and along quiet bays of the reservoir.

The nearby city of Lawrence was founded in 1854, soon after Kansas Territory was opened for settlement. With a pro-abolitionist population, the city played a leading role in the conflicts over slavery that dominated Kansas politics before the Civil War. Today, Lawrence is a dynamic city, featuring a well-restored downtown area, many cultural attractions, and the University of Kansas.

General location: About 5 miles west of Lawrence in Douglas County.
Elevation change: This is moderately hilly terrain, with an elevation variation of almost 100′ above the normal lake level of 875′. As a result, the trails feature frequent ups and downs.
Season: The trails should be accessible most of the year except during times of winter snow, spring thawing, or significant rains.
Services: The state park has water, rest rooms, swimming, and picnic and camping facilities available. All commercial services can be found in Lawrence.
Hazards: This is a technical trail system. Rocks, roots, tight corners, and steep descents will be encountered. Watch for traffic when you're crossing the park roads.
Rescue index: There is almost always help available in the park.
Land status: Kansas Department of Wildlife and Parks.
Maps: A map with biking information and a trail description is available from the park office or from many of the bike shops in the region.
Finding the trail: From Lawrence, take Clinton Parkway or US 40 west to CR 13. The state park entrance is just to the north of the Corps of Engineers Information Center and overlook. Several trail access points are possible. The east end of the trail departs from the overlook area. Access can be made near the state park office on the road into the marina, or from a dirt road and parking spot that branches off from the service road into a maintenance area on the marina road. There are several access points near the boat ramp at the west end of the state park. Spur trails also descend to the trail system from various loop roads through the campgrounds and picnic areas.

Sources of additional information:

Clinton State Park
798 North 1415 Road
Lawrence, KS 66049
(913) 842-8562

Rick's Bike Shop
916 Massachusetts Street
Lawrence, KS 66044
(913) 841-7181 or (800) 452-7604

Sunflower Bike Shop
804 Massachusetts Street
Lawrence, KS 66044
(913) 843-5000 or 843-6884 fax

Notes on the trail: The 2 trails are marked with white or blue blazes, and generally the blue trail stays closer to the water line and is somewhat more level. The white trail usually climbs higher into the woods and presents a more technical challenge, particularly in the section just west of a small dam near the

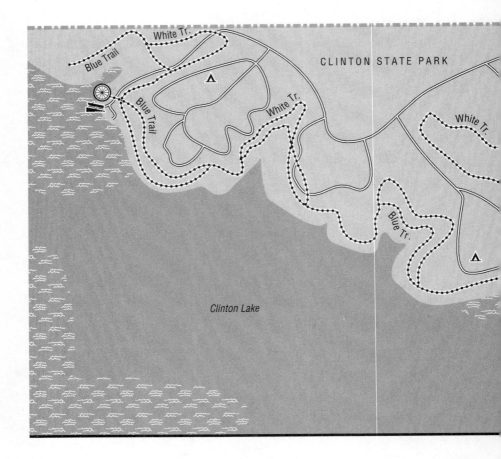

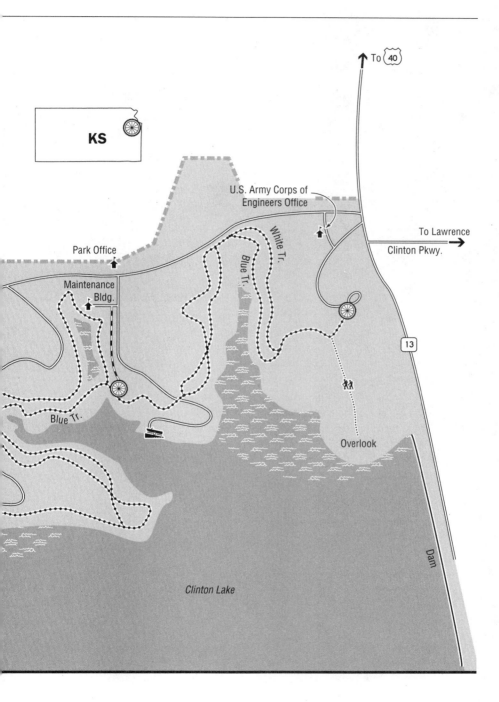

KS

To ⑳ 40

U.S. Army Corps of
Engineers Office

To Lawrence
Clinton Pkwy.

Park Office

White Tr.

Blue Tr.

Maintenance
Bldg.

13

Blue Tr.

Overlook

Dam

Clinton Lake

Clinton State Park has some of the most technically challenging single-track trails in Kansas.

marina road access. A mile-long straight section along the lake on the central peninsula of the park allows you to cruise for a few minutes before reentering the hilly woods. Both trails cross the park road near the boat ramp and continue for a ways on the north side of the road, forming a loop. Watch for periodic access trails to the park loop roads where you can bail out of the trail system if you wish.

These trails are still shared with hikers and casual walkers, so please show courtesy when encountering pedestrians. Other parts of the Clinton Lake project area are off-limits to mountain bikes; Rockhaven is designated for horseback use only, and Woodridge has been set aside for hikers and backpackers. There is a daily parking fee for vehicles entering the state park. Annual parking permits are also available.

RIDE 33   *DORNWOOD PARK*

This small, 110-acre city park and nature preserve has a surprisingly extensive little network of interconnected trails in a mostly wooded setting on the edge of Topeka. A core group of walking trails has been expanded with the assistance of a local bike shop to include a collection of technical single-track paths

RIDE 33 *DORNWOOD PARK*

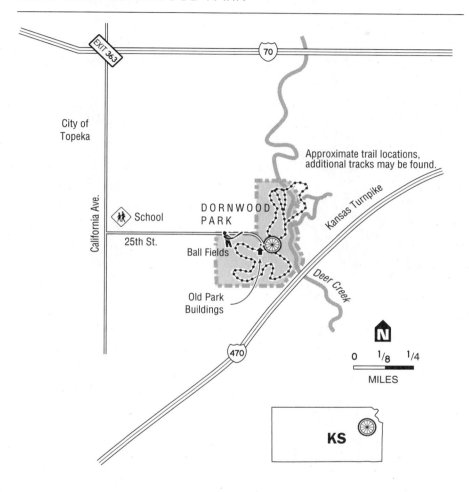

that zig-zag around a creek channel in a small woodland. The original, wider trails, which are mostly packed dirt, offer some quiet scenery as well as a few challenging descents, corners, and obstructions along the course of Deer Creek. As many as three to four miles of relatively easy to moderate biking can be squeezed out of the loops of trails here.

Around the park you will see remnants from earlier times; an old dam, some rusting machinery, and a few old buildings all hint of a time when this piece of land was used as a quarry or mill site. Some mountain biking events have been held here periodically, and local riders regularly use the trails and help with maintenance.

A variety of enjoyable trails can be found in Topeka's Dornwood Park.

General location: In the city of Topeka in Shawnee County.
Elevation change: Small bluffs along Deer Creek provide some short, steep climbs.
Season: Most of the year except during winter snows, spring thawing, and periods of rainfall.
Services: All services are readily available in Topeka.
Hazards: Steep descents, logs, rocks, and sharp corners will be encountered. Keep alert for other park trail users.
Rescue index: Help is available in the city.
Land status: City of Topeka.
Maps: The map in this book is the only one presently available.
Finding the trail: From the California Avenue exit off Interstate 70, drive south 1 mile, then east (left) on 25th Street past a school to the park. Continue to the trailhead past the softball fields.

Sources of additional information:

Capp's Bike Shop
813 Southwest Croix
Topeka, KS 66611
(913) 266-5900

Topeka Parks–Recreation and Maintenance
(913) 272-5900

Notes on the trail: Several trails take off from the trailhead near the old buildings. Head to the south toward the wooded area near the turnpike to reach the newest, most technical trails. To the north, several routes gain some elevation onto a rise, then make some steep drops into an old river channel where Deer Creek is now located. A bit to the south of the steep spots there is a bridge that leads to a few more trails in the woods on the east side of the creek.

This is a popular walking and jogging area, so be prepared to slow down and yield the trail. Avoid riding when the trail conditions are wet and muddy. A volunteer effort is under way to spread wood chips on sections of the trail to help prevent erosion. Courtesy and common sense when biking here will help assure that future use of the park by mountain bikers remains possible.

RIDE 34 FORT LEAVENWORTH NATIONAL RECREATION TRAILS

This 30-plus-mile trail system, all within the confines of the Fort Leavenworth Military Reservation, offers one of the most unusual and interesting places to mountain bike in eastern Kansas, particularly if you enjoy exploring an environment of history and tradition along with some scenic hills and woodlands. Three trail routes, all designated as National Recreation Trails, have been designed to encompass a variety of historical and natural features found on this 168-year-old base. Utilizing paved and unpaved roads and old double-track and single-track trails, the routes provide generally easy to moderate riding through the old historic fort district, the hilly upland areas to the west, and the floodplain along the Missouri River.

A trail handbook put together by the natural resource staff on the base is a good introduction to this trail system. You can follow the routes they suggest or put together various sections into your own tour; in any case, this guidebook is helpful and informative. The eight-mile Blue Trail is mainly a tour of the historic district and the wooded hills immediately to the west. The Yellow Trail adds several loops in some hilly upland forest terrain which eventually meet up with the Blue Trail, and the Orange Trail starts out along the hills of the Yellow route, then branches off into the flat Missouri River floodplains, referred to as the Bottomlands in the guidebook. Riders interested primarily in biking the off-road terrain will probably want to concentrate on the hilly outer sections of the Yellow Trail and the Bottomlands portion of the Orange Trail.

Established in 1827, Fort Leavenworth is the oldest continuously used fort in the west, a national historical landmark that has seen generals from Custer to Patton stationed here. Everywhere you poke around, you will find tidbits

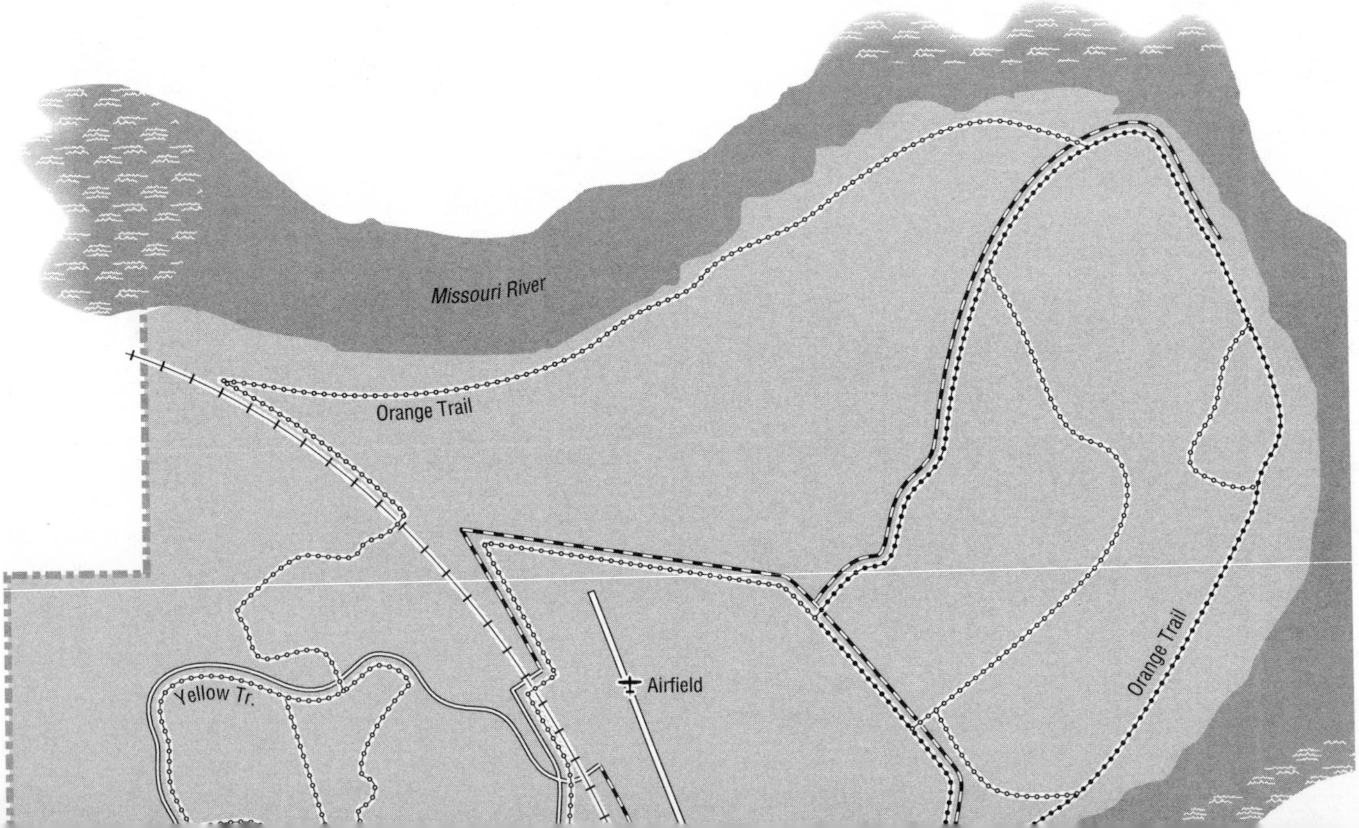

Missouri River

Orange Trail

Orange Trail

Airfield

Yellow Tr.

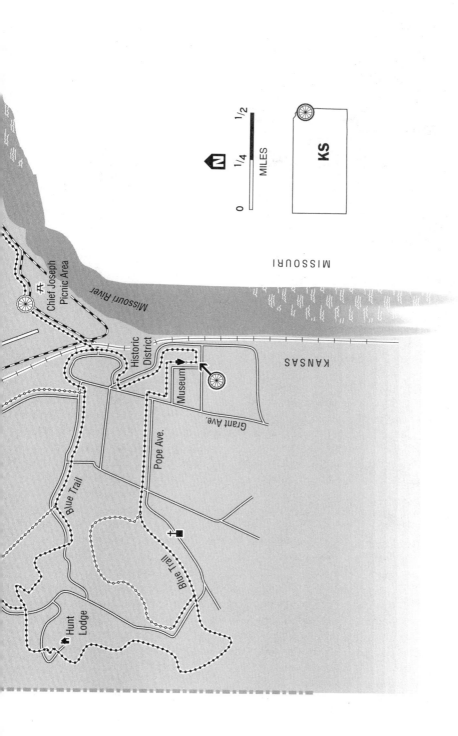

Chief Joseph Picnic Area

Missouri River

MISSOURI

Historic District

Museum

Grant Ave.

KANSAS

Pope Ave.

Blue Trail

Blue Trail

Hunt Lodge

N

0   ¼   ½
MILES

KS

Fort Leavenworth Military Reservation has a series of designated trails that include an extensive wooded area along the Missouri River.

from the past. On the way down to the river bottomlands, on Riverside Avenue, there is a cut in the hill where wagons starting out on the Oregon and Santa Fe Trails were hoisted up from the river. Statues abound, and a recent addition is the monument, initiated by General Colin Powell, honoring the "Buffalo Soldiers," the black cavalry regiments that fought many battles on the Great Plains in the war with the Indians. From the trail on the ridge near Sheridan Drive there are views to the west into the valley of Salt Creek, where William "Buffalo Bill" Cody's family settled in 1854. It was from the Fort Leavenworth area that Buffalo Bill moved on to his famous career in the "Wild West." The Fort Leavenworth Museum, near the historic district, presents a "frontier army" theme with a display of horse-drawn vehicles and other memorabilia from the fort's earliest days up to World War II.

The hilly uplands that cover much of the military reservation are largely comprised of loess, a fine, wind-blown soil that is quick to get muddy in wet weather. Much of this area used to be prairie grassland; now, with human prevention of grass fires, these hills are mostly forested, which also contributes to muddy conditions in times of ample rainfall. Older roads where vehicle use had caused ruts and erosion are being stabilized by the return of vegetation. Mountain bikers should be aware of these conditions and avoid areas prone to erosion during wet weather.

General location: Fort Leavenworth Military Reservation is immediately north of the city of Leavenworth in Leavenworth County.

Elevation change: The reservation consists of an upland and a lowland section, with a total elevation range of almost 350′ from the Missouri River to the tops of the bluffs.

Season: Trails should be open most of the year except during times of winter snow, spring thawing, or significant rainfall. The soil in some areas is particularly slippery and prone to erosion in wet weather.

Services: You can find most basic needs on the base. All other services can be found in the city of Leavenworth.

Hazards: Eroded areas, steep, slick spots, and areas of low maintenance may be encountered on the trails. Use caution when crossing the railroad tracks or the various roads on the base. Stay out of restricted areas. Hunting or military maneuvers may be under way at various times and places; check with the military police on base for specifics.

Rescue index: Help is close by in this area.

Land status: Fort Leavenworth Military Reservation.

Maps: A very complete, mile-by-mile guidebook, *Fort Leavenworth: Gateway to the West,* is available at no charge from the Post Museum on Reynolds Avenue. It is chock-full of historical and environmental information and is invaluable if you want to follow the trails closely.

Finding the trail: The main entrance to the military reservation is off US 73 (Metropolitan Avenue) on the north end of Leavenworth. Proceed north on Grant Avenue to the historic district, where you will find the museum and the starting point to the trails listed in the guidebook. Rides in the Bottomlands area can be started at the Chief Joseph Picnic Area on Nez Perce Way past the south end of the airfield.

Sources of additional information:

Fort Leavenworth Military Reservation
The Forestry Department
Directorate of Engineering and Housing, Building 85
Fort Leavenworth, KS 66027
(913) 684-2749 or 2993

Notes on the trail: Many sections of the trails are not specifically marked, so use the descriptions in the guidebook to keep track of your position. It is important to stay out of the various restricted areas marked with signs and mentioned in the trail guidebook. Do not climb over fences, especially the one surrounding the Fort Leavenworth Federal Penitentiary. Avoid biking in rainy weather and when the trail conditions are muddy.

ADDITIONAL MOUNTAIN BIKING OPPORTUNITIES
IN EASTERN KANSAS

Johnson County, in the metropolitan Kansas City area, is developing an extensive network of hike-bike trails that will form a series of interconnected loops through most of the suburban parts of the county. The existing sections of this network are mostly paved corridor trails providing easy urban commuter and recreational routes, good for a few hours of pleasant urban riding. The Streamway Park System, of which the existing Mill Creek Streamway Park (see Ride 30, Shawnee Mission Park) is a part, is a planned series of linear parks running along eight of Johnson County's stream courses. More miles of hike-bike trails will be developed along with this system. For more information, contact Johnson County Park and Recreation District, 6501 Antioch Road, Shawnee Mission, KS 66202, (913) 831-3355.

Also in Johnson County, the cities of Overland Park and Leawood have a paved, 13-mile hike-bike path system comprised of the Indian Creek Hike/Bike Trail and the Tomahawk Creek Greenway. These trails meander along wooded creek drainages in a suburban setting. For more information, contact Overland Park Planning/Parks and Recreation, (913) 381-5252. There are other similar, shorter trails in other parts of the county as well.

The John Redmond Reservoir near Burlington in Coffey County, about 25 miles southeast of Emporia, has an off-road-vehicle area that can be used by mountain bikes. There are about 3.5 miles of trails at the Otter Creek Recreation Area in a flat grassy to weedy area between the reservoir and the upstream side of the dam. Other sections of the Corps of Engineers land may have bikeable areas, but there are no current plans for future trail development at this time. For more information, contact John Redmond Project Office, 1565 Embankment Road SW, Burlington, KS 66839, (316) 364-8614.

Elk City Lake State Park near Independence in Montgomery County has a small trail system in some challenging and scenic terrain in an oak and hickory forest overlooking the Elk City Lake reservoir. Some of this is rocky, craggy terrain and may require some carrying and climbing. The trails are designated as National Recreation Trails by the U.S. Department of the Interior. The 15-mile-long Elk River Hiking Trail in the adjacent Corps of Engineers land is not open to mountain bikes at this time. For more information, contact Elk City State Park, P.O. Box 945, Independence, KS 67301, (316) 331-6295.

Bike Shops and Clubs

Earthriders Bicycle Club
7405 North Woodland
Gladstone, MO 64118

Johnson County Bicycle Club
Box 2203
Shawnee Mission, KS 66201

Kansas Bicycle Alliance
P.O. Box 2031
Shawnee Mission, KS 66201
(913) 967-7100

Kansas City Bicycle Club
P.O. Box 412163
Kansas City, MO 64141

Lawrence Bicycle Club
P.O. Box 3596
Lawrence, KS 66046

Mt. Bike Lawrence
c/o 2708 Lockridge Drive
Lawrence, KS 66047

The shops mentioned below provided me with useful information. There are a number of other good bicycle shops in the Kansas City area; check the area yellow pages for more information.

Bike Source
11912 West 119th Street
Overland Park, KS 66213
(913) 451-1515 or
(800) 728-8792

Bicycles, Etc.
311 South Broadway
Pittsburg, KS 66762
(316) 231-7727

Bike Rack
7945 Santa Fe Drive
Overland Park, KS 66204
(913) 642-6115

Capp's Bike Shop
813 Southwest Croix
Topeka, KS 66611
(913) 266-5900
club: Kansas Rough Riders
(913) 266-0055

Sunflower Bike Shop
804 Massachusetts
Lawrence, KS 66044
(913) 843-5000 or 843-6884 fax

Tri Tech Sports
12948 West 87th Parkway
Lenexa, KS 66215
(913) 894-5588

Central Kansas

There are several distinct regions of hills in central Kansas that add a bit of variety to the vast expanse of plains in the state and give it some of its more rugged terrain. The most dramatic of these regions is the Flint Hills, an open land of hilly vistas, escarpments, and remnants of the original tall-grass prairie. Now generally used for cattle grazing, much of this area presents the westbound traveler with a visual change, signaling the transition from the east to the west. To the west and north of Flint Hills is the Smokey Hills region, where more rolling hills gradually increase in elevation to the west, dotted with periodic sandstone and limestone rock formations. The central part of these hills, around Wilson Lake, is known as Post Rock Country, where the lack of trees forced the early settlers to make fenceposts out of the local soft limestone.

The Arkansas River valley cuts a wide arc through central Kansas, leaving a flat, sandy plain leading into the vicinity of Wichita, the largest city in the state, where cattle drives on the Chisholm Trail went as far as the railroads. The other major towns of this region include Hutchinson, on the Arkansas River, and Salina, Junction City, and Manhattan, all located on the Smoky Hill River–Kansas River valley.

Mountain biking in central Kansas falls into two rough categories: You can bike on the established trails of the most popular recreational sites, or head out to the hilly, more challenging back roads in the area. This part of the state is dotted with flood-control reservoirs, and a number of these places have trails or off-road-vehicle areas that can be used by mountain bikers. On the other hand, the wide-open spaces of Kansas have inspired a certain number of fat-tire enthusiasts to take to the many miles of hilly back roads. The Flint Hills region in particular has developed a following among hard-riding mountain bikers who enjoy the lonely and haunting beauty of the hill country.

RIDE 35   *SANTA FE LAKE*

This small park on the outskirts of Wichita is a fun spot to go for an hour or two of technical riding or just to get a good workout. There are about 1.5 miles of trails interwoven in a wooded section of land straddling a creek that flows out of Santa Fe Lake. The NORBA-designed trails consist of moderate to difficult single-track with some short climbs and descents, tight corners, rocks, roots, and man-made stone embankments. Competitive races are occasionally

RIDE 35 *SANTA FE LAKE*

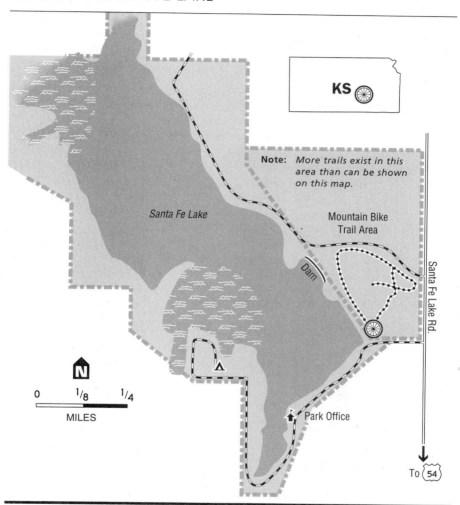

Note: *More trails exist in this area than can be shown on this map.*

Santa Fe Lake

Mountain Bike Trail Area

Dam

Santa Fe Lake Rd.

KS

N

0   1/8   1/4
MILES

Park Office

To 54

held here. The park caretakers have been very receptive to the mountain biking community, and future plans have been made for additional trails to be added to the north of the present system.

The park has facilities for camping, boating, and swimming. The town of Augusta, just to the east, features a historic 1935 theater, the first of its kind to be lit entirely with neon lights. The town of El Dorado, 20 miles northeast, was the site of the first major oil field developed in Kansas, and the Kansas Oil Museum there features equipment from the early drilling days. Nearby

Wichita has many attractions for visitors, including a number of good bike shops that can help with ideas for additional biking in the urban area.

General location: About 15 miles east of Wichita near Augusta in Butler County.

Elevation change: There are various short, steep ups and downs around the banks of a creek in an otherwise flat area.

Season: The trails should be rideable most of the year except in times of occasional winter snow, spring thawing, or significant rainfall.

Services: The adjacent park has water, camping, and other recreational facilities. All commercial services are available in Augusta or Wichita.

Hazards: Steep drops, rocks, and other obstructions may be encountered, and there is poison ivy in the brushy areas of the woods. The clay soil could be slippery when wet. Park rules require riders to wear helmets. Be alert for possible hikers in the area.

Rescue index: Help can be obtained at the park office.

Land status: City of Augusta.

Maps: The trails are self-contained in a small wooded area. Other than the map in this book, no specific trail map is available.

Finding the trail: Santa Fe Lake and Park is located 1.7 miles north of US 54 on Santa Fe Lake Road, 4 miles west of Augusta. The trailhead is well marked as you drive into the park.

Sources of additional information:

Santa Fe Lake Park
RR 1, Box 113
Augusta, KS 67010
(316) 775-3728

Bicycle Exchange
1516 East Central
Wichita, KS 67227
(316) 264-6427

Notes on the trail: A $3-per-vehicle fee is charged to use the park.

RIDE 36   *THE CENTRAL FLINT HILLS*

There is an area in central Kansas where the roads thin out and the towns become few and far between. The neat, orderly grid of rolling farmlands gives way to a more dramatic, open hill and bluff country where human creations

RIDE 36 *THE CENTRAL FLINT HILLS*

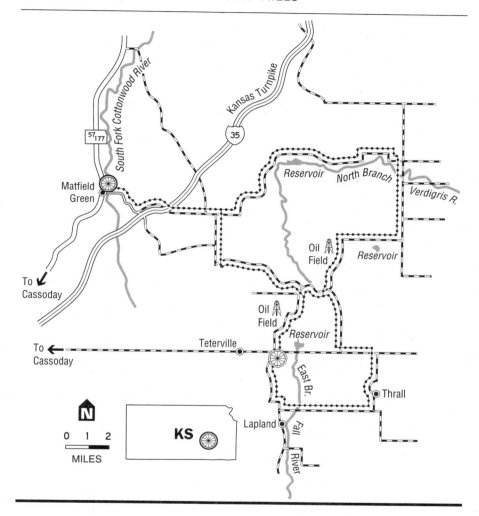

are only isolated monuments in the vast sea of grass. This is a section of the Flint Hills, a band of unique prairie lands that has resisted development since the days of the Santa Fe Trail. Hundreds of miles of back roads and four-wheel-drive tracks zigzag delicately through this hill country, offering dozens of loop and through-ride possibilities for the adventurous mountain biker.

More than just a place to ride, the Flint Hills evokes a particular feeling among the bikers who have tackled this region. Aside from periodic steep hills, rutted roads, and inevitable wind-blown, weather-beaten conditions, there is a freedom of open space and self-reliance here that you will not find within the confines of many other midwestern parklands. Here, your challenge is spread out before you, all the way to the horizon, and there are few places to pull out early. Much of the adventure riding in this region is centered in Chase County in the area around Cottonwood Falls, south to Mattfield Green, and in the area south of Interstate 35 and east of Cassoday in Butler and Greenwood Counties. Many of the back roads are not marked, and some roads and stream crossings may not be passable at various times, so be sure to obtain local advice and good maps before doing a long tour. The loops described below are only a few of many options in the Flint Hills.

This is primarily ranch country, and this remnant of the once vast tall-grass prairie is ideal for cattle grazing. Sections of the Flint Hills were once productive oil-producing lands, and there are still a few oil rigs here and there pumping away. The remains of old farms and boom towns from the 1920s and earlier are still evident here and there along the silent roads. The route of the historic Santa Fe Trail passes north of this area near the town of Council Grove, and it's not difficult in this area to imagine coming over a ridge and seeing a dusty wagon train far below. The ornate 1873 courthouse in Cottonwood Falls is the oldest courthouse in Kansas still in use. The Flint Hills host several guided bike tours and races each year, including the Matfield Green 100K, an ambitious two-day "death ride" designed to prove that the Great Plains region is just as challenging for mountain bikers as other parts of the country.

General location: This is a whole region of back roads in an open, hilly setting, located west of Emporia and north of El Dorado in Chase County and northern portions of Butler and Greenwood Counties.

Elevation change: This is hilly country, with elevation variations of over 500′ between the highest ridge tops and the river bottoms to the east.

Season: Most of the roads should be rideable all year except during times of occasional winter snows or significant rainfall. The midwinter months are chilly, with temperatures ranging from the 20s to the 40s. Midsummer brings temperatures in the high 90s and high humidity.

Services: Services are few and far between in the midst of the remote Flint Hills. There are a few services in Cassoday, Matfield Green, and Madison. All services are available in the larger towns of Council Grove, Cottonwood Falls, Emporia, Eureka, El Dorado, and Newton.

Hazards: Most of the hazards relate to the openness and remoteness of the landscape. The hot sun, threatening weather, and distance help make potential problems that are much more serious. Water in the various small reservoirs and streams is not safe to drink. Be cautious around cattle; give them as much space as possible. Watch for rocks, ruts, cattle guards, and occasional vehicles while riding on the roads.

The back roads of the rugged Flint Hills region offer
many miles of biking opportunities.

Rescue index: Plan carefully and be as self-sufficient as possible on long rides
into this area. Help is available in the larger towns mentioned above.

Land status: Mixed ownership; much of this area is private ranchland.
Respect private property when you rest or explore on the roadsides.

Maps: Individual county road maps are available at the various county seats
and show all of the local road systems. The USGS 7.5 minute quadrangles
covering this area are Eureka Northeast, Lapland, Shaw Creek, Teterville,
Thrall, and Thrall Northwest.

Finding the trail: If you are not familiar with this area, it is advisable to get
local advice on current road conditions and the latest sights to see. The bike
shops listed below can give you further information. The figure eight of loops
described below can be started in Cassoday or Matfield Green on KS 177
off I-35 (Kansas Turnpike)/exit 92. You can park in the towns or save some

miles by driving east on the unpaved roads to the loop area. Vehicles with low clearance may have trouble traversing some of the roads on the loop route.

Sources of additional information:

Pedal Revolution
725 Commercial
Emporia, KS 66801
(316) 343-7180

Great Plains Bicycle, Inc.
308 West Broadway
Newton, KS 67114
(316) 283-6055
Sponsors of the annual Matfield Green 100K "Flint Hills Death Ride."

Notes on the trail: Since much of this area is private ranchland, restrict your riding to public roads, or ask locally for permission and know where you are going before following other routes. Plenty of extra water in addition to sun, wind, and rain protection are necessities on tours in this area. Good maps are essential, and a bicycle odometer can be a very useful tool in this sometimes featureless area.

The total distance around the figure eight–shaped loop described here is about 53 miles; the north half of the loop can be done in 33 miles, and the south half, in 23 miles. The town of Matfield Green is 6 miles from the north loop, and the town of Cassoday is 12 miles from the south loop. You can cut out these miles by driving out to the loop roads, but you will have to improvise for a roadside parking place. From Matfield Green the access road heads east out of town for 2.5 miles to the second turnpike crossing, then continues east 3 more miles to a T intersection with a road coming in from the south.

This is the start of the north loop; continuing east (clockwise) gets you to the first long descent the fastest. A couple of miles east and north from the T intersection, the road will begin a 300′ descent into the partially wooded valley of the North Verdigris River. Head east down the river valley for 7 miles, past a reservoir, to a 4-way intersection. Turn south (right) and you will cross the river and the lowest point on the route, at 1,150′. Continue south from the 4-way intersection for 4 miles, then turn west near the south branch of the Verdigris River. Keep in mind that these river crossings may not be possible in times of high water. Now the steady climb back to the ridge tops begins. The road will pass a ranch and a reservoir, and turn south after 3 miles, continuing to climb to over 1,650′. You are entering the Browning oil field area, where there are some old foundations near the road. Three miles from where the road turned south, there is an obscure junction where the 23-mile south loop meets the route you are on. Turn west and follow the ridge to stay on the north loop. In 1.5 miles the south loop turns south down the hill, and there are good views over the valley of another oil field to the

Teterville Hill area. Continuing 5 miles west, then 3 miles north will get you back to the start of the north loop and the road to Matfield Green.

Twelve miles west of Cassoday is the start of the south loop, just down a big hill from the site of an old village called Teterville. A watershed district sign marks a 4-way intersection. Turn north (left) on a rutted, one-and-a-half-lane road that winds through the old Teterville oil field, past small reservoirs, and steadily climbs onto a ridge with great views of the surrounding treeless terrain. Four miles from the 4-way intersection you will meet the north loop; turn east here and wind along the ridge 1.5 miles and watch for the road turning south (right). Follow this road for a bit over 3 miles, then turn east at the crossroad. (Turning west here will return you to the 4-way intersection at the start.) Ride east 1.5 miles, then south 2.5 miles to the old village of Thrall, where there is a pumping station. Just south of there, turn west, and almost 4 miles farther, you will cross the east branch of the Fall River, at 1,220′, the lowest point on the south loop. Less than one mile ahead is a T intersection; 1 mile south is the site of the village of Lapland, and 3.5 miles north is the 4-way junction at the start.

These loops are just a portion of what can be done in this large region. With some good maps and lots of time and perseverance, you can discover many more lonely ridges and quiet valleys.

RIDE 37 *KANOPOLIS STATE PARK*

Kanopolis State Park is the starting point for a 12-mile-long multi-use trail system that meanders in and out of the sandstone canyons and open prairie ridges of the central Kansas Smokey Hills region. A series of connected loops in the state park and adjacent U.S. Army Corps of Engineers land makes possible a number of rides of 3 to 12 miles that could occupy several hours to a day of enjoyable riding. An additional 11-mile trail is under development along Alum Creek at the northwest side of the present trail system that will provide more open, grassy terrain to ride in. Most of the "Horsethief Trail" loop in the state park is single-track, following old cattle paths on open, grassy ridge tops or brushy, partially wooded canyons. There are also sandy and rocky sections and low water crossings to watch out for. The sandstone bluffs and occasional stands of cottonwood, cedar, and oak add to the visual interest of the terrain. Much of the two loops (called the "Prairie Trail") on the Corps of Engineers land is on an upland grassy plateau with good views of the Kanopolis reservoir.

After an initial visit to this area, I was unable to return for a closer look because of a bicycling injury, but the trail system should be of moderate difficulty, with some of the climbs and descents and the sandy, rocky, and rough

RIDE 37 KANOPOLIS STATE PARK

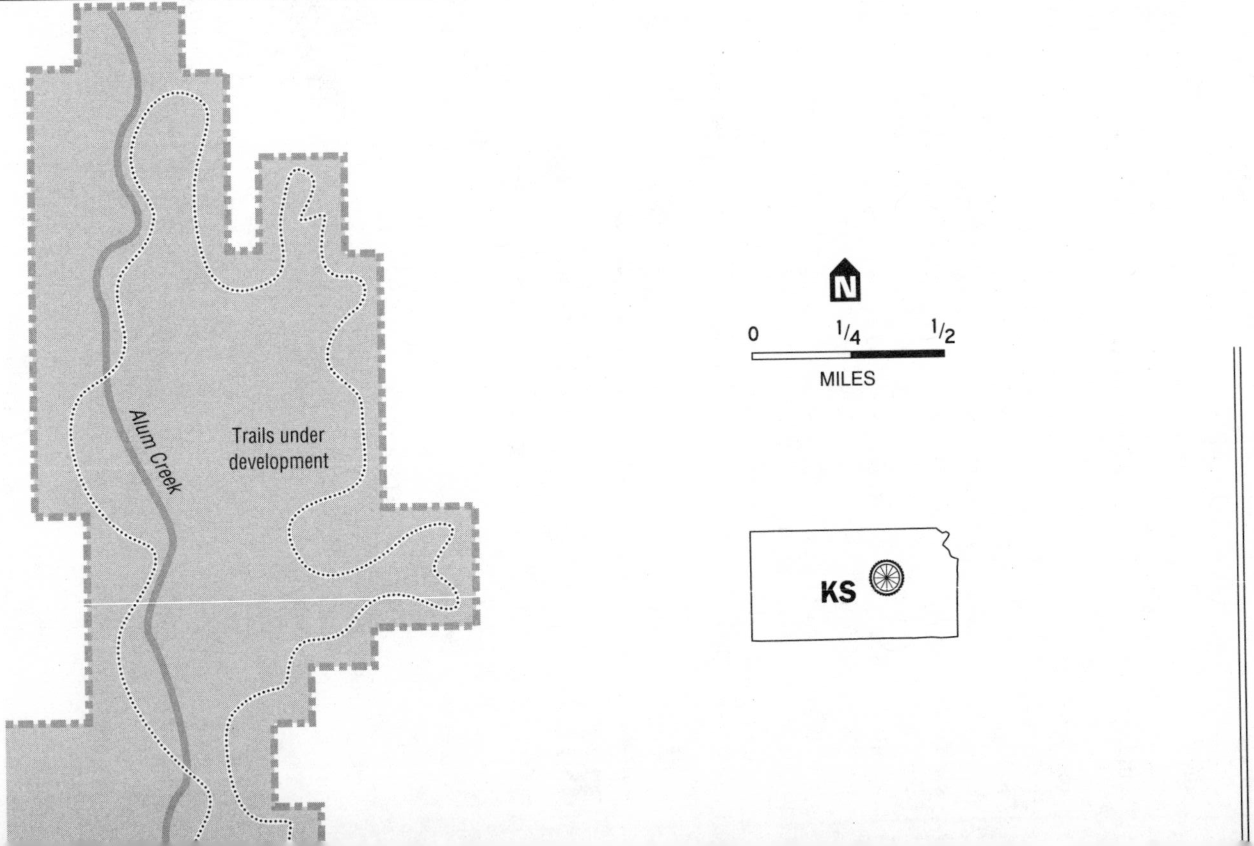

N

0   1/4   1/2

MILES

KS

Trails under
development

Alum Creek

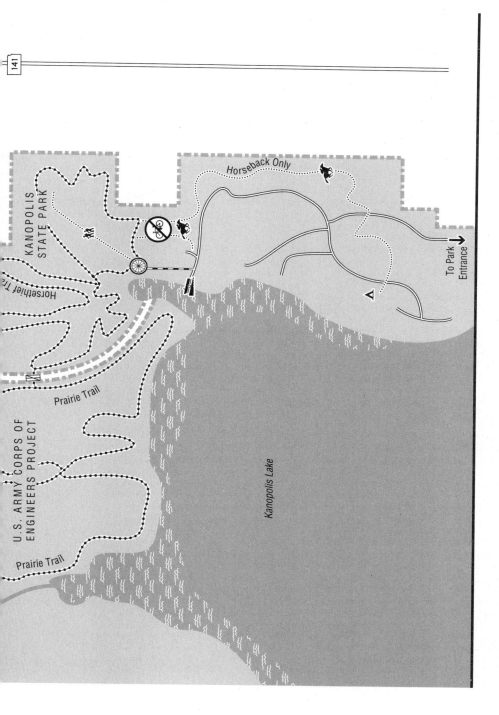

KANOPOLIS
STATE PARK

Horseback Only

Horsethief Trail

To Park
Entrance

Prairie Trail

U.S. ARMY CORPS OF
ENGINEERS PROJECT

Prairie Trail

Kanopolis Lake

spots providing some technical challenges. With the addition of the new trails, and the support of several mountain bike groups, the Kanopolis trails should become one of many classic mountain biking locations in Kansas.

Other points of interest in the area include Mushroom Rock State Park, north of Kanopolis Lake, which has an unusual collection of spherically eroded rock formations that has been a local attraction since the days of the wagon trains. In the town of Lindsborg, which has a Swedish heritage, the Old Mill Museum displays Swedish and regional pioneer exhibits, including several nineteenth-century buildings and a railroad locomotive.

General location: About 25 miles southwest of Salina in Ellsworth County.
Elevation change: There is a range of about 200′ in elevation from the normal lake level of 1,460′ to the tops of the ridges north of the lake.
Season: Trails in the state park section are open all year. The Prairie Trail section is closed November 1 through January 31 during the hunting season. Periods of winter snow or rain may make the trails impassable.
Services: The state park has water and picnic and camping facilities. All other services can be found in Ellsworth, Salina, or McPherson.
Hazards: Certain crossings of low areas in the canyons may be hazardous in times of heavy rains or high lake water. Note the hunting season restriction mentioned above. Watch for and yield to hikers and horseback riders.
Rescue index: There are generally park personnel and other visitors in the state park.
Land status: Kansas Department of Wildlife and Parks and U.S. Army Corps of Engineers, Kansas City District.
Maps: A trails brochure with a map is available at the state park.
Finding the trail: The trails must be accessed from Kanopolis State Park. The entrance is on KS 141, about 10 miles south of KS 140. Drive north through the park to the Buffalo Tracks Trailhead.

Sources of additional information:

> Kanopolis Public Lands Office
> Route 1, Box 26D
> Marquette, KS 67464
> (913) 546-2565
>
> Bike Tek
> 645 East Crawford
> Salina, KS 67401
> (913) 825-7314

Notes on the trail: These are multi-use trails; bikers should stay on the developed trails and yield to horseback riders. During times of high water, portions of the trail may not be accessible. Call the park for up-to-date information before making a long trip to bike here. Access to the various sections of the trail system are controlled by gates, so please heed trail signs and leave all fences as you find them. The Buffalo Tracks trail is designated for hiking use only. Camping is not allowed along the trail system at this time. A state park vehicle permit is required for entrance into the park.

RIDE 38 *SPILLWAY CYCLE AREA*

The Spillway Cycle Area is one of a variety of recreational facilities at Tuttle Creek Lake, located in the northern Flint Hills region of central Kansas. Although designed for motorcycles, the two or so miles of interconnected trails here provide moderate to very difficult technical riding for the mountain biker looking for a good workout. Located on a wooded slope overlooking the spillway channel of the Tuttle Creek dam, the cycle area trails consist of well-packed dirt with occasional roots and rocks and some very steep climbs and drops. Along with the Tuttle Creek ORV Area (see the next ride) near the north end of the lake, the Spillway Cycle Area can be part of a good day of hard riding and exploration around the second largest lake in Kansas.

Authorized in 1938, construction of the dam creating Tuttle Creek Lake began after some serious flooding in 1951 and was completed in 1962. The disastrous floods of 1993 filled the reservoir to a record capacity, and with all spillway gates open, the outflow reached 60,000 cubic feet per second, washing away almost 400,000 cubic yards of channel sediment. The resulting exposed bedrocks are dramatically visible from the cycle area.

Manhattan, home of Kansas State University, has a good zoo, an active arts community, and many other attractions. Aggieville is a shopping district near the campus, where there are two bike shops that can give you more information on bicycling in the area.

General location: At the southeast end of Tuttle Creek Lake, 5 miles north of Manhattan in Pottawatomie County.
Elevation change: There are a few steep climbs located on the bluffs above the river.
Season: The trails should be usable most of the year except during times of winter snow, spring thawing, or significant rainfall.
Services: There are rest rooms and picnic tables at the trailhead and half a dozen campgrounds around the lake. All other services are available in Manhattan.
Hazards: There is a steep drop-off where the river bluff is eroding away. Do not venture beyond the marked barricades. Steep descents, rocks, and trees

RIDE 38 *SPILLWAY CYCLE AREA*

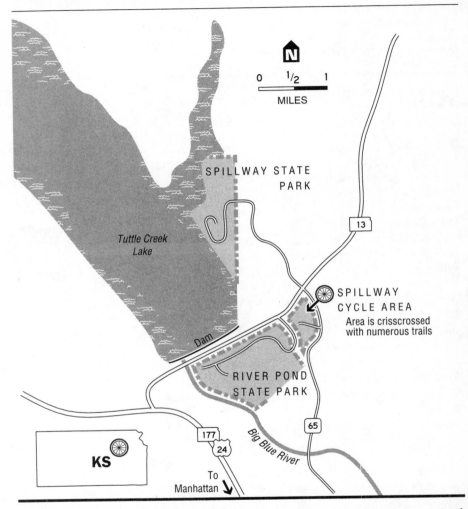

are among the usual trail hazards. As with any area where there is motorized use, be alert and listen for fast-moving cycles; and avoid times of heavy motor vehicle use. Helmets are a must in these areas.

Rescue index: Help can be found at the Corps of Engineers visitor center or in town.

Land status: U.S. Army Corps of Engineers, Kansas City District.

Maps: There is a general map of the area in the Army Corps of Engineers pamphlet covering Tuttle Creek Lake. The map in this book is sufficient to locate the trail area and begin your ride.

The Spillway Cycle Area overlooks the flood-damaged channel of the Big Blue River.

Finding the trail: Take US 24 north from Manhattan and cross the dam on KS 13. Just beyond the end of the dam, turn south (right) on Dyer Road and continue one-half mile to the cycle area.

Sources of additional information:

U.S. Army Corps of Engineers
Project Office
(913) 539-8511

Aggie Bike Station
1217 Moro
Manhattan, KS 66502
(913) 776-2372

The Pathfinder
304 Poyntz Avenue
Manhattan, KS 66502
(913) 539-5639

Notes on the trail: Be sure to bring plenty of water with you on hot days; there is none at the trailhead.

RIDE 39 *TUTTLE CREEK ORV AREA*

This undeveloped area is designated as an off-road-vehicle area by the Corps of Engineers and has at least three to four miles of meandering double-track trails on an upland ridge and through a wooded and grassy valley near the floodplain of the lake. Steep climbs, rocky and rutted tracks, stream crossings, and low, wet spots combine to present some moderate to difficult riding—great for bikers who like variety. As in most motorized-use areas, the trail surface is packed down, making the area a good alternative place to ride in times when trail systems elsewhere are too delicate for mountain biking.

This section of the Flint Hills is a land of open, hilly farm and range country, with considerable woodlands along water courses and deeper valleys. Riding here presents a good cross section of the variety of landscape in this region. There are nice views out over the long expanse of Tuttle Lake and a good mixture of sun and shade.

General location: About 25 miles northwest of Manhattan on the west side of Tuttle Creek Lake in Riley County.

Elevation change: This is fairly hilly terrain, with bluffs rising over 200′ from the lakeshore.

Season: The trails should be accessible most of the year except during times of occasional winter snow, spring thawing, or significant rains.

Services: There are no facilities at the site. There is a store and a park with water in the village of Randolph, and all other services are available in Manhattan.

Hazards: Steep descents, rocks, and some creek crossings are among the trail hazards found here. Tall brush in some spots may obscure views of oncoming vehicles. As in any area where there is motorized use, be alert and listen for fast-moving vehicles; and avoid times of heavy motor vehicle use. Hunting is allowed on much of the public land around the lake.

Rescue index: The village of Randolph, on US 77, is the closest source of help.

Land status: U.S. Army Corps of Engineers, Kansas City District.

Maps: There is a general map of the area in the Army Corps of Engineers pamphlet covering Tuttle Creek Lake. The map in this book is sufficient to locate the trail area and begin your ride. The USGS 7.5 minute quadrangle, Olsburg NW, will be of help for those who might want detailed information on the layout of the area.

Finding the trail: KS 177 and US 77 lead north from Manhattan to Randolph. Just south of Randolph, take CR 893 right (northeast) to the gravel access road into the ORV area. The 1.5-mile access road is relatively rough.

RIDE 39 *TUTTLE CREEK ORV AREA*

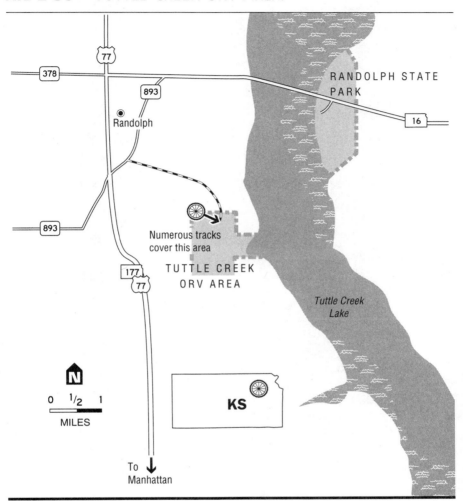

Sources of additional information:

Corps of Engineers
Project Office
(913) 539-8511

The Pathfinder
304 Poyntz Avenue
Manhattan, KS 66502
(913) 539-5639

A variety of double-track trails wind through the Tuttle Creek ORV Area.

Notes on the trail: The upper ridge area has many grassy and rocky tracks, with some that drop off to the small valley below. Many of the trails wind around in the wooded creek lowlands that occasionally flood in times of high water in the reservoir. A few other trails travel east along the lakeshore through high brush and along the remains of old paved highway.

RIDE 40 *SCHOOL CREEK ORV AREA*

This off-road-vehicle area is a hardened site with lots of challenging ups and downs, wooded and brushy corridors, and some lakeshore riding in a maze of trails. There are at least five miles or more of narrow to wide single-track trails, ranging from easy to difficult and good for anything from casual

RIDE 40 *SCHOOL CREEK ORV AREA*

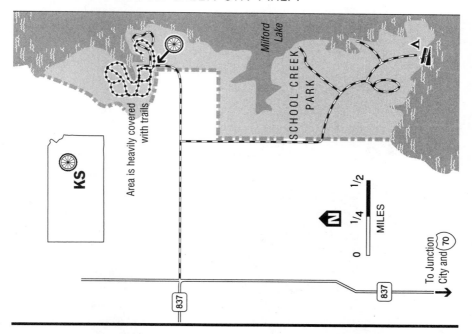

exploration to hard-core stuntmanship. The trail surfaces vary from sandy to packed dirt, with some gravel, rocky, and grassy spots. Some of the trails go in and out of steep pitlike areas that were sections of old quarries.

Milford Lake is the largest of a series of U.S. Army Corps of Engineers reservoirs in Kansas that provide flood control and manage water resources. Recreational opportunities are a secondary benefit that continue to be expanded upon since the lake was created in the 1960s. Fort Riley Military Reservation, located just to the east of the reservoir, was founded during the period of early white settlement and the resulting Indian warfare. Lt. Col. George A. Custer was stationed here in 1866, and it was here that his 7th Cavalry was organized. Before 1853 it was called Camp Center because it was believed to be near the geographical center of the United States. The U.S. Cavalry Museum is located here in the original 1855 hospital building.

General location: On the west side of Milford Lake, about 15 miles northwest of Junction City in Geary County.

Elevation change: Hills and steep banks in an old quarry in the area provide up to 25′ of relief.

Season: The trails should be usuable most times of the year except during times of winter snow, significant rain, or high water in the reservoir.

Numerous wide single-track trails zigzag through the
brush and along the slopes of an old quarry at School
Creek Park ORV Area.

Services: Water and camping facilities are available at the south end of the
School Creek unit and other Milford Lake parks. All commercial services can
be found in Junction City.

Hazards: Many of the trails and hills have blind corners or short sight lines,
so be alert and listen for fast-moving vehicles; and avoid times of heavy motor
vehicle use. Hunting is allowed on COE lands outside of the School Creek
Park.

Rescue index: Help can be reached at one of the Milford Lake parks or at the
Information Center near the dam.

Land status: U.S. Army Corps of Engineers, Kansas City District.

Maps: There is a general map of the area in the Army Corps of Engineers
pamphlet covering Milford Lake. The map in this book is sufficient to locate
the trail area and begin your ride.

Finding the trail: From Junction City, take KS 57 and KS 244 north and west to CR 837, then follow that road for 10 miles to the point where it turns west. There, turn east onto a local, unpaved road and follow it 1.5 miles to the off-road-vehicle area. There are signs to aid in direction.

Sources of additional information:

Milford Lake Project Office
U.S. Army Corps of Engineers
4020 West K57 Highway
Junction City, KS 66441-8997
(913) 238-5714

Notes on the trail: Water levels in the lake may vary, and some of the trails may be under water during times of flooding.

ADDITIONAL MOUNTAIN BIKING OPPORTUNITIES IN CENTRAL KANSAS

The city of Manhattan is partially surrounded by a flood levee, which is incorporated into the Manhattan Linear Park, a five-mile paved and limestone-surfaced trail along the Kansas River and the Big Blue River. First opened in 1988, the trail connects several city access points with the wooded Blue River Recreation Area, where there are picnic facilities and views of the river. A recreational master plan includes extending the trail all the way around the city. For more information, contact the Manhattan Parks and Recreation Department, (913) 58-PARKS.

The Arkansas River bed at the south end of Wichita near the Kansas Turnpike is an unofficial riding area in that city. The River Bike Path is a paved bike trail that runs along the Arkansas River in the middle of town and extends north to Sedgewick County Park, forming a 12-mile linear route. Sedgewick County Park has a 4.5-mile paved path and fitness trail. Maps of the Wichita area bike route and trail system are available at most Wichita bike shops.

Lakewood City Park in Salina, one-quarter mile east of Ohio Avenue on North Street, offers about 1.5 miles of easy dirt and wood-chip paths winding around a restored prairie area, a small lake, and picnic grounds.

Many of the towns of any size in central and western Kansas have city parks or local recreation areas where mountain bikers have formed unofficial trails. If you find yourself in some of these places, check with the folks at the area bicycle shops to learn about the local bike scene. Respect private property and local regulations, and have fun.

Bike Shops and Clubs

The shops mentioned below provided me with useful information. There are a number of other good bicycle shops in Wichita, Hutchinson, McPherson, and Manhattan; check the yellow pages for more information.

Bicycle Exchange
1516 East Central
Wichita, KS 67227
(316) 264-6427

Bicycle Pedaler
330 North Rock Road
Wichita, KS 67206
(316) 685-4545
Club: Oz Bicycle Club

Great Plains Bicycle, Inc.
308 West Broadway
Newton, KS 67114
(316) 283-6055

Harley's Cycle Supply
629 North Main
Hutchinson, KS 67501
(316) 663-4321

The Pathfinder
304 Poyntz Avenue
Manhattan, KS 66502
(913) 539-5639

Western Kansas

From the hilly regions of central Kansas, the high plains flatten out and begin to rise imperceptibly to the west toward their dramatic meeting with the Rocky Mountain front range. In western Kansas, these plains lack the variety that you'll see in the three Great Plains states to the north. Many rivers and stream beds make their way east across this area, but few carry water all the way across it. Even the mighty Arkansas River, a whitewater spectacle in Colorado, is a dry, sandy corridor much of the time. Yet, even in this land of exquisite geographical uniformity, there are some spots of natural diversity.

Irrigated agriculture and cattle ranching are the mainstays of the western Kansas economy, and although the rough-and-tumble days of the wild west are long gone, the lore of western history still leaves its mark on this region. Dodge City was the end of the trail for many a cattle drive, and its colorful history is re-created from Boot Hill to the old Front Street. Other prairie towns such as Cimarron, Garden City, Goodland, Hays, Liberal, Meade, and Ness City feature old buildings, landmarks, and museums that quietly tell the story of this region.

In a sparsely populated region such as this there are naturally few mountain bikers to inspire trail development, and its proximity to Colorado implies that if you're this far across Kansas already, it's only another five hours to the Rockies. Nevertheless, there are several rides here worthy of a stop; spend an hour—or a day—exploring the area. The Cimarron National Grassland, in particular, is a unique out-of-the-way corner of the west worth a visit.

RIDE 41   *CIMARRON NATIONAL GRASSLAND*

Cimarron National Grassland provides a variety of mountain biking opportunities in a unique, remote part of Kansas. Only a few miles from the old boundary markers where the state meets Oklahoma and Colorado, this area is the most arid corner of the five-state Great Plains area covered in this book. Here, the open expanse of the high plains is accented by the wooded Cimarron River corridor and the adjacent route of the historic Santa Fe Trail. Two trail systems take advantage of these features and make a journey "off the beaten track" to this area worthwhile.

149

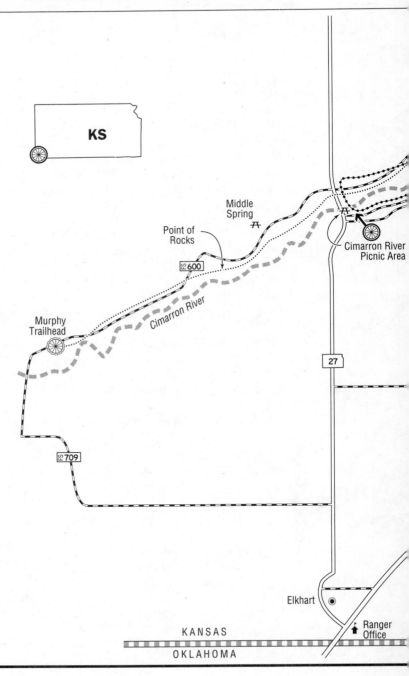

KS

Middle
Spring

Point of
Rocks

F2 600

Cimarron River
Picnic Area

Murphy
Trailhead

Cimarron River

27

F2 709

Elkhart

KANSAS

OKLAHOMA

Ranger
Office

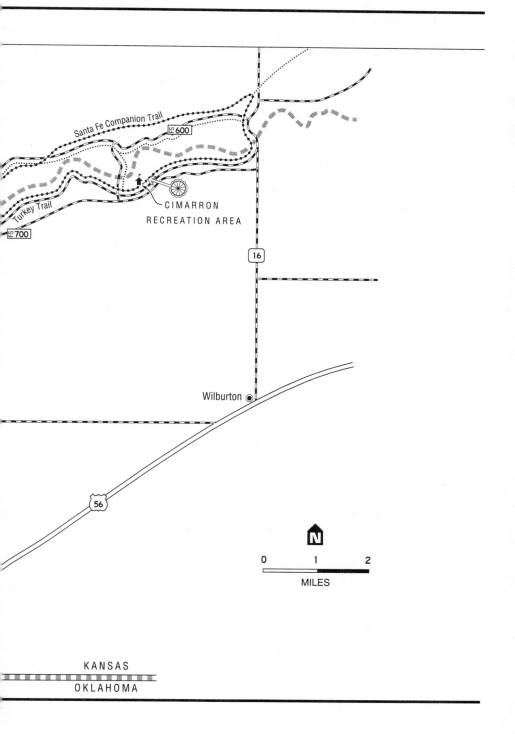

Santa Fe Companion Trail

SC 600

Turkey Trail

SC 700

CIMARRON
RECREATION AREA

16

Wilburton

56

N

0   1   2
MILES

KANSAS
OKLAHOMA

151

The Turkey Trail is a nine-mile double-track trail that parallels the cottonwood-forested Cimarron River bed. Although sandy in spots, this trail provides generally easy biking in a parklike setting with enough shade for the hot, sunny days of summer and protection on the cool, windy days of winter. Named for the wild turkeys found in the area, the trail provides a good chance to see other wildlife as well. It can be ridden as an out-and-back ride or combined with parts of the Santa Fe Companion Trail or other grassland roads to form various loops.

A recently completed addition to the Cimarron grassland is the Companion Trail to the old Santa Fe Trail route. This 19-mile mowed track either follows the original wagon route or closely parallels it, where it leaves the old wagon ruts and trail remnants still visible. Two major landmarks on the Santa Fe Trail are accessible from the Companion Trail: Point of Rocks, which was a rock formation used by Native Americans and travelers to observe the surrounding valley, and Middle Spring, which was the first reliable source of water for westbound trail users for almost 40 miles. The Companion Trail is open to hikers, horseback riders, animal-drawn vehicles, and bicycles, so the surface may be somewhat rough, but it nonetheless offers an exciting experience for those wishing to ride and daydream about life on the trail in the days of wagon travel.

In addition to these two options, there are several dozen miles of gravel and unimproved roads zigzagging around the grassland past stock watering tanks, moisture collectors, and operational oil pumping stations, connecting various points on the windswept high prairie. There are as many miles of riding possibilities in this area as any avid biker is willing to explore.

This seemingly barren prairie region is quite rich with wildlife; deer, antelope, elk, coyotes, and reptiles, including snakes, lizards, and box turtles, can be seen. There is also a wide variety of prairie bird life here, such as pheasants, quail, wild turkey, and the lesser prairie chicken. The grassland habitat is described as a midgrass prairie, with a mixture of short and tall grasses as well as sagebrush, yucca, and some cactus species. The bed of the Cimarron River is generally dry, the region receiving an average rainfall of less than 16 inches, but the water table is just below the surface. This corridor supports a cottonwood forest and other river-bottom vegetation that provides a home for much of the wildlife.

The section of the Santa Fe Trail in the Cimarron National Grassland is the longest portion remaining on public land. The Cimarron Route through this region was the shortest way to Santa Fe, although lack of water sources and hostile Indians made this route more hazardous than the alternate route through the southern Colorado mountains. The trail was used primarily as a freight route for trading between old Mexico and the expanding United States. After the Mexican-American War of 1846–48 ended with the annexation of New Mexico, trade along the Santa Fe Trail expanded as a series of army forts were set up. By the time of the Civil War, conflicts with Native Americans forced many of those using the Santa Fe Trail to use the mountain route. After that, the trail gradually diminished in importance as the railroads pushed their way west.

The Cimarron National Grassland is one of many grasslands in the plains states established by a federal program in the 1930s to reclaim lands severely eroded during the dust bowl years of the Depression. (See Ride 71 for a discussion on the national grasslands.)

Today, the Cimarron National Grassland provides active grazing land for the cattle industry and oil and gas production, along with a nice mix of recreational opportunities in an area that was little more than a badly eroded desert 60 years ago.

General location: Eight miles north of Elkhart in Morton County.

Elevation change: With an overall elevation variation of about 500′, this area has generally level to gently rolling terrain.

Season: In dry weather, the roads and trails of the national grassland can be used throughout the year.

Services: There is one established campground and two picnic areas with water and rest rooms available along the Cimarron River corridor. Primitive camping is possible in other areas of the grassland; check with the district office in Elkhart for details. Other commercial services are available in Elkhart.

Hazards: Cactus thorns could be a problem if you veer off the established road and trail system. Watch for occasional vehicle traffic when using or crossing area roads. Hunting is allowed in the grassland; check locally for seasons.

Rescue index: Some areas of the grassland are not frequently visited, so plan ahead when venturing away from the main routes. Help can be obtained along the main highway or in Elkhart.

Land status: Cimarron National Grassland is a division of the U.S. Forest Service.

Maps: The $3 Forest Service map covering the Cimarron National Grassland shows the road system and adequate information on trail location. For detailed maps, use the USGS 7.5 minute quads for Elkhart North, Wilburton, Elkhart NE, and Rolla NW.

Finding the trail: From Elkhart, take KS 27 north 7.5 miles to the Cimarron Picnic Area, just south of the Cimarron River crossing. This is the southwest end of the Turkey Trail, which can also be reached by driving 5 miles east on the adjacent FS 700 to the Cimarron Recreation Area, where there is water, camping, and rest rooms. The Companion Trail can be accessed at KS 27 just north of the river crossing or at the Murphy Trailhead, which can be reached by traveling 2 miles north of Elkhart on KS 27 and turning onto FR 709, then traveling 9 miles west and north to FR 600, and then east 1 mile. Parking, water, and rest rooms are located there.

Sources of additional information:

District Ranger
Cimarron National Grassland
242 Highway 56 East, Box J
Elkhart, KS 67950
(316) 697-4621

Notes on the trail: Several loop rides are possible by combining the Turkey Trail with portions of the Companion Trail and/or FR 700 and FR 600. One such loop, which makes for a mildly ambitious 19-mile introduction to this area, involves riding the entire Turkey Trail from Cimarron Picnic Area to its east end at CR 16, then riding north to FR 600 or a bit farther to the Santa Fe Companion Trail. Either one of these, or parts of both can then be ridden back to KS 27 and the picnic area. There is a cutoff on the Turkey Trail just west of the Cimarron Recreation Area that leads north to FR 600, trimming about 7 miles out of the loop.

If you're venturing out onto other back roads, be sure to respect private property. Use the Forest Service map to determine what lands are under federal ownership. Limestone fenceposts have been used in some areas on the old Santa Fe Trail as trail markers. Plan ahead and carry plenty of water in hot weather. Water in stock-watering wells cannot be assumed to be safe. By getting an early morning start, you can avoid the hottest parts of the day, and you'll have a greater chance of seeing wildlife as well. The grassland is an active grazing area, so be sure to leave fences as you find them. In the event of heavy rain, be alert to possible flooding and to muddy back roads, which for most vehicles will be impassable.

RIDE 42   *LAKE SCOTT STATE PARK*

In the semiarid landscape of western Kansas, Lake Scott State Park provides a partially wooded setting in a quiet valley surrounded by small canyons and bluffs. Several natural springs and the sheltered lowlands have been attracting prairie travelers for centuries. A multi-use horseback and mountain bike trail about six miles long circles the lake and upper creek area in the park, providing some relatively easy to moderately challenging terrain. The trail varies from grassy to sandy with some rocks, and there are some overgrown, indistinct areas where you may need to search for the trail or detour to the park road. Plans for upgrading the trail system have been mentioned by several sources. Plan to spend a few hours of pleasant exploration in a setting with other outdoor facilities and attractions to enjoy.

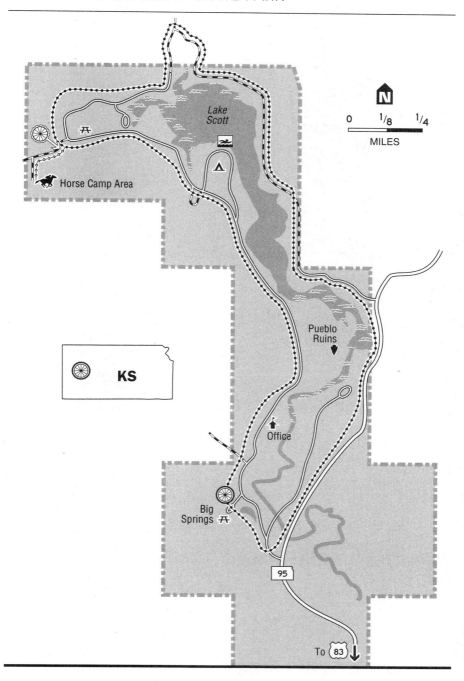

Lake Scott

Horse Camp Area

N

0   1/8   1/4
MILES

KS

Pueblo Ruins

Office

Big Springs

95

To 83

The Chalk Pyramids near Lake Scott State Park provide
an unusual break in the western Kansas prairie.

Lake Scott was created by a dam in 1929 and now is a popular regional fishing and boating spot. Of historical interest in the park is the partially restored El Cuartelejo Indian Pueblo, which a band of Taos Indians who escaped Spanish rule had established in about 1650. It was the northernmost pueblo dwelling built in the Southwest. After being excavated in 1970, this National Historic Landmark was made available to visitors. Close by is the Steele Homestead Museum, which is housed in a restored nineteenth-century pioneer farmhouse. Near the south end of the park is a privately maintained herd of buffalo.

Also worth a visit are the Chalk Pyramids, also called Monument Rocks, an unusual collection of erosion formations located near the Smoky Hill River, about 15 miles northeast of Lake Scott, an area sometimes referred to as the "Badlands of Kansas" by the locals. These groups of chalk pillars are surrounded by a few four-wheel-drive tracks, a possible short bike ride. Follow county roads in toward the east about seven miles from either side of the Smoky Hill River valley on US 83.

General location: About 13 miles north of Scott City in Scott County.
Elevation change: There is about 150′ of vertical relief here, from the 2,820′ level of the lake to the tops of the bluffs.
Season: The trails should be usable most of the year, except in very wet conditions.
Services: Water, rest rooms, a beach, and picnic and camping facilities are available in the park. Other services can be found in Scott City.
Hazards: Watch for vehicle traffic where the trail crosses the park roads.
Rescue index: The park is not always staffed, but help can always be found in Scott City.
Land status: Kansas Department of Wildlife and Parks.
Maps: A park brochure and map can be obtained at the park or by contacting the office listed below.
Finding the trail: The park can be reached by taking the KS 95 loop from US 83 north of Scott City. The trail encircles the lake and can be reached from a number of places along the nearby park roads. The Big Springs picnic area at the south end of the park and the campground and beach area on the lake near Horsethief Canyon are two good spots to begin your ride.

Sources of additional information:

> Lake Scott State Park
> Route 1, Box 50
> Scott City, KS 67871-1075
> (316) 872-2061

Notes on the trail: Yield to horseback riders on the trail. Improvements to the trail system may be in the works for the near future. A park entry fee is required for vehicles.

RIDE 43 *CEDAR BLUFF RESERVOIR*

Cedar Bluff Reservoir, formed by a dam on the Smokey Hill River, is just about the westernmost of the large reservoir recreation areas in Kansas; it's located on the western edge of the Smokey Hill region. Rolling prairie hills with some abrupt limestone outcroppings make for some typical western Kansas scenery, and quiet back roads in places around the reservoir provide some pleasant biking. The highlight of the area is an out-and-back ride to the highest of the bluffs on the south side, which offers a dramatic panoramic view of the reservoir from a limestone cliff. The gravel, dirt, and double-track

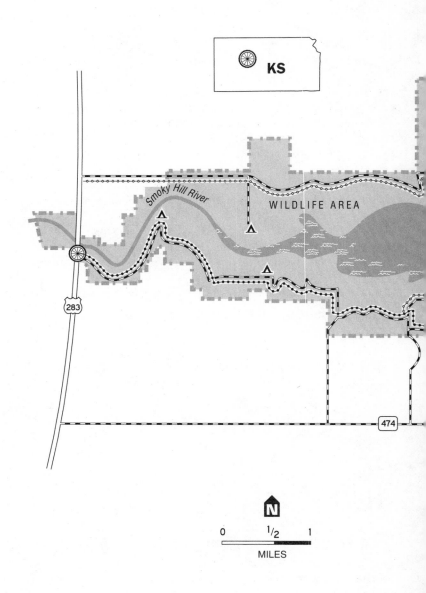

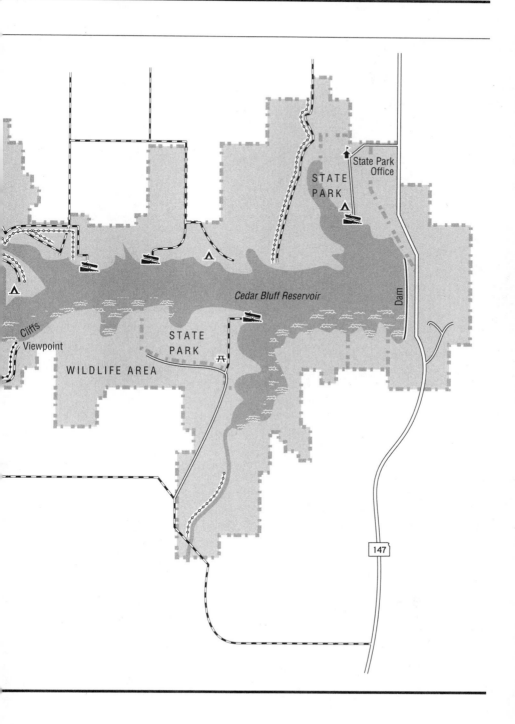

State Park
Office

STATE
PARK

Cedar Bluff Reservoir

Dam

Cliffs
Viewpoint

STATE
PARK

WILDLIFE AREA

147

The backroads on the south side of Cedar Bluff Reservoir lead to some interesting cliffs.

roads have generally easy grades and present no technical difficulties, except perhaps in wet weather. The out-and-back ride to the limestone cliffs from US 283 is about 6.5 miles (13 miles total) through stands of cottonwoods in the valley, along meadows, and past some cultivated fields to the cedar-dotted bluffs area. Ambitious bikers can circumnavigate the entire reservoir/park area with a 30-mile jaunt.

General location: In Trego County, about 25 miles southwest of Hays.
Elevation change: The bluff terrain on the south side of the lake has up to 150′ of vertical relief above the approximate lake level of 2,125′.
Season: Park roads and trails are accessible most of the year except during times of occasional winter snow or significant rains.
Services: Water is available in the park from April 15 to October 15. Rest rooms and campgrounds are located at several points around the reservoir. All other services can be found in Wakeeney or Hays.
Hazards: Approach the bluff lookouts with caution; there are abrupt drop-offs of over 100′. Be alert for motor vehicle traffic on most of the back roads.
Rescue index: There are usually other visitors to the park. During business hours, help can be obtained at the park office.
Land status: Kansas Department of Wildlife and Parks.
Maps: Diagram maps of the park and reservoir area can be picked up at the state park office.

Finding the trail: The two units of the state park can be reached on KS 147, 15 miles south of Interstate 70/exit 135. The back roads on the southwest side of the reservoir can be reached by US 283, about 15 miles south of Wakeeney. Watch for a turnoff just south of the Smokey Hill River crossing.

Sources of additional information:

> Cedar Bluff State Park
> Route 2, Box 76A
> Ellis, KS 67637-9403
> (913) 726-3212

> Bohm's Bike Shop
> 1011 Main
> Hays, KS 67601
> (913) 625-7447

Notes on the trail: The ride to the cliffs can be started at the information sign at the junction of US 283 and the local access road, just to the south of the Smokey Hill River, or at one of the parking spots or primitive campsites along the access road. Continue east, keeping left, through the seasonal road (still bikeable in the off-season), to the cliff access road. Go left up the hill onto the plateau to the top of the cliffs. The access road to the cliffs is marked with a sign from the east along CR 474 on the south side of the reservoir. Also on that road, south of the South Shore Camping Area at Page Creek, is a parking area with a double-track waiting to be explored.

ADDITIONAL MOUNTAIN BIKING OPPORTUNITIES IN WESTERN KANSAS

The dry Arkansas River bed in Garden City has several miles of accessible, flat terrain, criss-crossed with single- and double-track trails. A lot of it may be too sandy for many riders' preferences, but with the right amount of moisture in the soil or when it is frozen in the winter, this environment could be fun for a short spin. Check the local bike shops in the other towns along the river for more ideas on where to ride in this region.

Bike Shops

> Country Pedaler
> 109 Gunsmoke
> Dodge City, KS 67801
> (316) 227-2267

The Bike Rack
209 North Main
Garden City, KS 67846
(316) 275-8580
or 1-800-953-8580

Windy Plains Bike Shop
1118 Main Avenue
Goodland, KS 67735
(913) 899-3911

NEBRASKA

Most Americans have seen Nebraska only from the perspective of Interstate 80, flying past at 70 miles per hour. Yet this 77,350-square-mile slice of the Great Plains contains a surprisingly diverse array of natural areas of interest to outdoor enthusiasts and to mountain bikers as well. From heavily forested river bluffs along the Missouri River to the ponderosa-topped escarpments of the Pine Ridge, there is some challenging terrain that will make you want to veer off the freeway and explore the remote corners of the "Cornhusker" state.

The Missouri River forms the eastern and northeastern boundary of Nebraska and was the major corridor that defined the early development of the state. This region consists of low rolling hills made up of eroded glacial debris and wind-blown silt deposited near the end of the last Ice Age. A wide corridor of flat terrain along the Platte River stretches to the west; this is the level plain seen by most travelers on I-80. The many forested valleys and ridges of the Missouri River country gradually give way to the open prairie lands that stretch all the way to the Rockies. Most of the original tall-grass prairie has been replaced by farmland and grazing land, but remnants of this vast sea of grass can be found in many of the recreation areas and wildlife preserves.

About one-quarter of Nebraska consists of a unique region called the Sandhills. This vast rolling grassland is actually the western hemisphere's largest collection of sand dunes, covered with a veneer of prairie. Underlying much of this area is an extensive aquifer that provides water for a system of rivers that flows out of this area and allows for irrigated agriculture in the valleys. Although this source of water is gradually being depleted, the region is currently one of the finest beef-producing areas in the U.S.

Western Nebraska is decidedly more arid and rugged, with isolated buttes and pine-topped, meandering escarpments rising out of the short-grass prairie. These high plains blend right in with Wyoming to the west and the convoluted badlands perimeter of the Black Hills to the north.

Human beings have inhabited what is now Nebraska since the end of the Ice Age. Traditional cultures engaged in primitive agriculture and limited hunting until the introduction of the horse, which allowed for a more mobile lifestyle based on buffalo hunting. The first European explorers to reach the area were either the Spanish coming north out of Mexico, or the French following the river courses south into the prairies. "Ownership" of the vast plains region of North America was disputed for almost a century, as England, France, and Spain, influenced by political changes going on in Europe, made competing claims. In 1803 President Jefferson of the newly formed United States picked up the Louisiana Purchase territories from Napoleon, and in effect, doubled the size of the United States.

The Lewis and Clark Expedition brought back descriptions of this vast region, and after a series of forts were established, the Platte River valley became a major link in the series of wagon train routes, including the Oregon

Trail and the Mormon Trail, that brought settlers to the west. Almost a third of a million settlers moved over these trails to the Oregon Territory and other western destinations. Later, the Kansas-Nebraska Act of 1854 opened up the plains to settlement, and after the Civil War, steamboat and railroad transportation brought rapid development to the territory. Nebraska gained statehood in 1867. The rest of the century was generally a period of growth and prosperity, but in times of economic trouble, the farm economy would usually suffer the most. Nebraska was a center of populist politics, and William Jennings Bryan, a fiery Nebraskan, influenced U.S. politics for the first several decades of the twentieth century.

The Great Depression and the drought of the 1930s hit Nebraska hard, and it wasn't until after World War II and the introduction of widespread irrigation that the state returned to good times. Today, the state is a major producer of beef and corn and has a diversified service industry that adds stability to the economy. Nebraska is still a hub of east-west transportation for the northern and central United States.

Hot summers and moderate to cold winters create very distinct seasons in Nebraska. Precipitation and summer humidity tend to decrease as you travel west across the state, and much of the precipitation comes in the summer months, often in the form of thunderstorms. Winter brings periodic snowfall, which persists in the wooded areas, and occasional blizzards can virtually shut things down. The spring season is a fine time for bike riding, and, with local variations, most trails and roads should be dried out by mid- to late April. Autumn also can provide much pleasant weather for most outdoor activities, and unless there are long periods of rain or early winter storms, the biking season can extend into November and beyond.

Mountain Biking in Nebraska

Like the other plains states, there is a well-established community of road bicyclists in the larger towns and cities. Mountain biking is a much more recent phenomenon and is just beginning to get organized attention. Some of the local clubs and bike shops have sponsored races and rides and have worked with park officials to get mountain bikers accepted as valid users of public trails. These local bike shops and groups are your best source of information on the mountain biking scene in a given area. Nebraska has a strong network of state parks and recreation areas that provide many of the mountain biking opportunities throughout the state. The decision as to whether mountain bikes are allowed on trails in a particular park generally is made by the local supervisors, so check before using trails if you are unsure of their status.

Nebraska National Forest (yes, there really is one) has units around the central and western parts of the state that feature some unique trails in as much of a wilderness setting as there is available elsewhere in the state. There are also a number of city and county parks with small but fun places to ride.

Some of these rides are close to the interstate highway and make great places to stop for some exercise if you are just passing through the state with your bike. Many of these rides are worthwhile destinations in their own right, and I believe you will be pleasantly surprised by the diversity that is available in Nebraska's trails.

For Further Information

Nebraska Trails Council
Eastern Nebraska Trails Network
Elmwood Park Station
P.O. Box 6725
Omaha, NE 68106

Nebraska Travel and Tourism
Department of Economic Development
P.O. Box 94666
Lincoln, NE 68509-4666
(800) 228-4307, (402) 471-3796 or 471-3026 fax

Eastern Nebraska

The rolling hills and plains of eastern Nebraska contain most of the state's population, which is centered in the Omaha, Lincoln, and Platte River valley corridor. Much of the rest of the region is devoted to crop agriculture, which is still the foundation of the area's economy. The Missouri River forms the eastern and northern boundary of this region and was the original travel corridor for Native Americans, explorers, trappers, and settlers. Most of the region's state parks, recreation areas, and established trail systems, are along these major river courses.

Containing about one-third of Nebraska's population, Omaha is perhaps the most cosmopolitan city on the northern Great Plains. Anyone who misses the urban life will feel at home with the city's cultural, entertainment, and commercial opportunities. The Old Market district, the Union Pacific Historical Museum, Great Plains Black History Museum, Strategic Air Command Museum, and three other museums, as well as the Henry Doorly Zoo and horse racing at the Ak-Sar-Ben track, can provide a busy schedule for any visitors. North of Omaha at Fort Calhoun is Fort Atkinson State Historical Park, site of the first fort west of the Missouri River established in 1820 in a location recommended by the Lewis and Clark Expedition.

Not to be outdone, nearby Lincoln, Nebraska's capital and second largest city, features its own attractions. South Sioux City is the Nebraska part of the tri-state Sioux City area and is a major beef-processing center. Beatrice, Columbus, Fremont, and Norfolk are other regional centers firmly anchored in an agricultural economy.

Most of the mountain biking areas in eastern Nebraska are located in small, self-contained parks and recreation areas. In this section, I will describe six state park trail systems, two other trail systems operated by city and regional jurisdictions, and Nebraska's major rail trail.

RIDE 44   *INDIAN CAVE STATE PARK*

This is perhaps the premier mountain biking destination in eastern Nebraska, featuring over 15 miles of single-track riding on a combination of hiking and horse trails. The trail system consists of 11 numbered trails that form a series of loops in mostly moderate to difficult terrain. All the trails traverse a hilly oak hardwood forest with steep ravines cutting into the bluffs along the Missouri River, offering periodic vistas of the surrounding ridges and the wide

RIDE 44   *INDIAN CAVE STATE PARK*

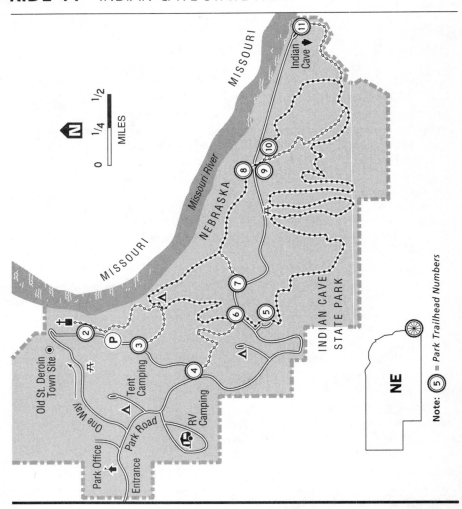

Missouri River floodplain to the east. Some steep climbs and descents, occasional obstacles, wet spots, and erosion add some technical challenges. Packed dirt, with some rocks, roots, and grassy spots make up the trail surface. You'll also encounter bumpy horse paths. You can enjoy anywhere from half a day to a couple of days biking here.

The wooded oasis of the park provides habitat for a wide variety of animal life. You may surprise some deer or see turkey vultures soaring over the ridges on warm days. In the spring and fall the Missouri River valley is a major waterfowl migratory route. Other attractions in the park include Indian Cave,

There are plenty of hills to climb in Indian Cave State Park.

Half-Breed Cemetery (a spur off Trail 2), and a restored log cabin, store, and schoolhouse at the site of St. Deroin, a colorful river community dating back to the 1850s.

The nearby historic town of Brownville, founded in 1854, was one of the first white settlements in the Kansas-Nebraska Territory. It was near here that the first claim of the Homestead Act, which gave virtually free land to settlers, was filed. The old downtown area features several restaurants, antique stores, and souvenir shops. Nearby are the Brownville Historical Society Museum and the Meriwether Lewis and Missouri River History Museum. In Nebraska City, you can visit a cave and passageway that were used to hide slaves escaping from nearby Missouri on the Underground Railroad.

General location: On the bluffs of the Missouri River, 15 miles southeast of Brownville between Nemaha and Richardson Counties.
Elevation change: Steep climbs and descents are common on the trails, with an elevation range of over 300′ from the Missouri River to the tops of the ridges.
Season: Midspring through late autumn. Off-season riding is possible during periods of moderate weather and when there is no snow on the ground. Spring thawing may render the trails too muddy for biking.
Services: Parking lots, water, rest rooms, and picnic and camping facilities are scattered throughout the park. Primitive campsites and Adirondack shelters

are available for hike-in or bike-in camping. The nearby town of Nemaha has a small store. All other services are available in Auburn and Falls City.

Hazards: Steep descents and occasional rocks and logs make riding under control imperative. When thunderstorms are possible, keep an eye on the sky when you're biking the ridges. Indian Cave State Park has an emergency siren system that warns of severe weather, fires, and other emergencies.

Rescue index: This is generally a busy park. The entrance gate and park offices are manned during the summer season.

Land status: Indian Cave State Park is managed by the Nebraska Game and Parks Commission.

Maps: An informative map/brochure is available at the park entrance.

Finding the trail: From NE 67, travel 5 miles east on NE S64E to the park entrance. There are parking lots on the paved park road near the various numbered trailheads. You may have to look closely for the trailheads; they are not all clearly marked.

Sources of additional information:

Indian Cave State Park
RR 1, Box 30
Shubert, NE 68437-9801
(402) 883-2575

Bike Rack
2528 South 130th Avenue
Omaha, NE 68144
(402) 333-1031 or 691-0080 fax

Thurman Bike & Sport Shop
1104 Third Corso
Nebraska City, NE 68410
(402) 873-7509

Notes on the trail: The various trailheads are numbered 1 through 11, with all but number 1 at the north end of the park open to biking. There are many possible trail loops in the park, but to get a good 10-plus-mile tour of the area, start with Trail 6, ride to the four-way junction, turn right, and continue east to trailhead 8, cross the park road and do part of the 9-10 loop, and return west to trailhead 5. Trail 6 starts at the north end of an open grassy area near a parking lot. Trails 6, 2, and 3 all descend and meet at the four-way junction in a thick ravine. Climbing to the east, the trail tops a ridge along the river and joins "Rock Bluff Run," for some great views of the river valley and across it to the state of Missouri. A steep drop brings you back to the park road near trailheads 8, 9, and 10.

The 9-10 loop does some steep climbing onto another scenic ridge, crosses some open meadows, and provides access to Trails 5 and 11. Trail 11 leads down to Indian Cave, site of some Indian petroglyphs. Trail 5 descends and climbs westward across several more ridges and meadowlands, returning to the park road near the trailheads of 4 and 6. Eroded ruts from horse use on Trail 5 make parts of it awkward to pedal, but the trail does provide a nice return route from the 3-8-9-10 combination. Additional riding can easily be added to the loop if you explore the other connecting trails, such as 4 or 7. Note the one-way direction on the paved park road loop that provides access to trailheads 2, 3, and 4.

As always, avoid riding when the trails are muddy, and yield the right-of-way to hikers and horseback riders. A state park sticker or daily entrance fee is required in Nebraska state parks.

RIDE 45   *IRON HORSE TRAIL LAKE AND RECREATION AREA*

Iron Horse Trail Lake is a relatively recent development that was created by a flood-control dam in 1983 near an old railroad route. The area opened for recreation in 1985, and about four miles of multi-use trails have been developed for use by hikers and other nonmotorized users. Two loop trails, one on each side of the lake, can be combined into an elongated figure eight–shaped route, or used to circumnavigate the lake. The trail system traverses a mixture of open meadows and thickly wooded hillsides over a five-foot-wide corridor of mowed vegetation, with occasional rocks, wet spots, thick grasses, and downed branches providing moderately easy to moderately challenging biking. These trails appear to get only occasional use, so you'll have to pay close attention to avoid wandering off on the many deer trails in the area. For mountain bikers wanting to explore a variety of riding areas in eastern Nebraska, the Iron Horse Trail has a relaxed, out-of-the-way atmosphere worth a visit.

Nearby, west of Humboldt, is Kirkman's Cove Recreation Area, a similar facility with a four-mile-long trail system. The nearby Pawnee City Historical Society Museum features a collection of pioneer artifacts contained in 16 buildings, one of which was the home of the state's first governor.

General location: In southeastern Pawnee County, 3 miles northwest of the town of DuBois or about 7 miles southeast of Pawnee City.
Elevation change: Gently rolling hills in this area provide some easy ups and downs.
Season: Spring through late autumn. Off-season riding is possible except during times of winter snow and spring thawing. Some spots may be flooded during times of high water in the reservoir.
Services: The recreation area has rest rooms, water, and picnic and camping facilities. There is a general store in DuBois, and other services are available in Pawnee City.

RIDE 45 *IRON HORSE TRAIL LAKE AND RECREATION AREA*

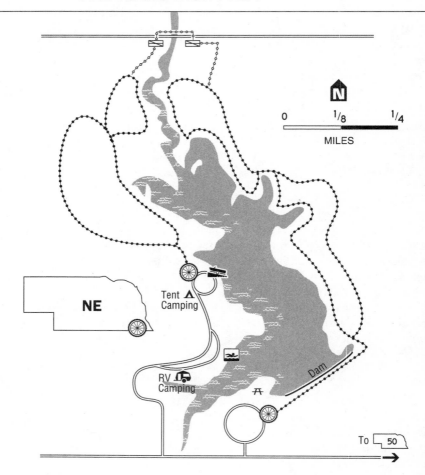

Hazards: Watch for vehicle traffic when using the park and local roads for trail access. The mowed stubble on the trail corridor in the woods can be sharp and therefore hard on tires.

Rescue index: Emergency help can be reached in DuBois.

Land status: Nemaha Natural Resources District.

Maps: A recreation area pamphlet is available from the Natural Resources District office.

Finding the trail: The two entrances to the recreation area can be reached from NE 50, one-half mile north of DuBois, then 2.5 miles west on a local gravel road; the turnoff is well marked. The trailhead and parking area are at

The forested trails in Iron Horse Lake Recreation Area make a quiet out-of-the-way destination.

the end of the park beach and campground access road near the boat ramp. The trails on the east side of the lake can be reached by crossing the dam from the day use area, which is the first park entrance you'll come to from the east.

Sources of additional information:

Nemaha Natural Resources District
125 Jackson
P.O. Box 717
Tecumseh, NE 68450
(402) 335-3325 or 335-3265 fax

Notes on the trail: The loop trails on the west side of the lake run through mostly forested terrain. Due to flooding, a bridge crossing over the creek to the east side is out, but it is possible to continue around the lake by heading north through some meadows to the county road at the north end of the recreation area. Cross the boundary fence at a cable gate, and on the other side of the creek re-enter at another gate and then follow the east boundary fence lines south to the trails. The east-side trail loops meander with a "high route" and a "low route" through a mixture of woodlands and open meadowlands. At the south end, you will need to cross an open, low area, which might be wet in times of rainy weather, and continue to the top of the dirt dam and return via the roads to the trailhead. There are no permits or camping fees required in the park.

RIDE 46   *MOPAC EAST RECREATION TRAIL*

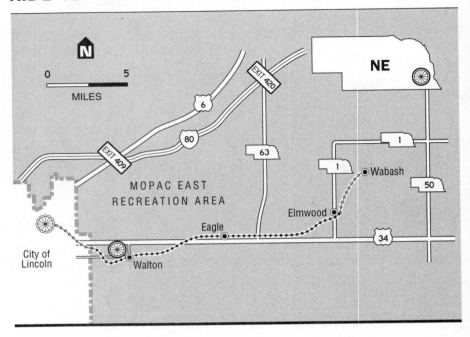

RIDE 46   *MOPAC EAST RECREATION TRAIL*

Running east from Lincoln into the rural countryside is Nebraska's major rail-conversion trail, the MoPac East Recreation Trail. This 25-mile, multi-use "linear" park runs along a corridor that alternates between a wooded canopy providing shade and wind protection and open vistas of farms and fields. About an 18-mile stretch of the trail surface is finished with crushed limestone as far east as Elmwood, but the unfinished roadbed is mountain bikeable to Wabash. As the railroad bed of the Missouri Pacific Railroad, the route provided passenger service from 1886 until 1954, and the grade was abandoned after flood damage in 1984. The land was acquired in 1991, and the MoPac East Trail Coalition was formed to coordinate development of the recreation trail. A volunteer effort helped to put the finishing touches on the 18-mile section in 1994. The MoPac Trail is an easy biking route that should prove to be a major asset to the Lincoln-area biking community, appealing to casual riders, families, and outdoor enthusiasts alike.

The MoPac East Trail, Nebraska's premier rail-trail,
connects rural villages with the capital city of Lincoln.

General location: The trail corridor runs from the eastern outskirts of Lincoln in Lancaster County to a point east of Wabash in Cass County.

Elevation change: There is very little elevation change in this area.

Season: The trail should be rideable most of the year except in times of winter snow and spring thawing.

Services: In Walton, the Walton Trail Co. offers bike service and refreshments. Eagle and Elmwood have stores and restaurants. All other services can be found in Lincoln.

Hazards: Watch for traffic when you're crossing roads. Keep an eye out for stormy weather during thunderstorm season.

Rescue index: Help can be found in the various towns along the route.

Land status: Lower Platte South Natural Resources District.

Maps: Information with basic maps can be obtained locally, from Great Plains Trails Network, or the Lincoln Parks Department.

Finding the trail: The western trailhead is located on 84th Street just south of O Street in Lincoln. Parking facilities there are not yet complete. The city of Lincoln has developed a concrete trail extension that begins at 33rd Street near Peter Pan Park, and this trail can be used as access to the MoPac Trail. Additional parking and trailheads can be found in Walton, Eagle, and Elmwood.

Sources of additional information:

Great Plains Trails Network
5000 North 7th Street
Lincoln, NE 68521

Walton Trail Co.
118th & A Streets
P.O. Box 246
Walton, NE 68461
(402) 488-5511

Notes on the trail: The Walton Trail Co., located in a 100-year-old building, offers refreshments and snacks as well as complete bike service. Information about volunteer opportunities to help further trail development is available from the Natural Resources District.

RIDE 47   *WILDERNESS PARK*

This wooded corridor along Salt Creek contains at least ten miles of single-track trails on either side of some old stream channels that wind through thick woodlands. You will be able to create round-trip rides of almost any length. The trail surface consists mostly of packed dirt with some grassy and low spots that could be muddy in wet weather; occasional bridge crossings, obstacles, and narrow sections keep you on your toes. A combined hiking and horse trail runs along a portion of the corridor. This is a good place for a few hours of relatively easy to moderate riding in a quiet setting.

Lincoln is the capital of Nebraska, and there is plenty to do in this lively city when you're not biking. The Haymarket District is an interesting shopping/restaurant area north of downtown in a century-old warehouse neighborhood. The Museum of Nebraska History features exhibits detailing the 12,000 years of human history of the plains region, and the State Museum of Natural History on the University of Nebraska campus has a great display of prehistoric mammals. Nebraska's unique state capitol building—with its landmark tower—houses the only unicameral legislature in the United States.

RIDE 47   *WILDERNESS PARK*

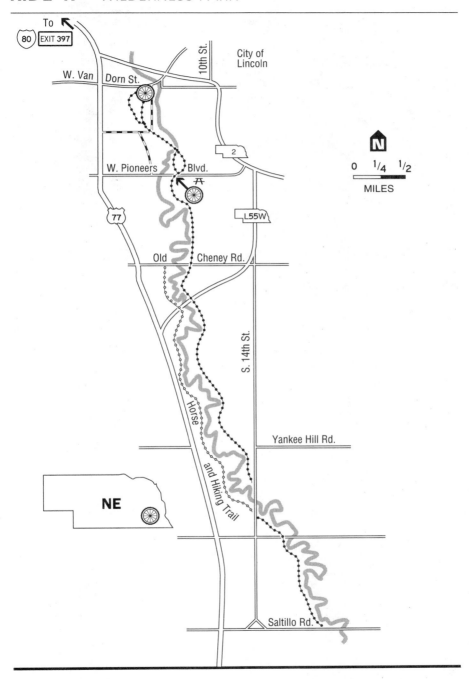

A well-developed trail system in Lincoln's Wilderness Park offers miles of pleasant riding.

General location: Adjacent to the city of Lincoln.

Elevation change: There are some short climbs and drops along old creek banks; otherwise, there is little elevation change in this area.

Season: Midspring through late autumn. Avoid riding when trails are muddy, during spring thawing, or when established cross-country ski tracks are present.

Services: All services are available in nearby Lincoln.

Hazards: Be alert for other trail users, especially when trail visibility is low in the thick woods. Watch for traffic at road crossings.

Rescue index: Help is always nearby in the city.

Land status: City of Lincoln Parks and Recreation.

Maps: A trailhead sign with a park map is posted in the parking lot on West Pioneers Boulevard.

Finding the trail: Parking lots are available just south of West Van Dorn Street on South 1st Street, on West Pioneers Boulevard, or on Old Cheney Road, which is on the southwest side of Lincoln, east of US 77.

Sources of additional information: Lincoln has an active bicycling community and a number of good bicycle shops (see listings at the end of this section of rides) that can provide more information on this area.

Notes on the trail: Heading south from the access road at South 1st Street, the main trail crosses to the east side of Salt Creek a quarter-mile north of

West Pioneers Boulevard, meanders along that side to South 14th Street, then crosses back to the west side and continues south to Saltillo Road.

This area is shared by runners, hikers, horseback riders, and skiers in the winter, and the trails are well marked for various uses. Ride cautiously and be prepared to yield the right-of-way if you cross paths with other trail users. Please follow other park rules to avoid user conflicts. It would be best to avoid biking here during wet conditions and the spring thaw period.

RIDE 48   *PLATTE RIVER STATE PARK*

Platte River State Park consists largely of a series of forested bluffs facing out over the broad expanse of the Platte River valley. There are about seven to eight miles of moderate to moderately difficult single-track hiking and horse trails intertwining on the hillsides and down in the quiet ravine of Stone Creek. Some steep grades, rocky and gravelly sections, and sharp corners add some technical challenges. A few longer climbs lead out of the ravine to various points on the park road, providing access to various park facilities or a return to the trailhead. A small waterfall on Stone Creek is the geologic highlight of the ravine area. Additional trails in a more remote part of the park can be reached by heading east from the ravine area along the river bluff trails toward Decker Creek. This "wilderness tract" provides some great vistas of the wide Platte River valley. You could easily spend several hours to the better part of a day in this park exploring the various areas.

General location: About 20 miles southwest of Omaha and 3 miles west of Louisville in Cass County.

Elevation change: The river bluffs in the park produce a variety of grades with a few steep climbs of up to 100´.

Season: The park is open all year, but check for trail conditions in the off-season. There is usually snow in the area in the midwinter months.

Services: The park has a variety of day use recreational facilities. Accommodations include cabins, a teepee village, and lodges. An observation tower next to the Scott Lodge/Restaurant provides views of the Platte valley. Louisville State Recreation Area (phone: (402) 234-6855), just north of the town of Louisville, offers camping with modern facilities. Additional services are available in Louisville and Omaha.

Hazards: Some steep grades require cautious descents. Don't cross the barbed wire fence into the railroad right-of-way along the river. Be alert for and yield to hikers in the park.

Rescue index: There are generally visitors in the park year-round. Further help can be found in Louisville.

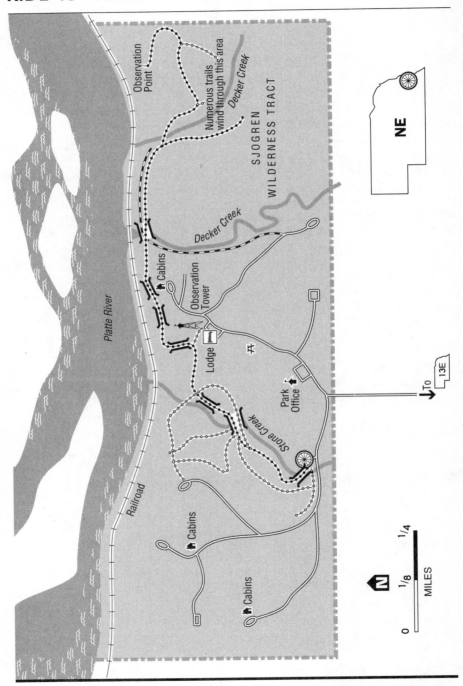

Observation Point

Numerous trails wind through this area

Decker Creek

SJOGREN WILDERNESS TRACT

Decker Creek

NE

Platte River

Cabins

Observation Tower

Lodge

Stone Creek

Park Office

To 13E

Railroad

Cabins

Cabins

N

0   1/8   1/4

MILES

A small waterfall on Stone Creek is a highlight in Platte River State Park.

Land status: Platte River State Park is managed by the Nebraska Game and Parks Commission.

Maps: A park map is available at the entrance station or park office.

Finding the trail: The park entrance is about 12 miles south of Interstate 80/exit 440 on NE 50, south of Louisville, and 2 miles west on NE Spur 13E. Parking and access to the trail system is just before the creek crossing to the left and downhill from the park entrance station. Water is available at that parking lot.

Sources of additional information:

Platte River State Park
14421 346th Street
Louisville, NE 68037-3001
(402) 234-2217 or 234-2520 fax

Notes on the trail: From the trailhead several miles of trails wind around the heavily wooded Stone Creek ravine, crossing several wooden bridges along the way. There are some additional trails northwest of the creek in the vicinity of the teepee village. Be sure to work your way east from Stone Creek along a trail above the Platte River, over a series of bridges to Owen Crossing, and to another trail system of several miles on the east side of Decker Creek. You'll be sharing this area with equestrians, but the good news is that this area offers some longer climbs and more remote loops. This is another busy state park, so please be courteous toward hikers and horseback riders, and avoid riding when the trails are muddy. A state park sticker or daily entry fee is required.

RIDE 49   *SCHRAMM PARK STATE RECREATION AREA*

This trail system consists of mostly moderate single-track trails that meander through some forested hills overlooking the Platte River. There are two loops of about 1.5 miles each, forming a figure eight and consisting of a gravel and packed-dirt surface. The recreation area is mostly wooded, with a mixture of hardwoods and evergreens, and is a haven for wildlife. This trail system has been developed primarily for walkers and other nature lovers, and with that in mind, you should bicycle here with respect for others using the trails. It would perhaps be best to avoid riding here at all during busy weekends and vacation time periods. A good strategy might be to check this area out early in the day as a warm-up ride before a tour of one of the other nearby parks, such as Platte River or Mahoney State Park (see Rides 48 and 50).

The self-guided tour on Trail 1 provides a good opportunity to learn more about the vegetation and history of the eastern Platte valley. Adjacent to the nature trails are the Ak-Sar-Ben Aquarium and the Gretna Fish Hatchery Museum, which was once an active fish hatchery—and Nebraska's first.

General location: Between Lincoln and Omaha, 6 miles south of Interstate 80, in Sarpy County.
Elevation change: This is an area of gently rolling hills and moderate grades.
Season: Midspring through late autumn. This area is usually snow covered in midwinter and too soft for biking during the spring thaw.
Services: Rest rooms and water can be found at the Ak-Sar-Ben Aquarium or the picnic area. Louisville State Recreation Area, just north of the town of Louisville, has camping with modern facilities. All other services are available in Gretna, Omaha, or Lincoln.
Hazards: There are some log stairs at several locations on the trail system. Be alert for and yield to hikers in the park. Watch for cars as you descend the gravel road from the Platte viewpoint/picnic area.
Rescue index: There are generally visitors around the area. In season, the Ak-Sar-Ben Aquarium is staffed during daytime hours.
Land status: Schramm Park State Recreation Area is managed by the Nebraska Game and Parks Commission.
Maps: An informative nature brochure and trail diagram is available at the aquarium.

RIDE 49 *SCHRAMM PARK STATE RECREATION AREA*

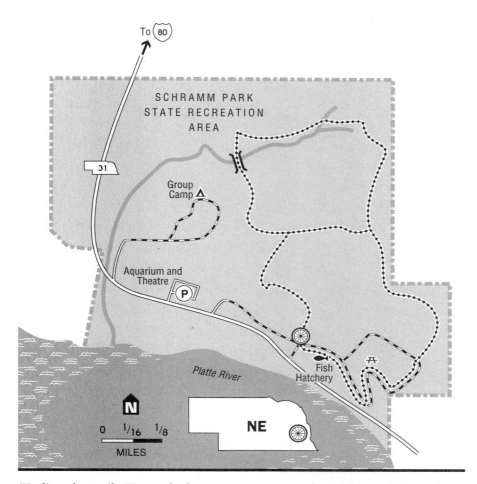

Finding the trail: To reach the recreation area, take I-80/exit 432 south on NE 31 for 6 miles. There is a small parking lot at the trailhead next to the Hatchery Museum, and more parking can be found in the picnic area. Additional parking is available at the aquarium, one-quarter mile west; a state park entry permit is not required there.

Sources of additional information:

Schramm Park SRA
21502 West Highway 31
Gretna, NE 68028
(402) 332-3901

A suspension bridge links some of the wooded trails in Schramm Park State Recreation Area.

Notes on the trail: The first trail loop is a marked nature trail climbing out of the river valley on a graveled path, over some log stairs, and meandering through a predominately oak and cedar woodland. The second loop veers left at a trail junction and is a bit less heavily traveled. The north side of the loop has some low areas along a creekbed that can be muddy in wet weather. Occasional side trails branch away, but the main trail is obvious. Several picnic shelters are available along the route. After the trails join, they emerge onto a gravel road at a viewpoint overlooking the Platte River. A sign located there describes the history of the river. From there the road returns to the trailhead via the old fish hatchery. A state park sticker or daily entry fee is required for vehicles entering the park.

RIDE 50 *EUGENE T. MAHONEY STATE PARK*

Mahoney State Park, open year-round, is Nebraska's most modern state park, offering three to four miles of single-track hiking trails situated in the oak-forested bluffs overlooking the Platte River. The well-used packed-dirt trails form an out-and-back ride with several short side loops and connecting links to the park roads. A number of bridge crossings, water bars, rocky spots, and short, steep drops in and out of small ravines provide some technical challenges in an otherwise moderately easy area.

Located halfway between Omaha and Lincoln, the park makes a nice week-end or daytime family outing that can include some introductory or more serious trail riding. For the interstate traveler, the park is convenient to the freeway and would make a nice rest stop and place to ride off some energy. Nearby, Schramm Park State Recreation Area and Platte River State Park offer additional riding and recreational opportunities.

General location: Just north of Interstate 80, between Omaha and Lincoln.
Elevation change: The hilly bluffs produce moderate grades with a few steep climbs.
Season: The park is open all year, but check for trail conditions in the off-season. There is usually snow cover in midwinter, and the trails will be too soft for biking during the spring thaw.
Services: This is a well-developed park with modern camping, restaurant, lodging, and conference facilities. A wide variety of recreational activities are available. Additional services can be found in Ashland, Lincoln, or Omaha.
Hazards: Watch for occasional steep drops, rocks, steps, and water bars. Don't cross the barbed wire fence into the railroad right-of-way along the river.
Rescue index: Park personnel are always available.
Land status: Mahoney State Park is managed by the Nebraska Game and Parks Commission.
Maps: A park map is available at the entrance station.
Finding the trail: The park entrance is just north of I-80/exit 426 on County Road 66. Parking and trail access are available at either the Riverview Lodge or the Kiewit Lodge.

Sources of additional information:

Eugene T. Mahoney State Park
28500 West Park Highway
Ashland, NE 68003-3508
(402) 944-2523 or 944-7604 fax

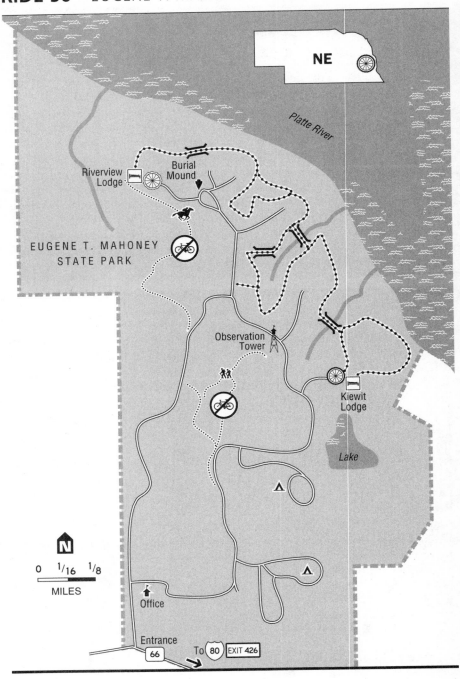

NE

Platte River

Riverview Lodge

Burial Mound

EUGENE T. MAHONEY
STATE PARK

Observation Tower

Kiewit Lodge

Lake

N

0   1/16   1/8
MILES

Office

Entrance
66
To 80   EXIT 426

Notes on the trail: The trail network runs along the wooded bluffs of the Platte River between the Riverview Lodge and the Kiewit Lodge areas of the park. Various side trails lead up to visitor cabins or other corners of the park. This is often a busy state park, so please be courteous toward hikers and avoid riding in wet weather or when the trails are muddy. Bicycles are not allowed on the horse trail system. A state park entrance sticker or daily entry fee is required.

RIDE 51 *PONCA STATE PARK*

Ponca State Park is located in a hilly, oak hardwood forest area overlooking one of the last naturally-flowing sections left on the central Missouri River. Over ten miles of hiking and horseback trails form several different loop systems in the center and southern sections of the park. The hilly terrain provides some nice ups and downs in thickly wooded ravines and ridges and occasional meadow areas. With all the hills, the single-track, packed-dirt, and grassy trails present a moderate to moderately difficult biking experience. The two horse trail loops, which give some nice views over the Missouri River valley, are available to mountain bike use when there are no organized trail rides underway. The hiking trails are open to bicycles—but be alert for walkers; they have the right-of-way. One of these trails passes a 351-year-old oak tree patiently guarding one of the many hillsides.

Other good biking opportunities nearby in the three-state area include Stone State Park in Sioux City, Iowa (Ride 25) and Lewis and Clark Recreation Area near Yankton in South Dakota (Ride 62). A 60-mile section of the Missouri River from Ponca State Park upstream to the Gavins Point Dam is designated as a National Recreation River because it is still roughly in the same condition as it was when Lewis and Clark passed through in 1804 and on their return in 1806.

General location: On the Missouri River, north of the town of Ponca in Dixon County, about 20 miles northwest of Sioux City, Iowa.
Elevation change: The Missouri River bluffs here are moderately rugged with a few steep slopes climbing almost 200′ in elevation.
Season: Midspring to late autumn. Avoid rainy periods, when the trails will be muddy.
Services: Park facilities include picnic and camping sites, a swimming pool, and modern cabins. Services are available in Ponca and South Sioux City.
Hazards: Watch for traffic when you're crossing or using the paved park roads. Yield to hikers and horseback riders.

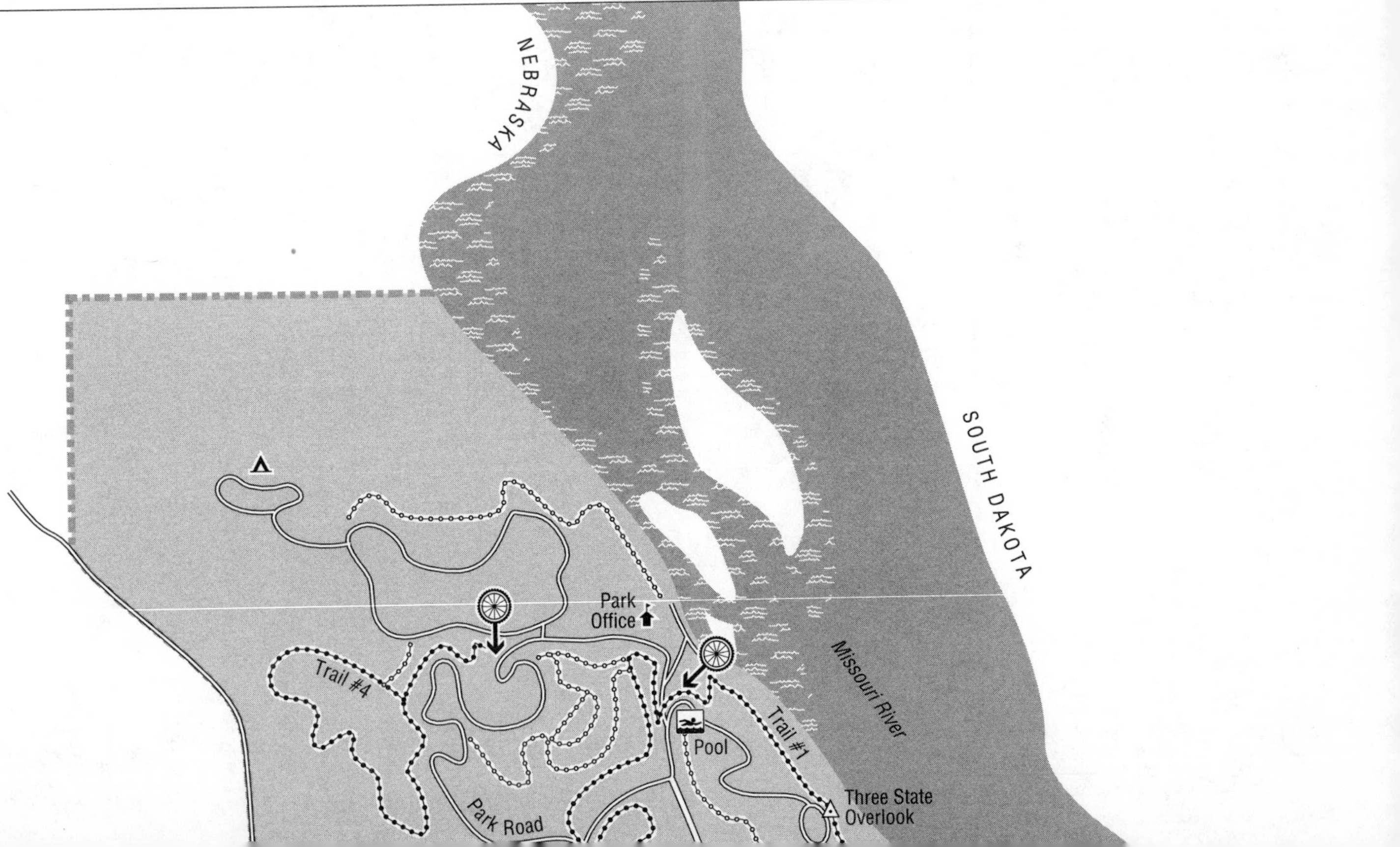

SOUTH DAKOTA

NEBRASKA

Missouri River

Three State
Overlook

Trail #1

Pool

Park
Office

Park Road

Trail #4

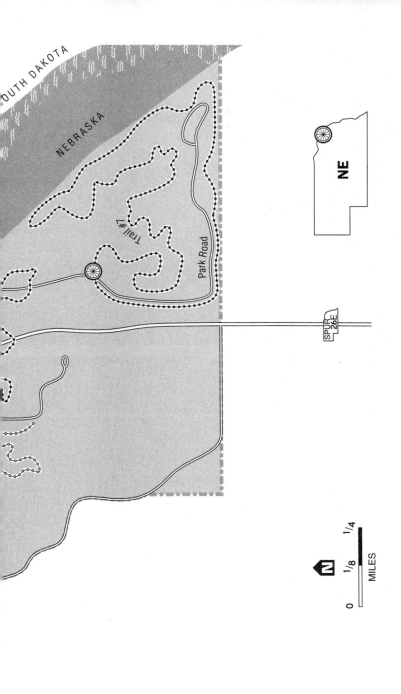

SOUTH DAKOTA

NEBRASKA

Trail #7

Park Road

SPUR
26E

NE

N

0   1/8   1/4
MILES

A trail in Ponca State Park passes under a 351-year-old oak tree.

Rescue index: Help is usually close by in this area.
Land status: Ponca State Park is managed by the Nebraska Game and Parks Commission.
Maps: An informative color map/brochure is available at the park entrance.
Finding the trail: The park entrance is 3 miles north of the town of Ponca on NE Spur 26E. Access to the trail system can be made from a number of points on the park roads. Check at the park office on the current status of the trails to determine the best place to start riding.

Sources of additional information:

> Ponca State Park
> P.O. Box 688
> Ponca, NE 68770-0688
> (402) 755-2284

Notes on the trail: There are two trail loops used by horseback riders. One originates in the park headquarters area and climbs onto the ridge above the river, where it passes the Three-State Overlook on the park road. You can park in the lots near the swimming pool to start this loop. At the south end of the park is an additional 3.5-mile horse-trail loop. Several pulloffs on the park road can be used to start that loop. The state park requests that you avoid using the equestrian trails when they are in use for organized trail rides during the busy Memorial Day to Labor Day season.

Several parking spots along the meandering park road can also be used to access the hiking trails. The first parking pulloff on the switchback road south of the **H** intersection west of the park office provides access to Trail 4, which is a pleasant, more out-of-the-way part of the park. Some, but not all, of the trail junctions are marked with signposts, so remain aware of your surroundings and the direction you're in to stay oriented.

A state park sticker or daily entry fee to the park is required.

RIDE 52 *NIOBRARA STATE PARK*

A visit to Niobrara State Park provides one of the first wide-open, "western" settings as you travel up the broad expanse of the Missouri River valley. Here, the many-channeled Niobrara River meets the wide Missouri, and the open ridges of the state park provide a dramatic panorama like few others in the region. About six to eight miles of hiking trails wind up and down over the steep, partially wooded ridges and along the river backwaters on an old railroad grade. Most of the trails are relatively easy to moderate mowed grassy corridors winding through the cedar trees, connecting various facilities of the park.

Several loop rides are possible when you use the railroad-grade trail or the park roads to tie the trail sections together. The two-mile rail trail crosses the Niobrara River on an old trestle and leads to a trailhead at the north edge of the town of Niobrara. There are tent campsites among the cedars and cabins available in the park, making this a nice destination for a family outing.

General location: Niobrara State Park is located on the confluence of the Missouri and Niobrara Rivers just west of the town of Niobrara in Knox County.

Elevation change: The terrain here is hilly, with a range of almost 300′ from the river bottoms to the ridge crests.

Season: Midspring to late autumn. The wooded areas will often have snow cover during the winter months. Avoid the spring thaw and rainy periods, when the trails will be too soft for riding.

Services: Park facilities include picnic shelters, campsites and Adirondack shelters, cabins, a swimming pool, and rest rooms at the east end of the park. Most other services are available in the town of Niobrara.

Hazards: Watch for traffic when you're crossing or using the paved park roads. Yield to hikers and use caution when descending the steep bluffs.

Rescue index: Help is usually close by in this park.

Land status: Niobrara State Park is managed by the Nebraska Game and Parks Commission.

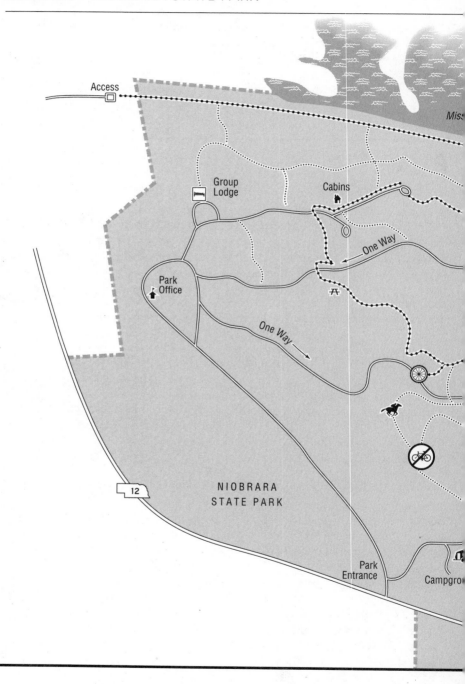

Access

Miss

Group
Lodge

Cabins

One Way

Park
Office

One Way

NIOBRARA
STATE PARK

12

Park
Entrance

Campgro

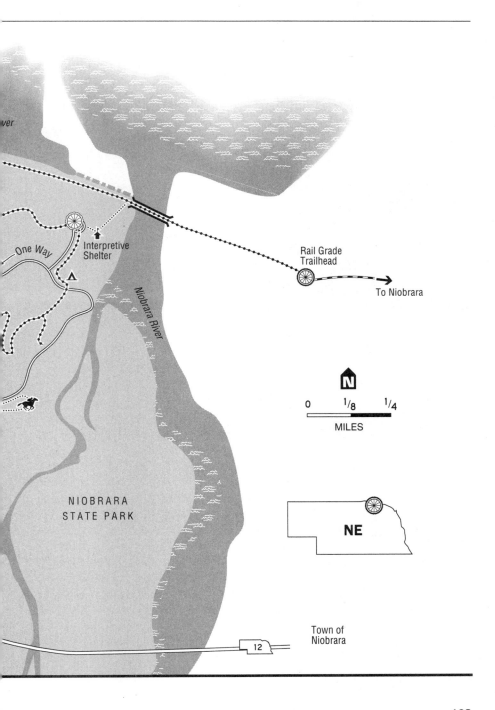

ver

One Way

Interpretive
Shelter

Niobrara River

Rail Grade
Trailhead

To Niobrara

N

0   1/8   1/4

MILES

NE

NIOBRARA
STATE PARK

Town of
Niobrara

12

Trails on the grassy ridges of Niobrara State Park provide excellent views of the vast Missouri River valley.

Maps: An informative map/brochure is available at the park entrance.
Finding the trail: The park entrance is located on NE 12, 1 mile west of the town of Niobrara. Trailheads for the hiking trails are located at several points on the 3-mile loop road running through the center of the park. The 2-mile railroad-grade trail has parking at the west end on NE 12 and on the east end, just west of the boat landing north of the town of Niobrara.

Sources of additional information:

Niobrara State Park
P.O. Box 226
Niobrara, NE 68760-0226
(402) 857-3373

Notes on the trail: The views from the trail that runs along the north side of the ridge in the center of the one-way park loop road make this section a must to include in your biking route. You can start at the third parking pulloff on the loop road and ride downhill to a 4-way trail junction. Continue straight ahead on the main trail through the cedar forest to the road near the tent area. Follow the road up to the Cramer Interpretive Center, and from there you can either drop down to the rail trail along the river or ride west along the open ridge to the cabin area or the Niobrara Group Lodge. Riding west along the rail trail you will find several uphill access trails back to the ridge. From the ridge, descend to the loop road on the access trail near cabins 3 and 4 and pick up the original ridge trail on the other side of the parking lot. Note the one-way direction of the 3-mile loop road when you use it to reach the trails.

An alternate starting point is at the east trailhead of the railroad-grade trail. Ride across the river to the west side, then make the climb up to the trail via the Cramer Interpretive Center. Please do not bike on the horseback trail system. A state park sticker or daily entry fee is required for vehicles in the park.

ADDITIONAL MOUNTAIN BIKING OPPORTUNITIES IN EASTERN NEBRASKA

A network of multi-use hike-bike trails is taking shape in the *Omaha-Bellevue metropolitan area*. Generally following the courses of local streams and rivers and the levees that run along them, these mostly concrete routes will total around 100 miles. Major sections currently completed include the Bellevue Loop in Bellevue, and the Keystone Trail in Omaha. Wehrspann, Zorinsky, Standing Bear, and Cunningham, four reservoir lakes on the western outskirts of the metro area, that currently have trails around them, will be connected to this larger trail system. Connections to trails in Council Bluffs, Iowa, and the Wabash Trace Rail Trail (Ride 22) are envisioned.

Kirkman's Cove Recreation Area, which is managed by the Nemaha Natural Resources District, as is Iron Horse Trail Lake (Ride 45), has a four-mile trail system that circles a 160-acre lake and connects a variety of park facilities. The recreation area is located 2.5 miles west of Humboldt in Richardson County.

Organizations and Clubs

Eastern Nebraska Trails Network
Elmwood Park Station
P.O. Box 6725
Omaha, NE 68106

Great Plains Bicycle Club
P.O. Box 81564
Lincoln, NE 68501

Omaha Pedalers
Box 648, Downtown Station
Omaha, NE 68101

The shops mentioned below provided me with useful information. There are a number of other good bicycle shops throughout eastern Nebraska; check the yellow pages for more information.

Bike Pedalers
1353 South 33rd
Lincoln, NE 68510
(402) 474-7000

Bike Rack
2528 South 130th Avenue
Omaha, NE 68144
(402) 333-1031 or 691-0080 fax

Blue's Bike & Fitness Center
427 South 13th Street
Lincoln, NE 68508
(402) 435-2322 or 435-2958 fax
There is an additional location at 3321 Pioneers Boulevard.

Cycle Works
720 North 27th Street
Lincoln, NE 68503
(402) 475-2453

Grandpa's Bicycle Shop
8901 Maple Street
Omaha, NE 68134
(402) 392-2390

Olympia Cycle
1324 North 40th Street
Omaha, NE 68131
(402) 554-1940
There is an additional location at 4910 South 135th Street.

Walton Trail Co.
118th & A Streets (P.O. Box 246)
Walton, NE 68461
(402) 488-5511

Bibliography

Streight, Dan, *Eastern Nebraska & Western Iowa Trail Guide,* third edition, Bike Rack, Omaha, NE, 1994.

Central Nebraska

Two main geographical features dominate the central Nebraska region. The wide Platte River valley, which has been a major corridor for human travel for perhaps thousands of years, is the flat agricultural landscape that most travelers see as they cross the region. And to the north lies the Sandhills region, an extensive area made up of sand dunes covered by prairie grasses and drained by rivers flowing southeast toward the Platte. These river and creek valleys are often wooded with elm and cottonwood and shelter a variety of wildlife. Much of the country between the rivers is treeless, open, moderately hilly range land.

Under much of the western part of the region is a vast aquifer that provides adequate groundwater for the rich grasslands, the rivers, and a district of shallow lakes. This area was largely bypassed as settlers moved through on their way westward during the wagon train era from about 1830 to 1860. The advance of railroads after the Civil War provided access to more remote areas and the local population grew steadily after that time. The agricultural economy of Nebraska was hard hit by the dust bowl years and the Depression but recovered as the use of irrigation increased across the area after World War II. Today, central Nebraska is a prime beef-producing region, and the ranching way of life is at the heart of most of the communities in the area.

The caravans of wagon trains rolling up the Platte valley have been replaced by caravans of trucks and cars on I-80. The major commercial centers of the region, including Grand Island, Kearney, Lexington, and North Platte, are along this corridor. These communities have small but growing numbers of bicycling enthusiasts, and the region's rural highway network is ideal for road biking. Mountain biking opportunities are a bit harder to find. Park management personnel are just beginning to look at mountain biking as a recreational alternative to be considered when improvements are made on public lands. I will describe three rides in this region: a popular city park trail area, a short rail trail route, and the unique Nebraska National Forest.

RIDE 53   FORT KEARNY HIKE-BIKE TRAIL

This is an easy two-mile linear trail on an old railroad grade that crosses the Platte River on two long trestles. The crushed-stone and double-track trail traverses a mixture of woodlands and open fields on its way to crossing the

RIDE 53 *FORT KEARNY HIKE-BIKE TRAIL*

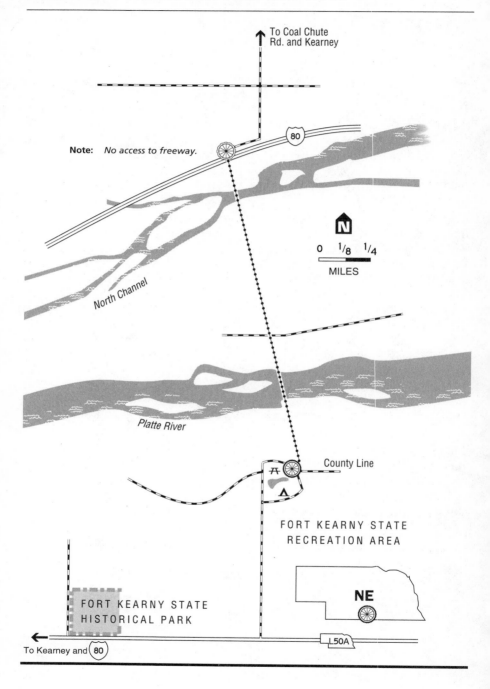

To Coal Chute
Rd. and Kearney

Note: *No access to freeway.*

80

N

0   1/8   1/4
MILES

North Channel

Platte River

County Line

FORT KEARNY STATE
RECREATION AREA

FORT KEARNY STATE
HISTORICAL PARK

NE

To Kearney and 80

L50A

wide channels of the river. The area along the river is one of the key spots for viewing the sandhill crane migration that gathers in the Platte River valley in the springtime. Fort Kearny State Historical Park two miles away is a reconstruction of one of the major forts that were located along the Oregon Trail and the Pony Express route. It was from here that these famous trails began their long westward ascent of the Platte River valley into what is now Wyoming and beyond. About ten miles away in Minden is Harold Warp's Pioneer Village, where a renowned collection of thousands of pioneer antiques is housed in 30 buildings dating back to the 1800s.

General location: In Fort Kearny State Recreation Area, 9 miles southeast of the city of Kearney, in Kearney and Buffalo Counties.
Elevation change: This is a very flat part of the Platte River floodplain.
Season: Midspring to late autumn.
Services: Camping and water are available in the recreation area. The city of Kearney offers all services.
Hazards: Use caution when passing hikers.
Rescue index: Help is usually close by.
Land status: Fort Kearny State Recreation Area is managed by the Nebraska Game and Parks Commission.
Maps: The map included here is sufficient.
Finding the trail: The recreation area is located 2 miles south of Interstate 80/Exit 272/Kearney on NE 44, and 5 miles east on NE L50A. The southern trailhead is at the northeast end of the recreation area across from the picnic area. You can reach the north end of the trail, which passes under I-80, from Kearney via US 30 and O Avenue, by traveling 3.7 miles east on Coal Chute Road and then 1.5 miles south on an unmarked dirt road. Watch for the freeway overpass and a large billboard.

Sources of additional information:

Fort Kearny State Historical Park
RR 4, Box 59
Kearney, NE 68847-9804
(402) 234-9513

Notes on the trail: This trail and park would be a good base of operations for families and history and wildlife enthusiasts. It would also be a good place to camp in conjunction with a visit to the Kearney area and a ride at nearby Cottonmill Park (see below). Future plans, although indefinite, call for additional miles of trail in this area.

RIDE 54 COTTONMILL PARK AND RECREATION AREA

Cottonmill Park is a pleasant facility in an otherwise flat, agricultural area of central Nebraska. About four miles of mostly single-track trails loop around a forested hillside and out into an open, treeless prairie preserve. Most of the riding is relatively easy to moderate, but there are enough short hills and thickly wooded trails to add some excitement to a one- or two-hour ride here. In addition, a 2.6-mile flat bike trail connects the park with the city streets of Kearney. If you are driving across Nebraska and have your mountain bike along, Cottonmill Park would be a great, accessible spot to take a break and burn off some energy.

Kearney features several museums and historical sites. Fort Kearny State Historical Park south of town on NE 44 is a reconstruction of one of the major forts that were located along the Oregon Trail. Two miles to the northeast of that park is Fort Kearny State Recreation Area, one of the observation sites of the spring sandhill crane migration. See the description of the Fort Kearny Hike-Bike Trail, Ride 53.

General location: Adjacent to the city of Kearney in Buffalo County.
Elevation change: Low hills in this area provide a few short, steep climbs.
Season: Midspring through late autumn. Off-season riding is possible, weather and trail conditions permitting.
Services: Rest rooms, water, picnic shelters, phone, and a swimming beach are available in the park. Camping is available at the Fort Kearny State Recreation Area, 9 miles from Kearney. The city of Kearney offers all services.
Hazards: Watch out for low, thick branches and downed logs in the forested trail area.
Rescue index: Help is never far away in this area.
Land status: Kearney Park and Recreation Department.
Maps: An informative brochure with a diagram map is available at the park office.
Finding the trail: The park is located on the west side of Kearney, 1.3 miles west of NE Spur 10A on US 30, then one-quarter mile north on Cottonmill Road. Once you're inside the park, a paved road curves around the south end of a small lake. All of the parking areas on the east side of the lake are adjacent to the trails.

Sources of additional information:

Cottonmill Park and Recreation Area
P.O. Box 1180
Kearney, NE 68848
(308) 237-7251

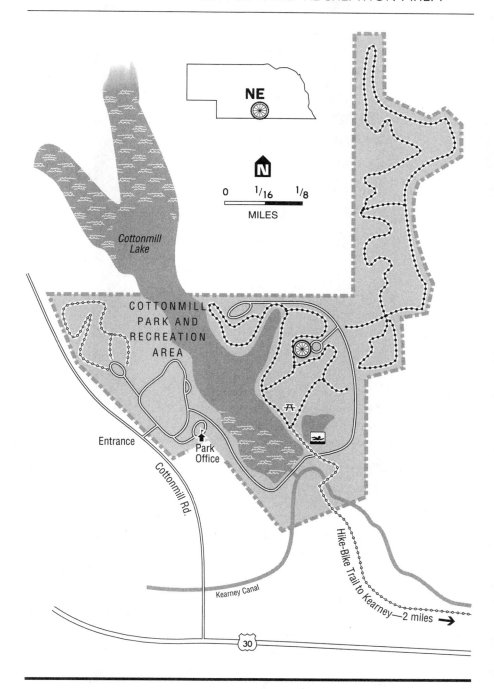

NE

N

0   1/16   1/8

MILES

Cottonmill
Lake

COTTONMILL
PARK AND
RECREATION
AREA

Entrance

Park
Office

Cottonmill Rd.

Kearney Canal

Hike-Bike Trail to Kearney—2 miles →

30

Trails alternate between wooded hillsides and an open prairie preserve in Kearney's Cottonmill Park.

Kearney Park and Recreation Department
(308) 237-4644

Western Schwinn Cyclery
2216 Central Avenue
Kearney, NE 68847
(308) 234-3822

Notes on the trail: There are three main parts to this trail system. A flat, crushed-stone bike trail leaves from 19th Avenue near the Kearney Country Club and parallels US 30 west to the park, where it crosses a bridge and joins the park road and the rest of the trail system. The wooded hills on the east side of the lake, north of several picnic shelters, contain at least 2 miles of dirt and grass trails circling around between the lake and the park road.

A number of side trails, obviously the work of local bikers, branch off here and there, providing some interesting riding in the thickest of the forest cover.

The third section of the trail system is a series of loops through a marked natural prairie preserve on the east side of the park road. Several short, quick climbs and sharp corners keep you on your toes. Some nearby housing developments prevent a feeling of real remoteness, but this area is a nice place to put in an hour or two of fun riding on a variety of terrain.

RIDE 55 *NEBRASKA NATIONAL FOREST/ BESSEY DIVISION*

Much of north-central Nebraska is composed of a region called the Sandhills— a seemingly endless, rolling grassland that is actually the western hemisphere's largest collection of sand dunes. In the early 1900s, an ambitious tree plantation experiment was started in an area near the Dismal River in an attempt to provide forest resources for the sparsely populated region. After a number of years, a forest of ponderosa pine, jack pine, and red cedar began to successfully emerge. Now, almost a century later, in spite of the 1930s drought and a serious fire in 1965, over 21,000 acres of trees stand as a unique and bizarre contrast to the vastness of the plains. They provide cover for deer, antelope, wild turkeys, grouse, and other wildlife, as well as a variety of recreational opportunities.

The Bessey Nursery, adjacent to the recreation area, continues to produce millions of tree seedlings for planting around the Great Plains. The picnic, campground, and 4-H camp locations in the recreation area are included as part of the Bessey Arboretum; and many of the thriving plant species that are found here are labeled for identification.

The Sandhills region is the heart of Nebraska's cattle industry, and a vast underground aquifer provides ample water for rich grasslands and agriculture. Towns to the west, like Thedford, strongly reflect this proud ranching tradition. The spring-fed Dismal and Loup Rivers are popular canoeing destinations, and there is a canoe outfitter in Thedford.

A network of trails, gravel roads, and four-wheel-drive tracks contains over 40 miles of possible riding in this unique environment of North America's largest human-planted forest. The routes described below provide a 15- to 20-mile tour covering the highlights of this area. Generally easy to moderate riding, the sandy terrain creates some challenges, and "fat" tires are a necessity off the gravel roads.

General location: Two miles west of Halsey in Thomas County.

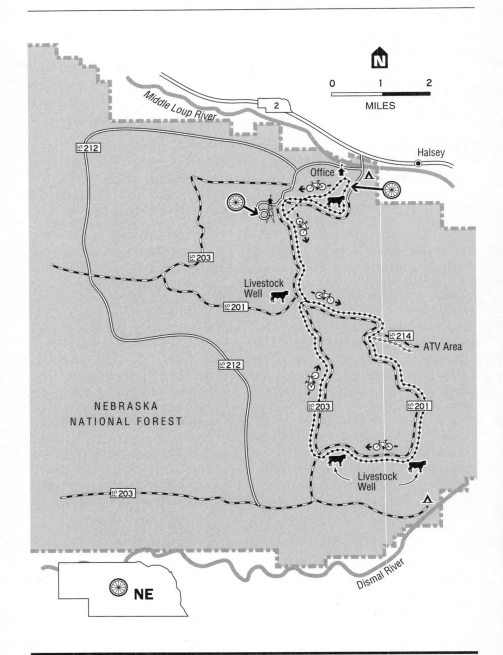

Elevation change: Elevation change of up to several hundred feet occurs throughout this region. Most of the trail climbs are gradual and short.

Season: Midspring through autumn. Winter may be a good time for hardy bikers to try this area if the weather is moderate and the ground mostly frozen.

Services: The recreation area at the entrance west of Halsey includes a campground, picnic area, water, a swimming pool, and the district offices. A store, restaurant, and gas station are available in the town of Halsey. Thedford, the county seat 15 miles west, and North Platte, 75 miles southwest, have all other services.

Hazards: Soft, sandy spots on the trails can quickly bring your momentum to a halt, so keep downhill speed under control. Watch for cattle that can be anywhere in the forest area. There may be fast-moving trucks and other vehicles on the gravel Circle Road. This is a popular hunting area in autumn, so be sure to check season dates.

Rescue index: In the summer season, there are generally staff people at the recreation area or the nursery, but the back roads and tracks in the forest can get rather remote. It is a good idea to leave word at the office or a note visible in your vehicle indicating your plans.

Land status: Nebraska National Forest is a division of the U.S. Forest Service.

Maps: A basic diagram map of the Bessey Division can be picked up free of charge at the campground or at the district office during weekday business hours. This map shows the roads, trails, fence lines, and windmill/stock water tanks. These tanks are numbered and can be used as a means of navigational reference. A $3 Forest Service map covering all sections of the Nebraska National Forest, including the Pine Ridge section near Chadron as well as the Oglala National Grassland is available. This map gives a good overview of these regions but contains less trail information than the free diagram map. For those wishing to supplement these maps with the USGS 7.5 minute series topographical maps, the Halsey and Halsey SE quads cover the area described below. The Natick and Halsey SW quadrangles cover the western side of the Bessey Division.

Finding the trail: The recreation area entrance is located 2 miles west of Halsey on NE 2. You can begin your bike tour at several starting points. See the trail notes below.

Sources of additional information:

Bessey Ranger District
P.O. Box 38
Halsey, NE 69142
(308) 533-2257

Notes on the trail: If you start at the picnic area/campground near the recreation area entrance, a paved road heads south, uphill, to either the start of the

The road to a fire lookout tower in the unique Nebraska National Forest offers a panorama of the largest human-planted forest in the United States.

Scott Lookout National Recreation Trail or, farther along, to a four-wheel-drive track (Forest Service Road 223) that goes in the same direction. The hiking trail is a more challenging single-track but has some soft sandy areas. It passes a windmill/stock water tank, crosses the four-wheel-drive track, and reaches FS 203 in about 2.5 miles. From here you can cruise south on FS 203. The four-wheel-drive track comes out on the paved road that leads to the lookout tower, and the start of FS 203 is just up the hill to the left a short ways. An alternate starting point is the Scott Lookout Tower, where there is some parking, rest rooms, and a great view of the surrounding pine forest/prairie environment. The hiking trail leaves the east end of the paved loop and descends a half-mile to FS 203.

FS 203, the "Circle Road," winds south through the mixed pine forest/prairie hills for several miles, where it meets FS 201, a four-wheel-drive track. Take the eastbound (left) section, which is a quarter-mile south of westbound FS 201. This track will meander through forest and prairie for about 8 miles back to FS 203. About a mile and a half along FS 201 is FS 214, a spur road that leads to a four-wheel-drive play area that might be fun if you are inclined to take on some steep hills. There are a few sandy spots to deal with on the way there. There are also some sandy hill climbs on the southwest corner of FS 201 that you probably will have to walk, but the surface improves as the road turns west toward FS 203. Windmill number 79 indicates that you are approaching the end of FS 201. Back on FS 203, the gravel/packed surface may be a relief, and you can cruise easily the 5 miles north on the return leg. Be alert for occasional fast-moving vehicles.

I found most of the trails and double-tracks to be adequately stable for biking, but some sandy sections will require walking or a delicate balance of speed and steering to avoid bogging down. Some sections can be bypassed through the grasses, but the best strategy for this area perhaps is to plan your visit in a period that has had moderate rainfall to settle the tracks and before much four-wheel-drive vehicle traffic has chewed up the soft spots. The Circle Road and other all-weather roads can always provide pleasant riding.

Be sure to carry plenty of water, especially in hot weather. The water being pumped by windmills is not guaranteed to be safe. Be aware of any restrictions that may be in effect due to fire danger in hot or dry weather. As with any multi-use area, be courteous to hikers and horseback riders, avoid spooking cattle and other animals, and be sure to leave any gates as you find them.

Mountain bikes are still newcomers to the recreation scene here, so there is much exploring yet to be done. The district officials here have indicated an interest in including mountain biking opportunities in their future recreational management plans, so be sure to take the time to find out what's new and share your thoughts about what you find.

ADDITIONAL MOUNTAIN BIKING OPPORTUNITIES IN CENTRAL NEBRASKA

Harlan County Lake, 23 miles south of Holdrege, is a reservoir managed by the U.S. Army Corps of Engineers that has camping and other facilities in several public use areas. This region was once a prime buffalo-hunting valley for the Pawnee, Cheyenne, and Dakota Indians. The terrain is predominantly open, rolling grassland, with wooded areas and heavier vegetation along the lake shore and river bottoms.

About a mile south of the dam, in the *Patterson Harbor Public Use Area,* there is a motorcycle/snowmobile area that can be used by mountain bikers. It goes without saying that caution should be exercised when there is motorized use going on. There are two areas of public land adjacent to the lake that have systems of graded dirt and low maintenance roads that might merit some exploration. Two of these areas are Prairie Dog Bay and White Cat Point on the south side of the lake, and another is in the Republican River lowlands west of Alma. Maps detailing the reservoir area are available from the administration office near Republican City. Local advice can be obtained from the bike shop in Holdrege, listed below. Contact: Harlan County Project Office, Republican City, NE 68971, (308) 799-2105.

Samuel R. McKelvie National Forest and the adjacent Merritt Reservoir State Recreation Area have over 50 miles of unpaved and four-wheel-drive roads in an area that is similar to the Nebraska National Forest. (See the Nebraska National Forest ride above.) Areas of the McKelvie National Forest feature small forests planted in the early 1900s in an attempt to demonstrate the benefits of forestation projects in the open prairie lands. The areas are located 25 miles southwest of Valentine in Cherry County. Contact: Bessey Ranger District, P.O. Box 38, Halsey, NE 69142, (308) 533-2257, or the Nebraska Game and Parks Commission, District II, Box 508, Bassett, NE 68714, (402) 684-2921.

The Southwest Reservoirs is a collection of recreation areas established around a series of lakes formed by Bureau of Reclamation flood-control and irrigation projects in the 1950s. All of the recreation areas are in the Republican River drainage in the general vicinity of the town of McCook, 70 miles south of North Platte and I-80. Each of these recreation areas has a series of unpaved roads that connect various recreational facilities and provide access to the bays and points of the lakes. In conjunction with the many camping and picnic opportunities in all of these spots, some pleasant riding can be done by families and others looking for some easy to moderate terrain. The Medicine Creek State Recreation Area contains the most forested land and a number of roads leading to quiet backwaters of the lake. The Swanson SRA and the Red Willow SRA are the most developed areas, and Red Willow includes a protected prairie dog town. The Enders SRA is the least developed of the four, with much of its land contained in a wildlife refuge traversed by the road systems. Contact: Southwest Reservoirs, 602 Missouri Avenue, McCook, NE 69001.

Bike Shops and Clubs

Cycle Sport
105 North Jeffers Street
North Platte, NE 69101
(308) 534-1033

Hastings Schwinn Cycling & Fitness
1719 West 2nd Street
Hastings, NE 68901
(402) 463-7118 or 463-7117 fax

Hilsabeck Sporting Goods Co.
408 East Avenue
Holdrege, NE 68949
(308) 995-5081 or 995-8840 fax

Wayne's Cyclery
309 North Pine
Grand Island, NE 68801
(308) 382-4223

Western Schwinn Cyclery
2216 Central Avenue
Kearney, NE 68847
(308) 234-3822
Club: Mid-America Bicycle Club

Western Nebraska

This part of Nebraska takes on a distinct western flavor once you leave the freeway and poke around the towns and back roads. Cattle ranching is the dominant industry, and crop agriculture is heavily irrigated. The North Platte River valley slices across this region of high, rolling plains and ridges, many topped with the ponderosa pine so common farther west. The western Sandhills region and its district of shallow lakes merges with this upland ridge country, separating the Nebraska "panhandle" from the rest of the state with miles of wide-open, rolling hills.

You are never far from reminders of western plains history in this region. The North Platte River was the corridor used by emigrants on the Oregon Trail, the Mormon Trail, and by the short-lived Pony Express. The landmarks that guided the wagon trains are still landmarks today, and ruts carved by the wagons can still be seen near the town of Harrison and at Scotts Bluff National Monument. Fort Robinson, now a state park, played a pivotal role in the battles between the U.S. Army and the plains Indian tribes after the Civil War (see Ride 61).

The Pine Ridge country in the extreme northwest corner of Nebraska is a rugged collection of ponderosa-topped ridges that provides the most extensive and challenging mountain biking terrain in the state. This unique area is a worthy destination in its own right, although it is often overshadowed by the popular Black Hills, fifty-some miles to the north in South Dakota. When biking the Pine Ridge, you may have to remind yourself occasionally that you are still in Nebraska. I will describe four rides in the Pine Ridge vicinity. If you make a trip to this region, I'm sure you will discover the enthusiasm that local riders have for this largely "undiscovered" area. State recreation and wildlife areas provide two other short but scenic rides in the Scottsbluff area.

RIDE 56   BUFFALO CREEK WILDLIFE MANAGEMENT AREA

This remote wildlife area is situated in the Wildcat Hills escarpment overlooking the North Platte River valley, offering a variety of rolling prairie hills sloping up to a series of ponderosa-topped ridges and cliffs. A series of four-wheel-drive and narrow single-track trails fan out from the trailhead area and climb into the hills, providing several short out-and-back rides into the scenic wooded canyons. Creekbed crossings, rocks, thick grasses, and steady elevation gains provide some of the challenges in the five or so miles of tracks here.

209

RIDE 56 *BUFFALO CREEK WILDLIFE MANAGEMENT AREA*

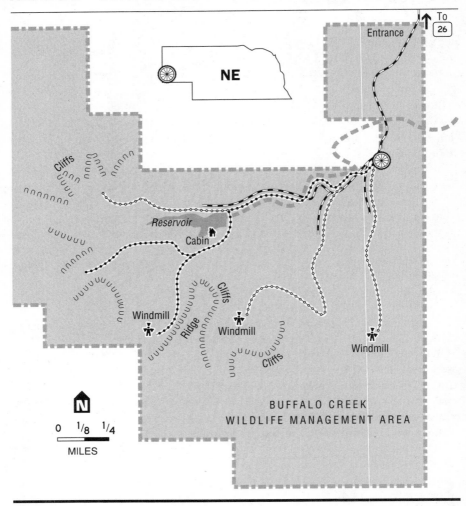

Surrounded by inviting groves of juniper and ponderosa pine on the bluffs above, this area's greatest asset is probably the quiet setting and sense of time-lessness you'll feel as birds soar overhead and old windmills creak in the wind. An old cabin near a small reservoir hints of days long past, when pioneers struggled to make a living on the harsh prairie. Today, life is not so difficult, and one can visit here and experience the beauty of our public lands.

General location: Nine miles southeast of Gering in Scotts Bluff and Banner Counties.

A double-track trail in Buffalo Creek Wildlife Area crosses a small earth dam.

Elevation change: Most of the tracks in the area climb gradually from the trailhead at about 4,125´, gaining up to 200´.

Season: Midspring through autumn.

Services: There are no facilities other than parking at the wildlife area. Commercial services are available in Gering and Scottsbluff.

Hazards: Hunting is allowed in season. Watch for cactus plants among the prairie grasses when you're following narrow tracks. Water in the various wells should not be considered safe to drink.

Rescue index: The nearest help may be as far as NE 92, 7 miles north.

Land status: Buffalo Creek Wildlife Management Area is managed by the Nebraska Game and Parks Commission.

Maps: The USGS 7.5 minute quadrangle covering this area is Wright Gap.

Finding the trail: From NE 92, 8 miles southeast of Gering, head 4.5 miles south on CR 26 (Wrights Gap Road), then west 1.5 miles, then south 1 mile to the wildlife area entrance. Small white signs help with directions on these unmarked roads. It is an additional three-quarters of a mile to a parking area.

Sources of additional information:

Wildcat Hills State Recreation Area
P.O. Box 65
Gering, NE 69341-0065
(308) 436-2383

Notes on the trail: Some of the more rugged sections of the wildlife area could make for good hiking, especially when the tracks peter out and the going gets too steep for bikes. Deer, wild turkeys, and rabbits are among the animal inhabitants of this area.

RIDE 57   *WILDCAT HILLS STATE RECREATION AREA*

This recreation area contains at least three miles of hilly hiking trails that switchback through rugged, pine-forested ravines on a prominent escarpment overlooking the vast North Platte River valley. Steep climbs and descents, loose rocks, and tight corners help create a moderate to difficult biking experience in an area with a distinct western feel. Ponderosa pine, cedar, prairie grasses, and even yucca and other cactus plants add to that atmosphere. The trails, a combination of single- and double-track, can be ridden as an out-and-back ride with several side loops. You can also return to the trailhead by the park road at the top of the ridge.

Many of the stone park buildings were built by the Civilian Conservation Corps during the 1930s. They provide interesting rest stops and nice overlooks of the canyons below. The adjacent wildlife preserve is a 350-acre fenced compound containing buffalo and elk, which may be viewed from the park road or state highway. Other wildlife that may be seen in the area include deer, wild turkeys, and coyotes. Just west of Gering is Scotts Bluff National Monument. This prominent stone outcropping was a major landmark for the wagon train emigrants on the Oregon Trail, and the deep wagon ruts are still visible here today. A museum and a road to the top of the bluff are part of the monument.

General location: Nine miles south of Gering and Scottsbluff in Scotts Bluff County.

Elevation change: Generally, the trails are either climbing or descending, with an elevation range of several hundred feet.

Season: Midspring to late fall. Snow could linger in the north-facing ravines in the early spring, keeping the trails muddy.

Services: Picnic shelters, water, toilets, and campsites are available. Gering and Scottsbluff offer all commercial services.

Hazards: There are some steep drop-offs beside the trail in places; watch your speed on the corners. There are a lot of low cactus plants on some of the grassy ridges, so stay on the trails to avoid trouble of the flat-tire kind.

Rescue index: While this area is not really remote, an accident in the steep terrain below the ridge crest could involve a difficult rescue.

RIDE 57 *WILDCAT HILLS STATE RECREATION AREA*

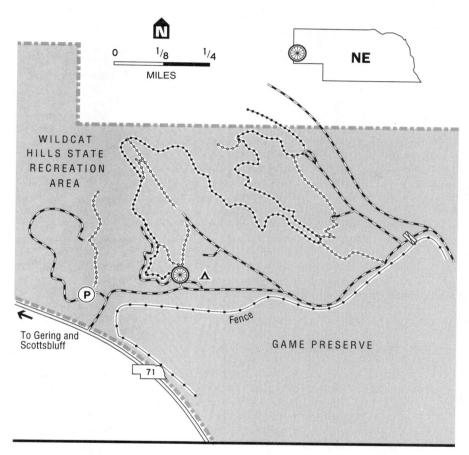

Land status: Wildcat Hills State Recreation Area is managed by the Nebraska Game and Parks Commission.

Maps: The map in this book shows the layout of the trails and is probably adequate for a few hours of fun riding. The USGS 7.5 minute quadrangle of this area is Wildcat Mountain.

Finding the trail: The recreation area entrance is about 9 miles south of Gering on NE 71 at the crest of the ridge. There is a parking area under construction at the entrance road, and there is also parking over the next hill at the campsites and water faucet. The main trail system drops down into the ravines at this camp area. A state park entry permit is required.

The rugged escarpment of Wildcat Hills has some great vistas and steep hills spiced with cactus plants.

Sources of additional information:

Wildcat Hills State Recreation Area
P.O. Box 65
Gering, NE 69341-0065
(308) 436-2383

Sonny's Bike Shop
1717 East Overland
Scottsbluff, NE 69361
(308) 632-3938

Notes on the trail: From the roadside campsite area you can bike most of the trails by heading down the westernmost (left) trail and keeping generally to the left as you ride up and down along the ridges and past the exposed rock outcroppings of the area. The side trails can be explored or used as access routes back up to the park road. The easternmost section of trail will contour an open hillside, then make a steep climb to a parking lot at the east end of the park road. From here, it is possible to ride out along the open ridge top a ways for a great vista of the surrounding escarpment and the wide North Platte valley beyond. Because they face north, most of the slopes provide some shady sections here and there for a break in hot weather.

RIDE 58 *PINE RIDGE TRAIL/EASTERN TRAIL GROUP*

This section of the Nebraska National Forest, east of US 385 and Chadron State Park, offers some of the greatest variety of Pine Ridge mountain biking in the area, providing numerous options ranging from easy to challenging. Over 30 miles of gravel and dirt roads, four-wheel-drive tracks, and single-track hiking trails can be pieced into a variety of loops of almost any distance you'd like. Trail conditions can vary from hard, packed dirt to soft, muddy and sandy spots. Sections of single-track trail can be relatively faint through the prairie grasses and woodlands, so map-reading skills can be an asset. A good introduction to the area is a moderate ten-mile loop, which is described in the notes below.

Like other sections of the Pine Ridge country, this area is made up of open, grassy ridges bordered by hillsides and small canyons of ponderosa pine and cedar and occasional rocky outcroppings. Steady climbs up the wooded slopes are rewarded with fine vistas of the surrounding bluffs and the vast arid prairie lands below. This is a multiple-use area where you may encounter cattle, deer, backpackers, and horseback riders. Several days could be enjoyably spent exploring this area, perhaps in conjunction with a stay at Chadron State Park and a ride on the trails there (see Ride 59) and in the Pine Ridge Recreation Area just to the west (see Ride 60).

General location: About 6 miles south of Chadron in Dawes County.
Elevation change: Elevation ranges from 3,650′ to over 4,300′.
Season: Midspring to late autumn. Summertime is usually pleasant but can get quite hot. Off-season weather can range from very mild to severe winter storm conditions.
Services: Nearby Chadron State Park has water and camping facilities. Most other commercial services can be found in the town of Chadron.
Hazards: Be alert for vehicles on the forest roads. Keep an eye on the sky during times of potential thunderstorm activity. Hunting is allowed here, in season.
Rescue index: Help is relatively close by on US 385 and at Chadron State Park.
Land status: Nebraska National Forest, U.S. Dept. of Agriculture.
Maps: "Pine Ridge Hiking Trails," a pamphlet that shows the general locations of the trails in the Pine Ridge vicinity, is available from various agencies in the area. The $3 USFS map covering all sections of the Nebraska National Forest and the Oglala National Grassland gives a good overview of the back roads in the region. An excellent map that shows the bike trails in Fort Robinson and Chadron State Parks and in the Pine Ridge Ranger District is

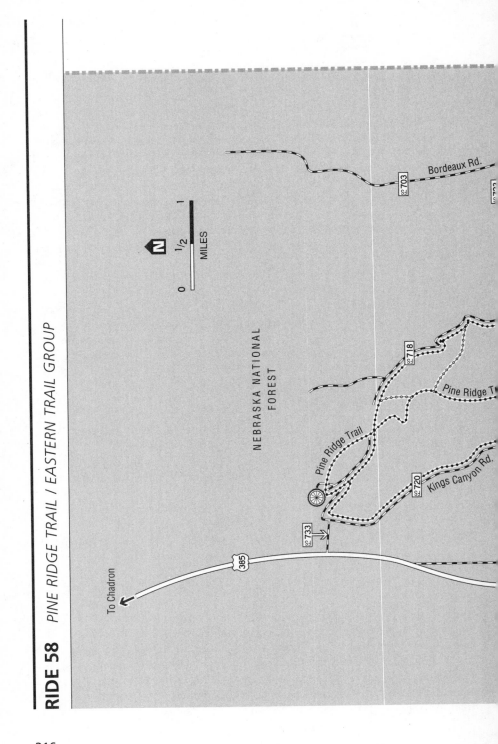

NEBRASKA NATIONAL FOREST

Bordeaux Rd.

FR 703

FR 718

Pine Ridge Trail

Pine Ridge T

FR 720

Kings Canyon Rd.

FR 733

385

To Chadron

N

MILES

0   ½   1

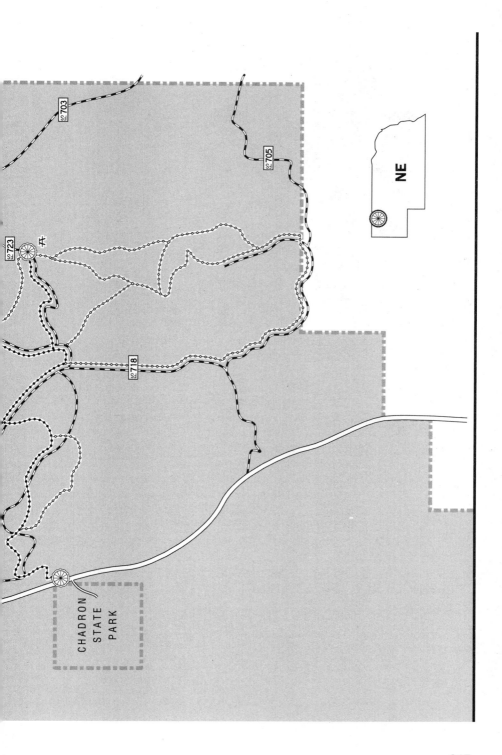

NE

703

705

723

718

CHADRON
STATE
PARK

The Pine Ridge Trail is part of a network of mountain bike routes on the eastern Pine Ridge escarpment in Nebraska National Forest.

published by *Trails Illustrated,* in part with a grant from the Nebraska Tourism Office. Including topographical information and suitable for trail navigation, this map features recommended trails that are color coded to indicate easy, moderate, and difficult riding. The map is printed on waterproof paper and is available from area bike shops and park agencies or the Chadron Area Chamber of Commerce for $6.95. The three USGS 7.5 minute topographic quadrangles covering the east trail area are: Coffee Mill Butte, Chadron 3 NW, and just a small corner of Chadron East.

Finding the trail: There is a parking lot and northern trailhead for the Pine Ridge Trail a little more than a mile east on Forest Service Road 733, about 5 miles south of Chadron on US 385. There is also a trailhead for the Pine Ridge Trail across the road from the entrance to Chadron State Park. Additional access points are available on the southeast side of the forest from FS 705 (Table Road) and FS 703 (Bordeaux Road).

Sources of additional information:

Pine Ridge Ranger District
RR 1, Box 13A9
Chadron, NE 69337
(308) 432-4475

Mountain Mania
361 Main
Chadron, NE 69337
(308) 432-3653

Notes on the trail: From the parking lot on FS 733, follow the road southeast over a ridge and down to the junction with FS 718. FS 718 will resume climbing for a few miles onto a largely open ridge in the center of the Forest Service lands. Several alternate loops branch off from this ridge top, including a steep descent to Bordeaux Creek and a picnic area. FS 718 swings to the west and meets FS 720 (Kings Canyon Road). Follow FS 720 northwest about a mile to where the road begins the descent into the canyon and crosses the Pine Ridge Trail. The trail provides a steep climb to the north, then a nice single-track ride through the pines and meadows back to FS 733 and the parking area. To the west, the Pine Ridge Trail takes two meandering courses with some good ups and downs for about 4 miles to Chadron State Park. Kings Canyon Road allows for a fast cruise downhill to the start at FS 733.

Several different trail-marking systems are used in the area, including white diamonds on most trails, and tree blazes and small posts on the Pine Ridge Trail. Be sure to leave fences as you find them. Cattle can be unpredictable; try to give them plenty of space to avoid you. Carry plenty of water and don't assume that water in any stream you happen upon is safe to drink.

RIDE 59 CHADRON STATE PARK

Situated near the center of the most extensively forested area on the Pine Ridge escarpment, Chadron State Park is a great base of operations for exploring this region. An excellent mountain bike loop of almost four miles has been established in the park and adjoining national forest lands, and it serves as a nice introduction to the Pine Ridge country. With a range of easy to difficult terrain, the trail offers a knife-edge ridge, steep descents and climbs, a rocky and wooded canyon, and views north to the Black Hills. Plan on an hour or more for taking in the scenery and negotiating the difficult spots.

Included in the park is an activities center, which contains a fur trade–era interpretive display. In Chadron, Wicahpi Vision features displays and sales of authentic arts and crafts from the Oglala Lakota (Sioux) and other Native Americans. Just east of Chadron is the Museum of the Fur Trade, which also covers history of the fur trade.

General location: The park is 8 miles south of the town of Chadron in Dawes County.

Elevation change: There is almost 400′ of elevation gain on the loop trail, reaching a high point of 4,225′.

Season: Midspring through autumn. The park is open all year, but winter conditions will probably keep parts of the trail impassable.

Services: The state park has water, picnic shelters, a campground, cabins, and a swimming pool. Other services are available in Chadron.

RIDE 59 *CHADRON STATE PARK*

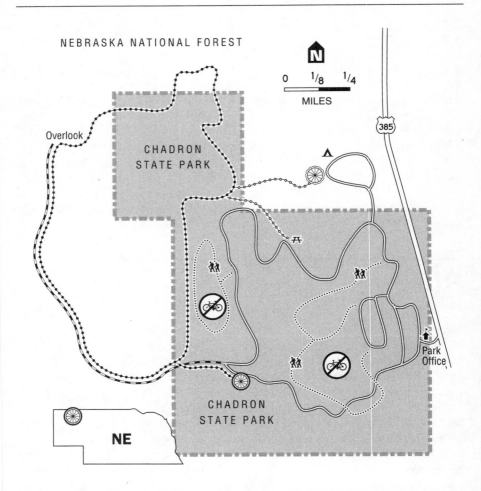

Hazards: The northern ridge section of the trail loop is narrow and has sharp drop-offs on either side. Ride with care and watch for hikers.

Rescue index: Park personnel or other visitors are generally present in the park.

Land status: Chadron State Park is managed by the Nebraska Game and Parks Commission.

Maps: A Chadron State Park brochure that shows the basic layout of the park facilities is available. The best map that shows the bike trail in Chadron

An inviting single-track leads up a breezy ridge in Chadron State Park.

State Park and in other parts of the Pine Ridge Ranger District is published by *Trails Illustrated*. See the discussion of maps under Ride 58.

Finding the trail: There is a parking lot and trailhead for the Overlook Trail on the park loop road past the campground and the swimming pool. An alternate starting point—if you want to start out on the easiest section first— is the parking lot at the top of the ridge on the loop road just east of the junction with the gravel Lookout Point Road.

Sources of additional information:

Chadron State Park
15951 Highway 385
Chadron, NE 69337-9312
(308) 432-6167

Mountain Mania
361 Main
Chadron, NE 69337
(308) 432-3653

Notes on the trail: From the parking lot near the start of the gravel road to Lookout Point, it is an easy mile and a half to the Black Hills Overlook. The fun begins here as you gradually descend along a sharp ridge with great views on either side. Nearby is an old burn area dating back to 1973. After a steep descent into an intermittent creek valley, the Overlook Trail heads left to the paved park road, but you can continue the mountain bike loop by following the trail markers up the creek valley into a rocky canyon, where you will probably have to carry your bike on the steep climb up. The trail will come out on the gravel road near a windmill, completing the loop.

Other trails in the park are reserved for hikers and horseback riders only. A state park sticker or daily entrance fee is required in the state park.

RIDE 60 *PINE RIDGE NATIONAL RECREATION AREA*

The Pine Ridge National Recreation Area is a nonmotorized use area, a good choice for riders who wish to experience the quiet and solitude that this whole region once offered. Traversing this area is the Pine Ridge Trail, which, including the Roberts Trailhead spur, provides almost 20 miles of moderate to difficult semiwilderness riding. This linear trail can be done as an out-and-back ride from several trailheads, or if you prefer to create a loop ride, you can use the various local dirt roads to return to your starting point. The Roberts Trailhead on the north end of the recreation area can be used to reach the center of the trail route most easily. The site of the trailhead was an old homestead in the 1930s, which was eventually donated to the park service.

The Pine Ridge Trail is a combination of single-track and old double-tracks following ponderosa pine–covered hillsides, steep, rocky valleys, and occasional open meadows that give nice views of the surrounding ridge country. Steady climbs out of the little canyons eventually give way to easier cruising on the ridge tops, followed by exciting descents into the next drainage. Occasional sandy spots, rocky slopes, water bars, and rutted sections give some additional challenges to the route, and even in hot weather, the pine-shaded canyons and breezy ridge tops will make most days pleasant. This is certainly one of the best mountain biking locations in Nebraska, as well as the Great Plains.

General location: The recreation area is approximately 20 miles southwest of Chadron, accessible on county and forest service roads from US 20.

Elevation change: The elevation range on this section of trail is almost 500′, topping out at about 4,400′ at the west end of the trail.

Season: Midspring to late autumn. July and August can be very hot. Off-season weather in western Nebraska can be quite variable, ranging from cool but pleasant sunny spells to howling, road-closing blizzards, so be cautious at that time of year.

Services: The Roberts Trailhead has picnic tables, rest rooms, and drinking water. The towns of Chadron and Crawford offer most services.

The Pine Ridge National Recreation Area provides a non-motorized haven in the Nebraska National Forest.

Hazards: There are steep downgrades, rocky spots, deeply rutted sections, and water bars on the trail. Keep an eye on the sky during times of potential thunderstorm activity. Hunting is popular in this region in the fall.

Rescue index: The Pine Ridge Trail traverses some semiwilderness where you may or may not encounter other people on a given day. Plan accordingly, and be sure to carry first-aid supplies and plenty of water.

Land status: Administered by the Nebraska National Forest, U.S. Forest Service.

Maps: See the discussion of map alternatives under Ride 58. The three USGS 7.5 minute topographic quadrangles covering the central trail area are: Chimney Butte, Coffee Mill Butte, and Coffee Mill Butte SW.

Finding the trail: The Roberts Trailhead provides the quickest access to the central part of the Pine Ridge Trail. From US 20, 9 miles west of Chadron, take FS 706 (Eleson Road) south 7.5 miles, then go east on FS 919. There is an old church and a sign at the turn. It is about 2 miles to the trailhead. The East Ash Trailhead on the west end of the trail is reached from East Ash Road, accessible from US 20, 9 miles east of Crawford, or from Bethel Road, starting just east of Crawford. The Coffee Mill Trailhead on the east end of the trail can be reached from Dead Horse Road, which runs south from US 20 near the Chadron airport.

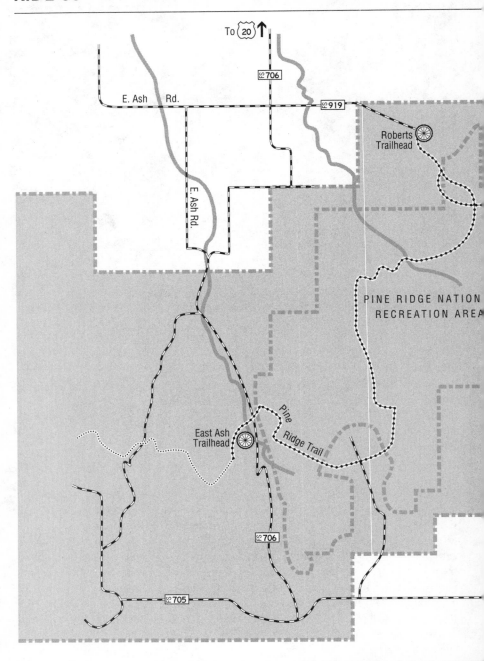

To 20

FS 706

E. Ash Rd.

FS 919

Roberts
Trailhead

E. Ash Rd.

PINE RIDGE NATION
RECREATION AREA

Pine
Ridge Trail

East Ash
Trailhead

FS 706

FS 705

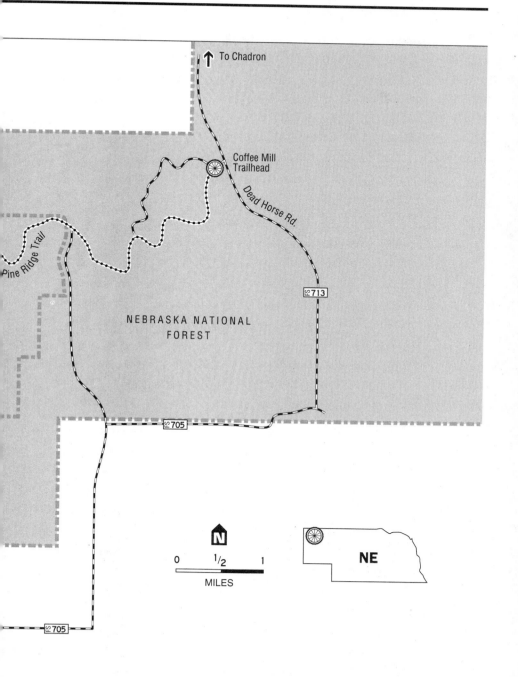

To Chadron

Coffee Mill
Trailhead

Dead Horse Rd.

Pine Ridge Trail

713

NEBRASKA NATIONAL
FOREST

705

705

N

0   1/2   1

MILES

NE

Sources of additional information:

Pine Ridge Ranger District
RR 1, Box 13A9
Chadron, NE 69337
(308) 432-4475

Notes on the trail: The Roberts Trail splits into two branches as it climbs up to meet the Pine Ridge Trail. The left (east) branch provides a steady climb with frequent water bars. Nice views of a cliff are the reward on that branch. The west branch provides a slightly more moderate climb, and both branches meet on the ridge at the Pine Ridge Trail, where there is easy riding for a ways in either direction. To the east, the Pine Ridge Trail skirts an open meadow before it drops into another drainage and leaves the recreation area. After about 4 miles of ups and downs, the trail reaches the Coffee Mill Trailhead. Continuing west from Roberts Trail, the Pine Ridge Trail makes a dramatic descent into the Indian Creek valley, only to climb again through an open area and then drop into the Cunningham Creek drainage. In a little less than 5 miles, the trail reaches the East Ash Trailhead. Another 5 miles or so of trail continue west from there. From the East Ash Trailhead, it is possible to return to the Roberts Trailhead via FS 706 and FS 919, creating a loop tour of about 17 miles.

The trail is marked with tree blazes or small posts in the open sections. Please leave any fence gates as you find them, and give cattle as much space as possible.

RIDE 61   *FORT ROBINSON STATE PARK*

Fort Robinson served as a military outpost from the time of the Indian wars in the 1870s until World War II, when it was used as a prisoner of war camp. It was here that Chief Crazy Horse was killed after he and his band of warriors surrendered to federal troops in 1877. The state park is now one of Nebraska's top park facilities, with picnic and camping areas, restaurant, swimming pool, two fine museums, and lodging in the old fort at the enlisted men's and officer's quarters.

One could spend days exploring this unique corner of Nebraska. Fifteen miles northwest of Crawford in Oglala National Grassland is Toadstool Park, site of some unusual rock erosion formations in Nebraska's section of the badlands. Agate Fossil Beds National Monument, 20 miles south of the town of Harrison, contains a bed of 19-million-year-old animal bones. The Chadron area has many more attractions and additional mountain biking trails. See the Chadron State Park Ride.

RIDE 61 *FORT ROBINSON STATE PARK*

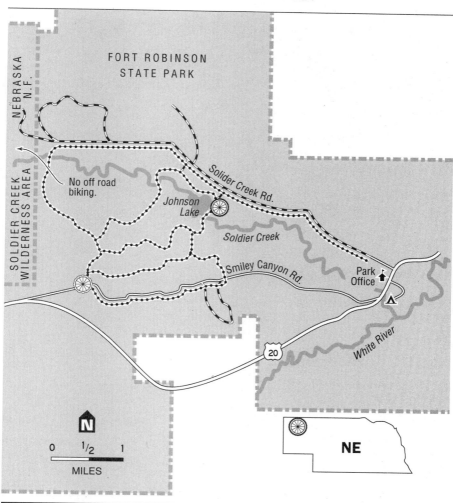

FORT ROBINSON
STATE PARK

NEBRASKA
N.F.

SOLDIER CREEK
WILDERNESS AREA

No off road
biking.

Solider Creek Rd.

Johnson
Lake

Soldier Creek

Smiley Canyon Rd.

Park
Office

White River

20

N

0   1/2   1

MILES

NE

An 18-mile trail network has been designated for mountain bike use in the Smiley Canyon–Soldier Creek area of Fort Robinson Park. It contains a series of three routes that descend over 600′ along four-wheel-drive tracks from the ridge tops, through rugged canyons, to the Soldier Creek valley below. An outer perimeter of roads and trails leads back to the upper ridge. Biking one of the descending trails with a return up one of the outer perimeter routes will result in a ride of from 6 to 12 miles, depending upon the combination chosen. With a mixture of open, grassy terrain, rocky ridges, and ample deadfalls from

The ridges overlooking the Soldier Creek valley in Robinson State Park allow several rugged 600-foot descents.

an old forest fire, there is a nice variety of challenges throughout the area, providing a moderate to difficult riding experience.

General location: Fort Robinson is 3 miles west of Crawford in Sioux and Dawes Counties.

Elevation change: Elevation varies from 3,950′ at Johnson Lake to over 4,600′ at the top of the ridge.

Season: Approximately April through mid-November, if seasonal weather cooperates.

Services: The town of Crawford has all basic services. There is a bicycle shop in Chadron, 25 miles east.

Hazards: As described below, fallen timber can be encountered all along the downhill sections. The rough spots on the trail and the variety of terrain may make the ride take longer than you anticipate, so bring plenty of water in hot weather.

Rescue index: There are always staff people at the fort area, but the back roads and tracks in the farther reaches of the park can be somewhat remote. It may be a good idea to leave word of your intended route at the park office or visible in your vehicle.

Land status: Fort Robinson State Park is managed by the Nebraska Game and Parks Commission.

Maps: The best map that shows the bike trail in Fort Robinson State Park and in other parts of the Pine Ridge Ranger District is published by *Trails Illustrated*. See the discussion of maps under Ride 58. The USGS 7.5 minute quadrangle covering the Fort Robinson trail area is Smiley Canyon.

Finding the trail: The Smiley Canyon Road turns off US 20 less than one-half mile west of the fort complex and climbs 2.5 miles to the base of Smiley Canyon. Soldier Creek Road, providing access to Johnson Lake, travels northwest out of the fort area 3 miles to the lake.

Sources of additional information:

Fort Robinson State Park
P.O. Box 392
Crawford, NE 69339-0392
(308) 665-2900

Notes on the trail: The key strategy for handling this trail system is to ride one of the 3 inner trails downhill west to east. If you prefer to get the uphill climb out of the way first, then start at the trailhead at Johnson Lake, 3 miles northwest of the fort complex, or at the base of Smiley Canyon on Smiley Canyon Road. If you're eager to do the descent first, there is a small pulloff for parking one-quarter mile beyond the trailhead at the top of Smiley Canyon. Head out across the open ridge tops, following the white blazes on posts and pick one of the 3 trails descending through the canyons, leading to Soldier Creek visible far below.

The tracks are sometimes rocky, sometimes steep, but they offer great views down the ridges. Occasional side tracks branch off from the marked trails, so keep an eye out for the white diamond posts. In 1989 a serious fire burned much of the park, including this ridge, resulting in a more open, austere landscape and creating a lot of dead trees that periodically fall onto the trail. Keeping your downhill speeds under control is therefore a necessity. When I rode this area, a major windstorm 5 days before had blown down hundreds of trees, making the process of climbing over logs and branches a real nuisance. However, park personnel said that they regularly try to keep the trails cleared out with a bulldozer for fire-access purposes. Learn to look at fire-scarred environments in a positive light, observing the succession of plant and animal life that quickly returns after a fire.

As the trails emerge from the canyons, they meet on a north-south grassy track that descends to Johnson Lake or meanders south to the paved Smiley Canyon Road. The northernmost of the three descending trails seems a bit less well traveled, and the section heading toward Johnson Lake is overgrown with low brush. From Johnson Lake, the northern outer loop returns to the top of the ridge by way of a 3-mile-long gravel road, a stream crossing, and a steady two-mile climb up another grassy canyon.

Other roads that are open to vehicles in the state park are also open to bicycling. There are some easy gravel roads along the White River valley in the vicinity of the fort. Trails in the Soldier Creek Wilderness Area west of the mountain bike trail system are open to hikers and horseback riders only. There are additional trails open to foot traffic only; avoid these as well.

ADDITIONAL MOUNTAIN BIKING OPPORTUNITIES IN WESTERN NEBRASKA

Part of the U.S. Forest Service administered lands in the Pine Ridge area is the *Oglala National Grassland,* which, like other grassland units discussed in this guidebook, is a checkerboard collection of prairie lands administered for grazing and other purposes. The roads through these lands are usually dirt and four-wheel-drive and are open to mountain bike exploration. The Oglala National Grassland has a number of these types of roads that should make for some interesting rides. A good place to start exploring this area would be the Toadstool Park picnic area, about 15 miles northwest of Crawford. This spot features some badlands-type erosion formations. Nearby is the Hudson-Meng Bison Kill Site, where prehistoric hunters drove some buffalo over a cliff 10,000 years ago.

For Further Information

Chadron Area Chamber of Commerce
P.O. Box 646
Chadron, NE 69337

Scottsbluff/Gering
United Chamber
1721 Broadway
Scottsbluff, NE 69361
(308) 632-2133

Bike Shops

Mountain Mania
361 Main
Chadron, NE 69337
(308) 432-3653

Sonny's Bike Shop
1717 East Overland
Scottsbluff, NE 69361
(308) 632-3938

SOUTH DAKOTA

South Dakota is almost evenly divided in half by the Missouri River, with relatively flat glaciated plains in the east and arid, rolling terrain culminating in the Black Hills in the west. The eastern side is primarily devoted to agriculture, and ranching dominates the western half. The state's 77,120 square miles are home to about 700,000 people, making it the 45th most populous state in the country, so South Dakota is another place with lots of elbow room.

South Dakota's flat eastern plains are broken up by a zone of low rolling hills consisting of glacial moraine deposits running from the southeast to the northeast corner of the state, just to the west of the Minnesota border. Many of eastern South Dakota's state parks and recreation areas are located in these hills, or what the early French explorers called "coteau," which are dotted with shallow lakes. Central South Dakota is a transition area dominated by the Missouri River, now harnessed into a series of giant reservoir lakes built to manage the water resource. The hilly country west of the Missouri is mostly treeless short-grass prairie, cut into periodically by small rivers meandering in from the west.

The western high plains of South Dakota are dotted with buttes and ridges and highlighted by the most spectacular geography of the plains states—the Black Hills. This dome of mountains is an isolated eastern extension of the Rockies, with a rugged igneous core surrounded by a ring of sedimentary ridges and hills cut by steep valleys. The predominate forest cover is dark green ponderosa pine, giving the hills a black appearance when viewed from the prairies below. The nearby badlands region on the plains to the east is the largest of these heavily eroded, semidesert outcroppings found in various spots around the western Great Plains.

South Dakota has a continental climate, with great temperature variations from summer to winter. Summers are humid in the east and drier with less rainfall in the west, and thunderstorms can be common across the state. Winters can be moderate to severe, with continuous snow cover likely in the eastern half of the state from December until March. The Black Hills region often generates its own local weather patterns and usually picks up a bit more summer rain and winter snow than the surrounding plains.

As did the other plains states, the area that is now South Dakota hosted nomadic and agricultural inhabitants for thousands of years. At the time of the first European exploration, the Dakota (Sioux) tribes were beginning to dominate the plains with their nomadic way of life. In 1743 the La Vérendrye brothers, sons of the great French explorer Sieur de La Vérendrye, reached the area near Fort Pierre and claimed the region for France. After the Lewis and Clark Expedition of 1804–6, the stage was set for almost a century of conflict over control of the Great Plains, as the Dakota tribes were pushed westward by settlers from the growing United States.

Yankton was the first white community and the original capital of Dakota Territory, and settlement of the region grew rapidly with the coming of the railroads after the Civil War. Along with North Dakota, South Dakota became a state in 1889. The eastern plains of the state developed an economic base of commercial agriculture, and the west became a ranching and mining region. After a period of populist politics around the turn of the century, the differences in temperament between the two halves of the state became more pronounced. This distinction, which is largely true for North Dakota as well, has brought about the observation that Dakota Territory should have been divided into East Dakota and West Dakota, instead of South and North. Economic hard times in South Dakota during the Depression and the dust bowl years were replaced by the boom years after World War II, and the state's economy has diversified into tourism, industry, and service-oriented business.

Mountain Biking in South Dakota

Most of the recreational opportunities in the eastern half of the state center around the state park system. A number of these parks have equestrian trail systems that have been opened to mountain bike use. These trails are generally moderately challenging, usually set in wooded, hilly terrain near lakes and rivers. In the central plains region around the Missouri River, there is little in the way of established trails, but there are many informal places to ride in the hills along the Missouri reservoirs, where much of the land is under the jurisdiction of the U.S. Army Corps of Engineers. Check with local bike shops for ideas in this region, and be sure to respect private property and Indian reservation land.

In western South Dakota, the Black Hills region should rank as one of the top mountain biking areas in the United States. There are several hundred, perhaps over a thousand, miles of forest back roads and trails spread throughout the meadows, hills, and canyons of this special place, ideal for mountain bikers of all abilities and interests.

State Park and Tourism Information

Department of Game, Fish, and Parks
523 East Capitol
Pierre, SD 57501-3182
(605) 773-3391

South Dakota Department of Tourism
711 East Wells Avenue
Pierre, SD 57501-3369
(605) 773-3301 or 773-3256 fax

Eastern South Dakota

Roughly paralleling the route of Interstate 29 stretch the "Coteau des Prairies," a line of rolling prairie hills and lakes, carved by the last Ice Age, and made up of rich soils that attracted the first settlers to this pastoral region. The lakes, ridges, and river courses of this area contain many of South Dakota's eastern state parks and trails.

Sioux Falls is South Dakota's largest city and is the economic hub of the eastern half of the state. Originally built around a waterfall on the Big Sioux River, which early industry tapped for power, Sioux Falls now has a diversified, modern base of shopping, services, and culture that regularly earns it a rating as one of America's most livable small cities. There is an active community of bicyclists and a number of good bike shops here. Other cities in the area with modern services and bike shops include Aberdeen, Watertown, Brookings, Yankton, and Mitchell. Synonymous with the city of Mitchell is the Corn Palace, a one-hundred-year-old building with a facade of corn and grain located downtown. It is a high-priority stop for tourists and, presumably, migrating birds.

In this section, I will describe trail systems in four state parks and three state recreation areas.

RIDE 62   *LEWIS AND CLARK RECREATION AREA/ GAVINS POINT UNIT*

Some of the most challenging mountain bike terrain in eastern South Dakota can be found in the wooded bluffs of the Lewis and Clark Recreation Area. Over four miles of mostly single-track trails form a loop with various offshoot trails that meander up and down the hardwood-forested slopes and ravines and over some open grassy uplands. Periodic challenges keep the riding interesting in this area of mostly moderate difficulty; you are likely to encounter sandy spots, muddy ravine crossings, downed branches, horse-trail ruts, and rocky spots. It pays to take the time to look around a bit and enjoy the view overlooking the limestone cliffs and the blue waters of the reservoir. You are likely to see deer and other wildlife in the mornings and evenings. Whether you spend an hour or the better part of a day here, this is a trail worth visiting; and with five other rides within about an hour's drive in three states, a pleasant weekend of mountain biking—Great Plains style—can be done. (See Rides 25, 51, 52, 63, and 64.)

RIDE 62 *LEWIS & CLARK RECREATION AREA / GAVINS POINT UNIT*

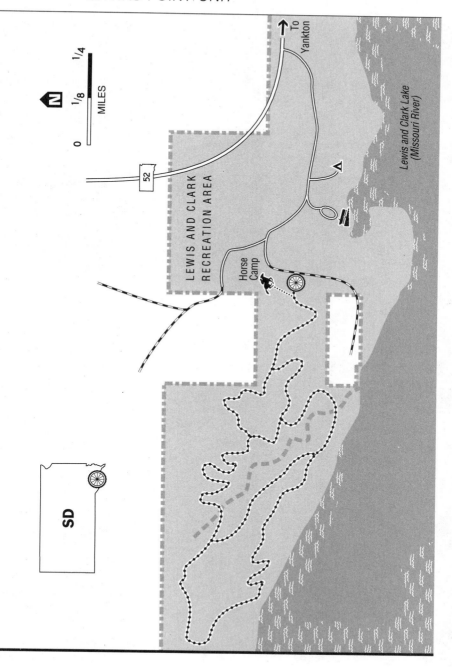

Views of the Lewis and Clark Reservoir are frequent from the trails at Gavins Point near Yankton.

The Gavins Point Dam, which created Lewis and Clark Lake, was completed in 1957 and is one of six dams that control the waters of the upper Missouri River. The dam is near the site where Lewis and Clark met with the Yankton Sioux tribe on their journey up the river in 1804. The Lewis and Clark Visitor Center, which features exhibits portraying the history of that time, is just north of that location, on the Nebraska side of the river. In Yankton, the Dakota Territorial Museum covers the history of the time when Yankton was capital of the Dakota Territory.

General location: Eight miles west of the city of Yankton in Yankton County.
Elevation change: High bluffs overlooking the river valley produce almost 200′ of elevation above the lake level of about 1,200′.
Season: Midspring to late autumn. There is often winter snow cover in the woodlands of this area.
Services: The park has picnic, camping, and swimming facilities. All other services are available in Yankton.
Hazards: Watch out for steep descents into ravines with sharp corners, water bars, and some spots with deep ruts.
Rescue index: In season, the recreation area is well staffed and usually busy.
Land status: Lewis and Clark Recreation Area is a unit of the state park system, managed by the South Dakota Department of Game, Fish, and Parks.

Maps: The map included in this book and the map signpost at the trailhead will get you started.

Finding the trail: The entrance to the Gavins Point Unit is located 8 miles west of Yankton on SD 52. Follow the park road past the beach area turnoff around to the equestrian staging area. Access to the trails can be made from the parking lot in the grassy area just beyond that staging area.

Sources of additional information:

Lewis and Clark Recreation Area
RR1, Box 240
Yankton, SD 57078-9207
(605) 668-3435

Coast Bike & Sport Shop
103 West 3rd Street
Yankton, SD 57078
(605) 665-2813

Notes on the trail: From the grassy area the trail climbs through the woods over some water bars onto the ridge overlooking the reservoir. The action continues as you make several descents into and out of ravines leading down to the water. Various side trails branch off here and there, so be prepared to explore around a bit. Near the west end of the area, the trail intercepts a four-wheel-drive road leading up from the lake.

Bikers and hikers share these trails with horseback riders. Be prepared to yield the trail and get well off to the side if necessary. There has been talk of expanding the trail system here, but plans are indefinite. A bicycle trail for casual riders runs along the waterfront of the campground area. A daily entrance fee or park sticker is required to enter the park.

RIDE 63   UNION COUNTY STATE PARK

This small park has three to four miles of multi-use trails in a mostly open, rolling prairie setting. The trails, which consist of a series of small, easy to moderate loops, do not seem to get much use and may be somewhat overgrown with tall grasses in some areas. Other sections of the trail have packed dirt, stones, and occasional muddy spots in the low areas. In season, wildflowers and autumn leaves will add some color to the prairie landscape, and in midsummer, the surrounding vistas of low hills present a sea of green. There is also an arboretum display in the park. A ride here of an hour or so might serve as a nice warm-up for bikers intending to do some harder riding at Newton Hills or Lewis and Clark Recreation Area.

RIDE 63 *UNION COUNTY STATE PARK*

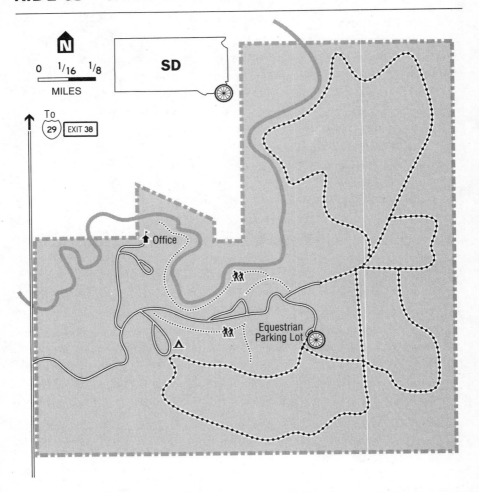

General location: Ten miles south of Beresford in Union County.
Elevation change: Gently rolling hills in this area provide some moderate ups and downs.
Season: Midspring to late autumn.
Services: The park has water, picnic areas, and camping facilities. Other services can be found in Beresford, to the north, or Vermillion, 20 miles southwest.
Hazards: Tall grasses on the open slopes can obscure rough and uneven terrain.

There are several miles of prairie riding on the grassy tracks in Union County State Park.

Rescue index: There is usually a staff person on duty in the park.
Land status: Union County State Park is managed by the South Dakota Department of Game, Fish, and Parks.
Maps: A basic diagram map is available at the park.
Finding the trail: Take Interstate 29/exit 38, then follow the signs to the park. The equestrian parking lot area at the end of the park road is the best starting point for most of the trails.

Sources of additional information:

Union County State Park
RR 1, Box 44
Beresford, SD 57004
(605) 253-2370

Notes on the trail: The trail loops fan out from the equestrian parking lot in several directions. These multi-use trails are used by horseback riders; please yield the trail when horses are present. There are other trails in the park reserved for hikers. A daily entrance fee or park sticker is required for vehicles in the park.

RIDE 64 *NEWTON HILLS STATE PARK*

Newton Hills State Park is situated in the southern end of a region of low glacial hills, forested valleys, and small lakes. About seven miles of equestrian trails forming a convoluted loop through several ravines and bluffs at the north end of the park are available for mountain bike use. These bluffs, which overlook the Big Sioux River and the Iowa border, contain some of the most rugged and scenic trails in eastern South Dakota. A number of steep grades, and muddy, rocky, and eroded spots make for some moderate to moderately difficult riding on mostly single-track trails. The most hilly terrain in the ravines of the western end of the loop is in a thickly wooded setting, providing cool shade on warm summer afternoons. The lower eastern slopes near Sargent Creek are more open, grassy meadowlands.

The thick oak and elm forest cover of this hilly region resisted agricultural development and gave birth to legends of Indian curses, bandits, and horse thieves in the area. This mixture of prairie and rich woodland also provides a prime habitat for wildlife; if you proceed quietly, you may encounter deer, foxes, wild turkeys, and other animals. Most bikers should enjoy this area, whether they ride hard for an hour or spend a leisurely half a day.

General location: Six miles south of Canton in Lincoln County.
Elevation change: The hilly terrain has many short, steep climbs and descents.
Season: Midspring to late autumn. The wooded areas are usually snow covered during the winter months.
Services: The park has picnic, camping, and swimming facilities available. A small store is located just outside the park. Other services can be found in Canton or Sioux Falls.
Hazards: You'll encounter some steep grades and muddy spots, as well as rocks and other debris on the trails.
Rescue index: In season, the park is staffed and visitors are usually present.
Land status: Newton Hills State Park is managed by the South Dakota Department of Game, Fish, and Parks.
Maps: An informative pamphlet with a diagram map is available from the entrance station.
Finding the trail: From SD 11 south of Canton, take CR 140 east several miles to the park; the main park entrance is just to the north on CR 135. Access to the trail system can be made from a parking area near Sargent Creek on the park loop road about 1 mile north of the campground entrance. The trail system also departs from an equestrian staging area north of the main park entrance on CR 135.

RIDE 64   *NEWTON HILLS STATE PARK*

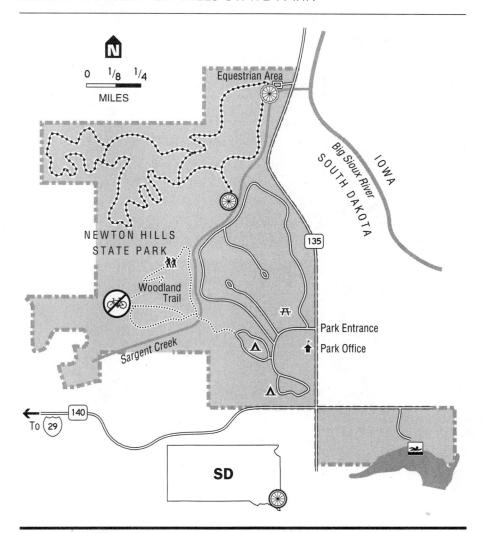

Sources of additional information:

Newton Hills State Park
Route 1, Box 162
Canton, SD 57013
(605) 987-2263

Open meadows and thick, hilly woodlands provide
plenty of variety in Newton Hills State Park.

Notes on the trail: From the parking lot on the park loop road, cross the
creek and join the trail loop a bit uphill from a clearing. Keeping to the left
will get you into the steepest terrain and allow you to tour most of the area.
Additional side trails may add some confusion as to the route of the loop;
don't be afraid to explore and backtrack. You will be sharing these trails with
horseback riders who have been using this area for years. Be prepared to yield
the trail and get well off to the side if necessary. The Woodland and Coteau
Trails are designed as nature hikes, so please avoid biking on these. A daily
entrance fee or park sticker is required for vehicles in the park.

RIDE 65   *BIG SIOUX RECREATION AREA*

Convenient to the Sioux Falls urban area, Big Sioux Recreation Area has almost four miles of relatively easy trails that make a nice one-hour tour (depending on your speed) in the morning or evening. Two main loops, one on each side of the Big Sioux River, wind through oak forests and open meadows on a mowed grass and packed-dirt trail. The northern loop meanders through a wooded slope overlooking the river and along the edge of some open fields. The west loop circumnavigates a prairie meadow and climbs onto a hillside for a nice view of the local river valley. Bridge crossings, water bars, narrow spots, and a few climbs add some challenges to the routes.

General location: Just east of Sioux Falls, 1 mile south of Brandon in Minnehaha County.
Elevation change: Bluffs along the river provide some climbs on the 2 main trail loops.
Season: Late spring to late autumn.
Services: Water, rest rooms, a picnic shelter, and a small campground are available at the recreation area. Other services are available in Brandon and Sioux Falls.
Hazards: In times of high water some parts of the trail system are likely to be flooded. There are some bridges, stairs, and water bars to watch for.
Rescue index: The park is not always staffed. Help is always present in nearby Brandon.
Land status: Big Sioux Recreation Area is managed by the South Dakota Department of Game, Fish, and Parks.
Maps: A trail map is posted at the picnic shelter near the central trailhead.
Finding the trail: Brandon can be reached on SD 11, off Interstate 90/exit 406. The park is about 1 mile south of town and three-quarters of a mile west of SD 11. Watch for the turnoff onto Sioux Boulevard from SD 11 near a race track; then follow the signs. Both the eastern and western trail systems can be reached from the picnic shelter area and parking lot.

Sources of additional information:

Palisades State Park
25495 485th Avenue
Garretson, SD 57030
(605) 594-3824

RIDE 65 *BIG SIOUX RECREATION AREA*

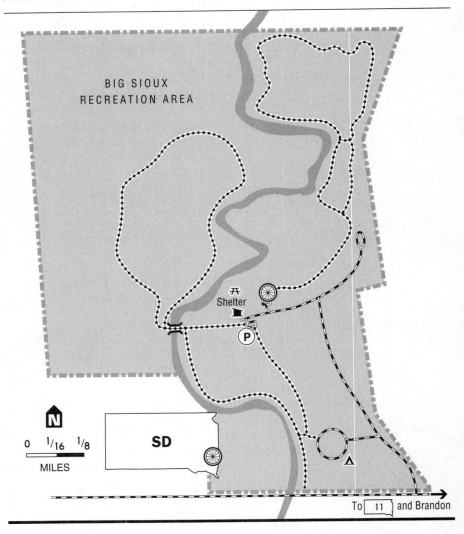

BIG SIOUX
RECREATION AREA

Shelter

P

N

0   1/16   1/8
MILES

SD

To 11 and Brandon

Notes on the trail: Horseback riders may be using the west trail loop. Other bikeable trails in the park meander south along the river and around the campground. There are future plans for development of an additional trail for bike use. A daily entrance fee or park sticker is required for vehicles in the park.

For centuries, the Oakwood Lakes were an oasis for Native Americans and explorers. Today, they make a pleasant place to ride.

RIDE 66 *OAKWOOD LAKES STATE PARK*

Oakwood Lakes State Park is situated in the center of a collection of lakes of glacial origin that have attracted human habitation for hundreds, or perhaps thousands of years. A collection of Indian burial mounds, several old cabins, and an 1857 fort site stand as reminders of the busy past this rich area had. Today, over five miles of trails parallel the fields, lakeshores, and wooded corridors that make up the park. Single-track equestrian trails as well as four-wheel-drive tracks that form several loops and short spur trails are open to bicycles here. The riding is generally easy and level, but thick grass, muddy ruts, and high water can create some obstacles.

General location: 18 miles northwest of Brookings in Brookings County.
Elevation change: This is a fairly level area, with just a few low rolling hills.
Season: Midspring through October.
Services: The park offers water and picnic, swimming, camping, and cabin facilities. Commercial services can be found in Volga or Brookings.
Hazards: Watch for traffic at points where the trails exit onto the local roads.
Rescue index: Park personnel are generally available in the park.

RIDE 66   *OAKWOOD LAKES STATE PARK*

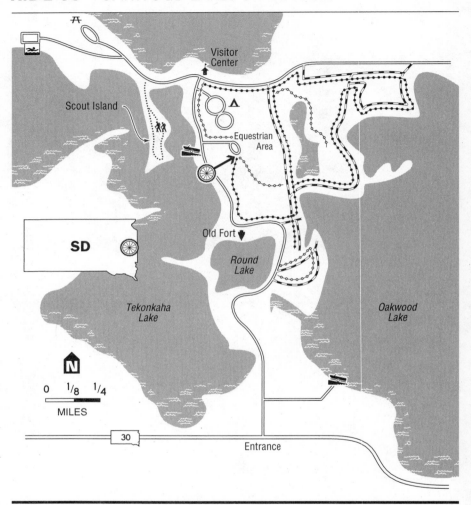

Land status: Oakwood Lakes State Park is managed by the South Dakota Department of Game, Fish, and Parks.

Maps: An informative brochure with a basic map is available, and a new, updated map is in the works. A park map with trail information is posted on a sign near the visitor center.

Finding the trail: From Interstate 29/exit 140, take SD 30 west about 11 miles to the park entrance. You can start biking at the equestrian area near the burial mounds to the south of the campground.

Sources of additional information:

Oakwood Lakes State Park
RR 2, Box 10
Bruce, SD 57220
(605) 627-5441

Notes on the trail: A mowed grass trail heads south from the equestrian area and provides access to the dirt roads and tracks that wind along the shorelines of the Oakwood Lakes. A short side trip can be made to the old fort site at the north end of Round Lake. You can cross a narrows at the northwest end of the big lake and follow a double-track through small woodlands and open meadows to the paved park road at the northeast end of the park. From there, it is probably most scenic to return the way you came, but some tracks along the edge of fields or the park road can be used to return to the campground area. Most of the routes are not marked, and some of the grassy tracks may be obscure, so plan on doing some exploring.

The addition of a short trail for casual biking is being planned for the future. Please do not bike on the Scout Island hiking trail loop. A daily entrance fee or park sticker is required.

RIDE 67 SICA HOLLOW STATE PARK

In the vicinity of Sica Hollow the "Coteau des Prairies" glacial hills region of eastern South Dakota reaches its highest and most dramatic point. The forested hillsides and secluded ravines of Sica ("she-cha") Hollow State Park offer some of the most rugged terrain in the eastern half of the state, and the open prairie uplands on the tops of the bluffs present great vistas of the rolling plains to the east. The Dakota Sioux people who once inhabited this region considered the valley to be a sacred spot, where you'll find a natural spring and abundant wildlife.

One of the major draws to this relatively undeveloped park is the almost ten miles of multiple-use trails that climb through the ravines and meander along the edges of the bluffs. The mostly dirt and grassy single-track trails are shared with horseback riders, hikers, and cross-country skiers in the snowy months. With one trail generally following the creek down the center of the park, and two trails following the bluffs on either side of the valley, there are several possible loop rides that are moderate to moderately difficult. There was a certain amount of erosion damage along the creek drainages during the 1993 floods, and there are still some rough spots and possible obstacles to watch for. A visit to Sica Hollow should provide an enjoyable

RIDE 67 *SICA HOLLOW STATE PARK*

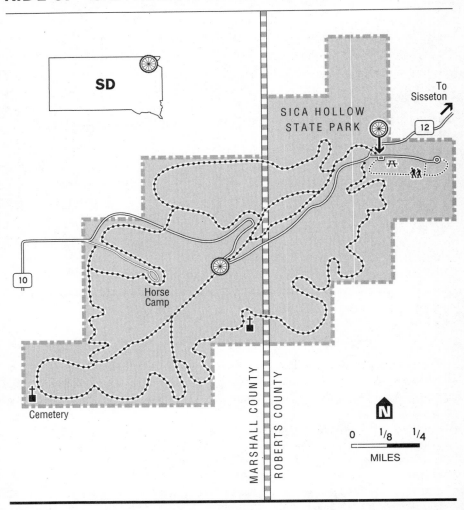

challenge to almost any mountain biker. But tread lightly and don't abuse this special place.

The Tekakwitha Fine Arts Center in Sisseton has a display of Native American art and a gift shop. Fort Sisseton State Park, southwest of Lake City, has one of the most completely preserved frontier forts on the Great Plains. It is listed as a National Historic Landmark and includes a museum and a campground.

Trails on the bluffs overlooking the wooded ravines of Sica Hollow allow some of the best panoramas of the prairie hills region.

General location: Sica Hollow is located about 16 miles northwest of Sisseton on the border of Marshall and Roberts Counties.

Elevation change: The bluffs and steep ravines have many good climbs and descents ranging in elevation of over 200′.

Season: May through October. Many of the shady ravine trails will be slow to dry out in the spring. Avoid biking in times of wet weather, when trails will be muddy.

Services: There are rest rooms and a picnic site near the springs. Camping is available in nearby Roy Lake State Park. Other services can be found in Sisseton.

Hazards: Watch for obstacles and control downhill speed on the various long descents.

Rescue index: This park does not always have staff personnel on site. The closest towns are Lake City and Sisseton.

Land status: Sica Hollow is managed by the South Dakota Department of Game, Fish, and Parks and administered from Roy Lake State Park.

Maps: Maps and park information can be obtained from the office at Roy Lake State Park.

Finding the trail: From SD 10, four miles west of Sisseton, take CR 6 north about 7 miles, then CR 12 west into the park. The easiest trail access point is at the first switchback on the park road less than 1 mile up from the park entrance. Park there or at the day use area near the entrance.

Sources of additional information:

> Roy Lake State Park
> RR2, Box 94
> Lake City, SD 57247-9704
> (605) 448-5701

Notes on the trail: From the switchback it is a steady ride uphill to the head of the valley. You can keep left and climb onto the southern bluffs and eventually pass an old settlers' cemetery. By keeping to the right you will gain the bluffs on the north side. The bluff trails return to the valley floor near the day use area. Several cutoff trails and short loops are also available. Visit the natural spring, but don't bike on the walking trail that surrounds it. This area is especially nice during the fall color season in October.

RIDE 68   *RICHMOND LAKE STATE RECREATION AREA*

The three-mile trail system here was designed for cross-country skiing, but it serves well as a pleasant, although rather flat, biking area. The single-track trails along mowed, wooded corridors are laid out in a series of small interconnected loops, allowing users the opportunity to double back and try different variations, thus extending the possibilities. The wide variety of human-planted and natural forest cover in the area makes for gorgeous trailside scenery and a multitude of colors in autumn. The recreation area, situated in a mostly agricultural region, is also a haven for bird life and other animals. This is a great quiet place to catch a bit of nature and get in an easy hour of riding.

General location: Ten miles northwest of Aberdeen in Brown County.
Elevation change: This area is mostly flat, with a few gradual hills on the west side near the lake.
Season: Midspring to late autumn.
Services: There are picnic and camping facilities in the park. All other services are available in Aberdeen.
Hazards: Use care when passing hikers in the area. Watch for vehicles when crossing the narrow Forest Drive road.
Rescue index: Park personnel are usually available at the office and maintenance area.
Land status: Richmond Lake Recreation Area is managed by the South Dakota Department of Game, Fish, and Parks.

RIDE 68 *RICHMOND LAKE STATE RECREATION AREA*

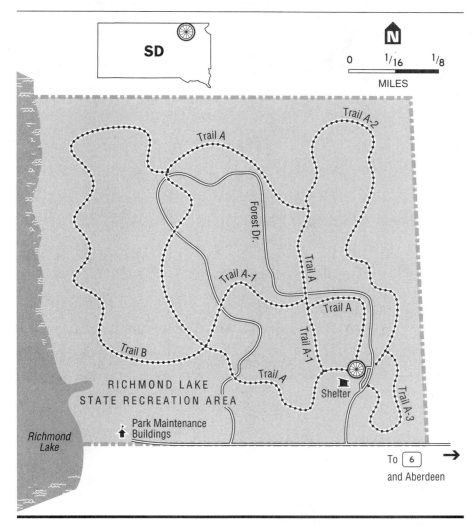

Maps: A map of the trails is usually available at the warming shelter parking lot.

Finding the trail: Take US 281 north from Aberdeen about 4 miles, then west on CR 13 for 4 miles and north on CR 6 for about 3 more miles to the turnoff. Follow the signs west into the park. Start your ride at the warming shelter parking lot on Forest Drive.

A variety of easy trails in Richmond State Recreation Area make a nice quick tour near Aberdeen.

Sources of additional information:

Richmond Lake State Recreation Area
RR 2, Box 500
Aberdeen, SD 57401
(605) 225-5325

Dakota Outdoors
402 North Main
Aberdeen, SD 57401
(605) 229-0123

Notes on the trail: The trails are marked with signs indicating the letter of the route. The "B" loop has some small hills along the west side and is the most challenging of what's available at this area. A daily entrance fee or park sticker is required for vehicles.

ADDITIONAL MOUNTAIN BIKING OPPORTUNITIES
IN EASTERN SOUTH DAKOTA

Many of the towns mentioned above have informal bike riding areas nearby used by local mountain bikers. You can get information on these areas from local clubs and bike shops.

Bike Shops and Clubs

Sioux Empire Bicycle Club
P.O. Box 90154
Sioux Falls, SD 57105

The shops mentioned below provided me with useful information. There are a number of other good bicycle shops throughout eastern South Dakota; check the area yellow pages for more information.

Bike Barn
100 South Cliff
Sioux Falls, SD 57103
(605) 338-4125 or 336-3603 fax

Dakota Outdoors
402 North Main
Aberdeen, SD 57401
(605) 229-0123

The Pedaler
112 North Main St.
Mitchell, SD 57301
(605) 996-0679
Club: Palace City Pedalers

Sioux River Cyclery
501 Main Avenue
Brookings, SD 57006
(605) 692-5022

Spoke N Sport
2101 West 41st Street
Sioux Falls, SD 57105
(605) 332-2206

41st Street Scheels
501 West 41st Street
Sioux Falls, SD 57105
(605) 334-7767 or 334-8936

Central South Dakota

French explorers and trappers, the Lewis and Clark Expedition, and eventually settlers arriving during the steamboat era all used the Missouri River to travel in and out of what is now South Dakota. When the railroads and highways shifted the emphasis of transportation to east-west travel, the Missouri River became a landmark symbolizing the crossing from east to west, moving from the farmlands of the Midwestern prairies to the ranches of the wide-open, arid high plains of the west. Today, the long, multi-span bridges that carry traffic over the wide river help to dramatize this transition.

This seemingly endless land is a rich area where the tall-grass prairie—or the remnants of it—begins to change over to the short-grass prairie environment. The Missouri River is in the heart of the central flyway for migratory geese and other waterfowl. The abundant wildlife, including antelope, deer, pheasants, and grouse, make this a popular hunting destination. The South Dakota section of the Missouri is now controlled by four flood-control dams that created reservoirs with over 3,000 miles of shoreline. These waterways have become a recreational resource in the state second only to the Black Hills area.

The centrally located state capital of Pierre is the major commercial center of the region. Fort Pierre, which is located across the river, was founded in 1832 during the waning days of the fur trade.

The massive Oahe Dam, four miles north, forms the largest of the reservoir lakes and produces electricity for a large area. The South Dakota Cultural Heritage Center in the hills above the city recreates the history of South Dakota.

Other major Missouri River towns include Chamberlain, which is at the Interstate 90 crossing of the river and home to the Akta Lakota Museum. The museum features displays of native art and scenes from the daily life of the Lakota (Sioux), as well as some props that were used in the filming of the movie "Dances with Wolves." Mobridge, on Lake Oahe, is another lake recreation center. Overlooking the river here is the grave of Chief Sitting Bull, who was the leader of the Sioux forces at the Battle of the Little Bighorn. A monument marking the grave was carved by Korczak Ziolkowski, who conceived of and began the construction of the Crazy Horse Memorial in the Black Hills. East of Mobridge is a wheat-growing region centered around Eureka that was settled in the late 1800s by German immigrants from Russia who had been forced out by the czar.

Miles of trails on LaFramboise Island are easily accessible from downtown Pierre.

RIDE 69   *LAFRAMBOISE ISLAND NATURE AREA*

Since the Oahe Dam has prevented the periodic cycle of flooding on the Missouri River, a diverse woodland habitat is developing on LaFramboise Island, which is adjacent to the city of Pierre. A mixture of young, thick stands of secondary trees and open meadows mingles with the dominant cottonwood forest, providing shelter for a population of deer, wild turkeys, and other wildlife. Some seven to ten miles of single-track and double-track trails are intertwined on the two-mile-long island. Although it is quite flat, with only a few small ups and downs along new and old river banks, the variety

RIDE 69 *LAFRAMBOISE ISLAND NATURE AREA*

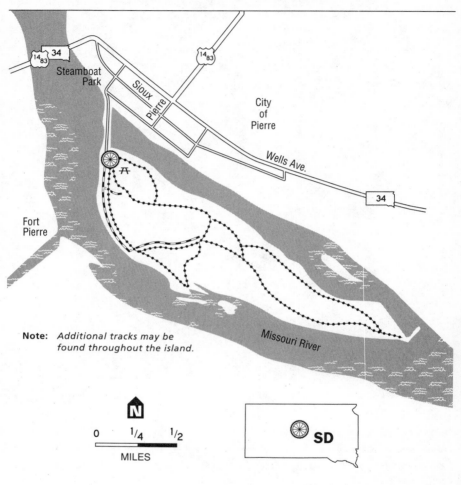

Note: *Additional tracks may be found throughout the island.*

MILES

SD

of habitats here make for some great riding. Several double-track and wide single-track sections run along the river and through the tall stands of cottonwood. A series of narrow, winding single-track routes in the thick woods offers some more technical options. Trail surfaces vary from packed organic soil to some loose sandy spots in old flood channels, and occasional logs and debris add some obstacles. Occasionally you will hear noises from the city, but generally this is a quiet place, nice for a quick getaway and relaxing ride.

General location: Adjacent to the city of Pierre on an island in the Missouri River.
Elevation change: This island is almost totally flat.
Season: Midspring through late autumn. Winter riding could be possible in times of little snow.
Services: All services are available in Pierre. Water, rest rooms, and picnic facilities are available at the trailhead.
Hazards: Watch for sandy spots, sharp corners, and occasional downed logs.
Rescue index: Help is close by in the city.
Land status: U.S. Army Corps of Engineers.
Maps: There is a large trail map painted on a sign in the park at the trailhead.
Finding the trail: From the riverfront park area in downtown Pierre follow the causeway out to the island. There is parking at the end of the paved road.

Sources of additional information:

Beckwith's Bicycles
413 South Pierre Street
Pierre, SD 57501
(605) 224-8955

Notes on the trail: This is a popular spot for hiking; be on the watch for and yield to people on foot. A few of the trails have signs, but be prepared just to explore and work your way back when you're ready to quit.

ADDITIONAL MOUNTAIN BIKING OPPORTUNITIES IN CENTRAL SOUTH DAKOTA

The U.S. Army Corps of Engineers has jurisdiction over much of the land adjacent to the reservoir lakes on the Missouri River and has established quite a number of recreational sites along the many miles of shoreline. Mountain bike use of some of these lands in the Chamberlain and Pierre areas has been reported by the local bike shops. Be respectful of local regulations and private property when you're exploring new areas. Check with the following shops for further information: Beckwith's Bicycles, 413 South Pierre Street, Pierre, SD 57501, (605) 224-8955, or The Pedaler, 112 North Main Street, Mitchell, SD 57301, (605) 996-0679.

A small community of mountain bikers is growing in the *Mobridge Area*. There are about ten miles of informal single- and double-tracks along the river south of town on Corps of Engineers land, as well as some four-wheel-drive tracks on the bluffs along the west side of the river. For specific information on this area, check with Motown Cycles, 502 East Grand Crossing, Mobridge, SD 57601, (605) 845-7345.

Farm Island Recreation Area, downstream from Pierre, is a 1,800-acre wooded island—a location free of prairie fires—originally used to grow crops. There are about three miles of easy to moderately challenging trails here that have been used by mountain biking groups for a number of years. Water and picnic and camping facilities are located here as well. Contact: Farm Island Recreation Area, 1301 Farm Island Road, Pierre, SD 57501, (605) 224-5605.

The National Grassland System, a division of the U.S. Forest Service, is a potential source for remote, undeveloped recreational opportunities. See the discussion of the grasslands in Ride 71, Buffalo Gap. The 116,000-acre Fort Pierre National Grassland, which is south of Pierre, has back roads that may be of interest to mountain bikers. For more information: Fort Pierre National Grassland, Wall Ranger District, P.O. Box 417, Pierre, SD 57501, (605) 224-5517.

Bike Shops

Beckwith's Bicycles
413 South Pierre Street
Pierre, SD 57501
(605) 224-8955

Motown Cycles
502 East Grand Crossing
Mobridge, SD 57601
(605) 845-7345

Western South Dakota

The sparsely populated western plains of South Dakota seem endlessly open. They act as a reminder even to modern travelers of the price in distance and time you need to pay in the Great Plains to get to your next destination. Isolated buttes, ragged ridge tops, and cottonwood-lined river bottoms break the monotony of the open prairie and hint in the incessant wind of their story-rich past. But eventually in your prairie journey you'll see the dark shadows of the Black Hills rising on the far horizon. They are South Dakota's mecca, once sacred to the Native Americans and now a magnet for recreational travelers.

Today, the ranching, forest products, and mining industries make up the mainstay of the western South Dakota economy. Tourism, however, is the most visible industry to travelers in the region, or at least to those reading billboards on Interstate 90. Outside the Black Hills region, there are many other areas of natural, perhaps more subtle, beauty, including Badlands National Park, Buffalo Gap National Grassland, several state parks, the Pine Ridge Reservation and three other Indian Reservations, and small units of other national forests and grasslands. Some of these locations have interesting terrain for mountain bike riding, so think beyond the Black Hills when you're visiting this region.

Rapid City is the commercial center of the western half of South Dakota. With the presence of the popular Black Hills and Ellsworth Air Force base, the city boasts many urban-quality shopping, cultural, and entertainment facilities. Popular attractions include the downtown shopping district, Rushmore Mall, the Sioux Indian Museum, and the Firehouse brew pub. The Museum of Geology at the School of Mines and Technology has an excellent fossil and rock collection. Dinosaur Park, the delight of generations of kids (as I know from my visit decades ago), overlooks the city.

No visitor to South Dakota can get out of the state without at least becoming aware of Wall Drug in the town of Wall, on I-90, 50 miles east of Rapid City. This quintessential tourist stop has been beckoning travelers for over 60 years with their far-flung network of billboards and bumper stickers. I have actually seen "Wall Drug" signs in the Yukon and in the Asian country of Nepal.

THE BLACK HILLS

The Lakota (Sioux) people named the "hills that are black" aptly, for when it is viewed from the hot prairie for miles and miles around, the vast, pine-covered uplift looks like a dark, shadowy cloud. The hills rise for over 4,000

259

feet from the plains to their highest point at Harney Peak (7,242 feet), the highest point in South Dakota, as well as in the United States east of the Rocky Mountains. The Black Hills is a land of many other regional superlatives as well. Custer State Park is by far the largest state park in South Dakota, and it is the second largest in the United States. The park has the largest buffalo (bison) herd in the United States. It is also home to an extensive herd of elk and bighorn sheep.

Most of the forested sections of the Black Hills fall under the jurisdiction of the U.S. Forest Service; three units are maintained by the National Park Service. Possibly the most familiar national monument of all is Mount Rushmore, one of the biggest tourist attractions in the United States. The faces of the four presidents were blasted out of the granite pinnacles of Mount Rushmore beginning in 1927 and ending in 1941, when the funding ran out. The original version envisioned by sculptor Gutzon Borglum was never finished beyond the stage we see today. Wind Cave National Park protects the more than 55 miles of caverns and passageways of Wind Cave, as well as a forest environment and an extensive natural prairie, which is home to buffalo, pronghorn antelope, and prairie dogs. Not to be outdone by Wind Cave, Jewel Cave National Monument, west of the town of Custer, contains over 80 miles of complex passageways, highlighted by deposits of crystals. Devils Tower National Monument, the original national monument, is located at the northwestern edge of the Black Hills region in Wyoming. Bicycling, including mountain biking, is restricted to established roads in all of these national facilities.

Sprawling over almost 2,000 square miles, the Black Hills National Forest links all these areas and contains many attractions of its own. The section surrounding Harney Peak between Custer, Hill City, and Mount Rushmore is the geological core of the region, made up of spectacular granite pinnacles and domes, which are popular with hikers and rock climbers. On the western edge of this core area, north of the town of Custer, is the Crazy Horse Memorial, a mountain being carved into a likeness of the Lakota chief that will eventually dwarf the Mount Rushmore carvings.

Wildlife, including bighorn sheep, elk, whitetail and mule deer, mountain goats, and wild burros, abounds in this section. Bighorn sheep were introduced in various areas of the western Dakotas to replace the original Audubon bighorn; the last one of that subspecies was killed in 1925. Elsewhere in the Hills, deer are everywhere, and pronghorn antelope can be found in open grasslands and the lower prairie lands. Prairie dogs, relatives of the ground squirrel, are found in large colonies in many locations of the protected lands of the western Dakotas, including the lower areas of the Black Hills and the badlands. There are no bears remaining in the Black Hills, but rattlesnakes, ticks, and poison ivy may be encountered.

The central and northern Black Hills contain a number of reservoir lakes featuring developed recreational sites and several of the best established trail systems. Towns within the National Forest include Custer, Hill City, and Deadwood, each of which cater heavily to the tourist business with western-theme downtowns and most other conveniences. Deadwood has casino gambling as well as an atmosphere reminiscent of the mid-1800s and the days of Wild Bill Hickok. The neighboring town of Lead is primarily a mining center and the location of the Homestake Mine, the richest gold mine in the United States. Spearfish and Sturgis are commercial centers on I-90 on the northern fringes of the Black Hills. Sturgis hosts the annual Sturgis Rally in August, at which many thousands of motorcyclists fill the city streets. About 40 miles north of Sturgis, near Castle Rock, is the geographical center of the United States.

Black Hills weather offers Midwesterners a reprieve from the hot, humid midsummer doldrums found to the east; here there is much lower humidity, temperatures are rarely above the 80s, and the nights are cool. October and May can be nice off-season times of the year for biking—and good times to avoid the crowds. Winter is usually a time of continuous snow cover, with the greatest amounts in the central and northwestern areas.

For thousands of years the isolated Black Hills region was a special place to Native Americans, a place of spiritual significance, and a place to meet without warfare. As the Lakota (Sioux) tribes were pushed westward by the expansion of the United States after the Civil War, the Black Hills and surrounding lands were "given" to the Lakota people by the Laramie Treaty of 1867. In 1874 General George A. Custer conducted an expedition to the Black Hills, where he discovered gold and other valuable natural resources, sparking a land rush into the area. The U.S. Army was unable to prevent the great influx of settlers, so the Lakota fought back and won the victory at Little Bighorn against Custer in 1876. But with the surrender of Crazy Horse in 1877, of Sitting Bull in 1881, and the Wounded Knee Massacre in 1890, Lakota control of the northern plains was ended. In 1897 the Black Hills Forest Reserve was established to help control excess timber cutting and the threat of forest fire.

Few scenic areas in the United States are more saturated with tourist facilities than the Black Hills, particularly in the vicinity of Rapid City and Mount Rushmore. To their credit, the majority of these services and attractions are of good quality, but that area has become popular to the point of excess during the peak summer vacation times. With a bit of planning, however, and by using a mountain bike for your exploration, it's possible to travel beyond this hectic zone into the back country and experience the quiet, special magic of the Black Hills. Let us all tread lightly, respect what we see and what once was, and allow the splendor of the "hills that are black" to remain for future generations.

With hundreds of miles of back roads and trails in the Black Hills, this guidebook can only touch on the highlights of the mountain biking scene here. Adventurous bikers with map-reading skills will most likely want to do some exploration on their own into the remote corners of this huge area. Local riders will undoubtedly know of additional hot spots that I didn't get to in several seasons of visits. Additional ideas for rides can be obtained from the several good bike shops in the region and from the active biking groups. Whether you spend a day or a month, you will never run out of mountain biking possibilities in the Black Hills and vicinity. In this section, I will describe twelve rides with over 333 miles of trails.

RIDE 70   *SHEEP MOUNTAIN ROAD*

Badlands National Park is one of the top scenic attractions in the Great Plains region. For the westbound traveler, this rugged, desolate moonscape of erosion formations is a stunning contrast to the endless rolling prairie of the Dakotas. The enchanting canyons and lack of vegetation beckon one to disappear into the backcountry of the park. Keep in mind that mountain bikes are restricted to the designated road networks, of which there are few. The Sheep Mountain Road in the western half of the Badlands Park provides an opportunity to do some serious biking in this spectacular area.

Located away from the main flow of park traffic, Sheep Mountain Road is a seven-mile dead-end, one-and-a-half lane dirt road that climbs onto a high tableland for some impressive views of the eroded badland valleys below. The view to the west from the plateau is of convoluted, empty land that was used as a gunnery range during World War II; beyond, you can see all the way to the Black Hills. More great vistas unfold to the east and south before the track comes to an end. Except for the long climb, this is a generally easy ride on a packed-dirt surface with occasional rocks, erosion channels, and ruts; but the unique geological environment is the key attraction here. It is possible to drive a ways in toward the plateau before setting out on bike, if you want to shorten the out-and-back distance of 14 miles. You may want to do this ride early in the morning to avoid vehicle traffic and the heat of the day and to catch the spectacular sunrise colors.

The badlands are a surprisingly rich habitat for wildlife, including mule deer, pronghorn antelope, coyotes, porcupines, jackrabbits, bats, and rattle-snakes. Reintroduced populations of buffalo (bison) and bighorn sheep are increasing in numbers. The visitor center at Cedar Pass at the east end of the park, where there are natural history exhibits, is open year-round. To the south of Sheep Mountain Table is the White River Visitor Center, located in a portion of the park that is on lands of the Pine Ridge Reservation. Here you can find water, information, and displays portraying the history of the Oglala Sioux or Lakota people.

Farther south into the reservation is the site of the 1890 Wounded Knee Massacre, one of the sorriest episodes in nineteenth-century U.S. history. This

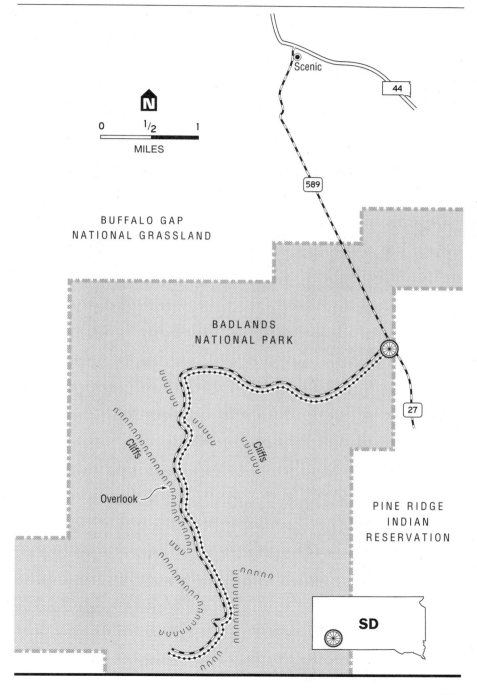

N

0   1/2   1

MILES

Scenic

44

589

BUFFALO GAP
NATIONAL GRASSLAND

BADLANDS
NATIONAL PARK

Cliffs

Cliffs

Overlook

27

PINE RIDGE
INDIAN
RESERVATION

SD

The Sheep Mountain Road leads into some of the remote corners of the vast Badlands region.

last "battle" of the U.S./Indian wars forever put to an end the way of life of the Lakota people. The endless sky and the ceaseless winds of the Dakota high plains seem a fitting memorial to that sad time.

General location: In Badlands National Park, 4 miles south of the small town of Scenic on CR 589.

Elevation change: A climb of almost 250′ onto Sheep Mountain Table is the major elevation change on the road, with 400′ of total variation on the route.

Season: Midspring through autumn. Check on current road conditions during the off-season.

Services: There is no water or any other services along the road. The village of Scenic has a few tourist facilities. The Cedar Pass area of Badlands National Park has a campground, lodge, and a store. The town of Wall on I-90 has most other services, and Rapid City has bicycle shops and anything else you might need.

Hazards: Motorized vehicles periodically use the road. There are steep and sudden drop-offs at the edges of the plateau. Pay close attention to changing weather patterns in the west or southwest. Lightning and thunderstorms can be a common hazard in the summer months. Rattlesnakes may be found in areas of the park.

Rescue index: The road is in a remote part of the park. There is regular traffic on the paved highway south of Scenic.

Land status: Badlands National Park is a unit of the National Park Service.
Maps: The map in the glossy Badlands National Park pamphlet shows the location of Sheep Mountain Road and is probably adequate as long as you stay on the road (which bicycles are required to do). For more detail the USGS 7.5 minute quadrangle covering this location is Sheep Mountain Table. A new Trails Illustrated map, *Badlands National Park,* has just been released; this map shows the Sheep Mountain Road and vicinity in detail, including topographical information.
Finding the trail: The road is slow but passable by most vehicles; find a parking spot off the roadbed as much as possible and take off.

Sources of additional information:

Badlands National Park
P.O. Box 6
Interior, SD 57750
(605) 433-5361

Notes on the trail: The first 3 miles of the road, which are partially graveled, head west through a variety of eroded formations that change color and texture with the surrounding cliffs. Once up on the top of Sheep Mountain Table, you will be back in a prairie grassland that is seemingly devoid of scenery until you reach the edge of the plateau and the view at Gunnery Range Overlook. More views, and even some scrubby trees, will greet you farther along.

This area is a semidesert, and in summer it can get very hot, so plan ahead—bring plenty of water and use sunscreen. Be cautious on the return descent from the Sheep Mountain Table, watching for loose rocks and washouts.

RIDE 71   *BUFFALO GAP NATIONAL GRASSLAND/ WARD DAM ROAD*

The national grasslands are a unique category of public lands found in the Great Plains states. These open stretches of prairie land have been administered by the U.S. Forest Service since 1954 for recreation, grazing, erosion control, watershed protection, and wildlife management. During the boom years of the early 1900s millions of acres of these marginal lands were homesteaded and developed. When the Depression and the dust bowl years of the 1930s hit, many of these farms were abandoned. In 1934 the federal government began buying back some of these lands to help control erosion and stabilize the rural plains economy. The "National Grasslands" designation came in 1960, and now the lands are managed in a similar fashion to the national forests.

RIDE 71 *BUFFALO GAP NATIONAL GRASSLAND / WARD DAM ROAD*

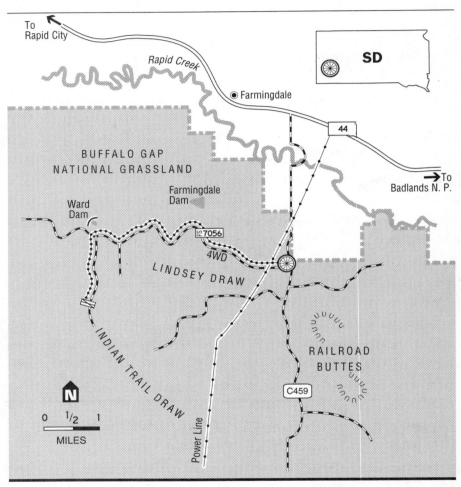

Primarily used for cattle grazing and public hunting, these now productive grasslands provide recreational potential for hikers and others willing to explore the prairie environment. Many of the areas within the grasslands have four-wheel-drive tracks and trails that are well suited for mountain bike use. The reacquisition process of these public lands over the decades left many private holdings scattered throughout most of the grassland jurisdictions, so it is important to be aware of and respect private property, fences, and other land uses. For those bicyclists who wish to explore "new" terrain, test navigational and outdoors skills, and are willing to appreciate the rich prairie environment, there are hundreds of miles of riding possibilities in our national grasslands.

This ride is but one of the dozens of possibilities on the public lands of the Buffalo Gap National Grassland. This location is conveniently accessible from Badlands National Park to the east and Rapid City to the west. The route described here is an out-and-back ride on four-wheel-drive dirt roads and double-tracks to the top of a hill providing views of the Rapid Creek valley to the north, the Railroad Buttes to the east, and the Black Hills to the west. The 13- to 14-mile round-trip is of moderate difficulty, involving a few steady climbs and descents on a packed-soil surface with ample spots of rocks and ruts, as well as some attentive navigational work. And in all likelihood, you will have a battle with one of the natural elements of wind, sun, or rain.

The Buffalo Gap National Grassland Visitor Center, in the town of Wall on I-90, can provide more information on this area and suggest other areas to explore.

General location: Public lands of the Buffalo Gap National Grassland are spread out over a 150-mile arc from east of the Badlands National Park southwest to the Wyoming-Nebraska border region. The ride is located 25 miles southeast of Rapid City near Farmingdale in Pennington County.

Elevation change: The draws, rolling hills, and buttes of this area have a variation of almost 500′ in elevation, with points along the route varying from 2,775′ to almost 3,200′.

Season: Midspring through autumn.

Services: There are limited services in Farmingdale. All services are available in Rapid City.

Hazards: Keep a reasonable distance from cattle when possible. Watch developing weather patterns closely, and be aware of the lack of natural protection in this environment. In the event of a lightning storm, get into the lowest spot possible, but avoid drainages that might flood. It is not difficult to become disoriented in a land where direction and a sense of scale are difficult to judge. Know your navigational skills and respect your own limits.

Rescue index: When you leave the all-weather roads in these areas, consider yourself to be on your own, and carry appropriate emergency supplies and plenty of water.

Land status: Buffalo Gap National Grassland is a unit of the U.S. Forest Service.

Maps: As they do for the forest areas, the Forest Service publishes detailed land-use maps of the national grasslands, available from district offices for $3. These show the general locations of roads and trails, land ownership, drainages, and other features. While they can be used as a navigational tool, serious exploration of the prairie backcountry should be done with the USGS topographical maps. The 7.5 minute quadrangles for the area of this ride are Caputa and Caputa NE.

Many miles of double-tracks penetrate the austere, yet intriguing, environment of Buffalo Gap National Grassland.

Finding the trail: From Farmingdale on SD 44, head east just over 1 mile to CR C-459 and go south 3.5 miles to the junction with FS 7056. Park here or nearby off the roadbed and start your ride.

Sources of additional information:

> Wall Ranger District, Buffalo Gap National Grassland
> P.O. Box 425
> Wall, SD 57790
> (605) 279-2125

Notes on the trail: Begin by riding west on FS 7056 toward the Ward Dam. A bicycle odometer can be a useful navigational tool in this type of terrain to avoid overestimating distances ridden and to help verify return landmarks. At about 2.5 miles, the track you want to be on will curve left in the vicinity of a small reservoir and eventually climb onto a rise where two possible tracks lead to Ward Dam. The clearest track goes through a fence, about 4 miles from the start, heads to another fence, then drops down to the small reservoir and wildlife preserve at the damsite. From the south side of the reservoir, a less distinct track begins the climb to the south toward a butte that has a small stand of cedar trees on the side. Keep that destination in sight as you follow tracks south for over 1 mile, keeping right, eventually making a rocky ascent onto that hill at another fence line. There will be great views of the Rapid Creek valley to the north and east to the Railroad Buttes. A powerline should also be visible several miles to the east. There are other possible places to explore from here. My attempt to continue south and return to the east on FS 7056 was curtailed because the route became too indistinct to describe. It is perhaps best to enjoy the view, have a snack, and return via the same route.

Remember to carry plenty of water, use sunscreen in sunny weather, leave gates as you find them, and keep your distance from cattle. National grassland rules require you to stay on the "roads," but watch for occasional cactus plants if you wander off the tracks. Keep at least mental notes on times, distances, and visual landmarks—large and small—to minimize becoming disoriented. Be additionally careful on overcast days with flat light conditions. With proper preparation and the right attitude, prairie grassland exploration by mountain bike can be a unique and rewarding experience. You will certainly earn your beer back at the brewpub!

Several double-tracks near this ride that run east from CR C-459 and lead toward the Railroad Buttes might be interesting to explore. A bit farther south on CR C-459, in Lindsey Draw there is an off-road-vehicle area that might be fun for some practice riding.

RIDE 72   *CENTENNIAL TRAIL*

The Centennial Trail, which was forged to commemorate South Dakota's statehood centennial in 1989, bisects the heart of the Black Hills' most rugged, heavily-forested interior as it climbs south from the plains surrounding Bear Butte State Park and winds 111 miles to the meadowlands of Wind Cave National Park. It is the longest continuous recreational trail in the Great Plains region, with numerous side trail connections adding to the network. Several relatively short sections are off limits to mountain biking, including the portions in Wind Cave National Park and the Black Elk Wilderness Area west of Mount Rushmore. Designed as a hiking, backpacking, and horseback trail, much of the Centennial Trail makes an ideal wilderness mountain bike route, with any number of one-way or out-and-back rides possible from the more than 20 trailheads and road crossings. The longest segment between intermediate trailheads is about 11 miles, and the longest climb (or descent) within a segment is almost 1,500´; both of these segments are in the relatively remote area between Interstate 90 and the Dalton Lake Campground.

Because of its length, you can expect to encounter a wide variety of trail conditions, levels of use, and states of repair. There are both double-track and single-track sections, and packed-dirt, grassy, and rocky surfaces to

Note: *The 111 mile Centennial Trail is a combination of single and double tracks connecting 20 trailheads.*

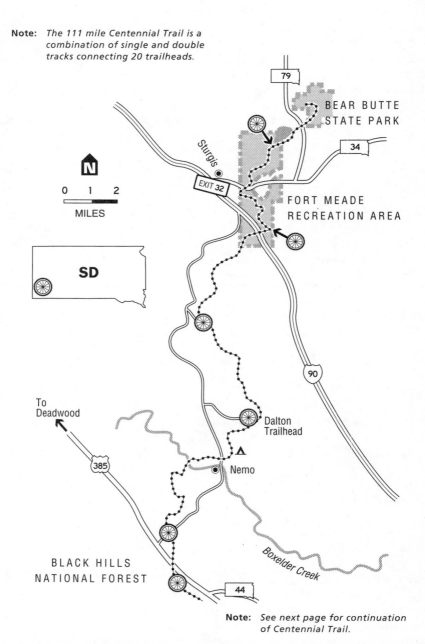

Note: *See next page for continuation of Centennial Trail.*

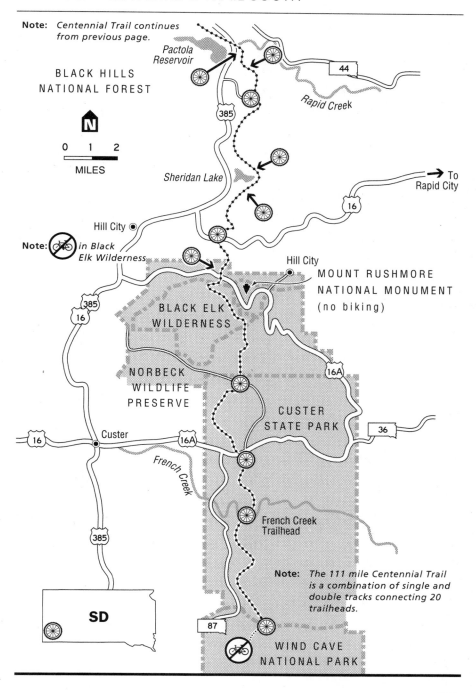

Note: *Centennial Trail continues from previous page.*

Pactola Reservoir

BLACK HILLS NATIONAL FOREST

44

Rapid Creek

0 1 2
MILES

Sheridan Lake

385

To Rapid City

16

Hill City

Note: *in Black Elk Wilderness*

385
16

Hill City

MOUNT RUSHMORE NATIONAL MONUMENT (no biking)

BLACK ELK WILDERNESS

NORBECK WILDLIFE PRESERVE

16A

CUSTER STATE PARK

36

Custer

16

16A

French Creek

French Creek Trailhead

385

Note: *The 111 mile Centennial Trail is a combination of single and double tracks connecting 20 trailheads.*

SD

87

WIND CAVE NATIONAL PARK

make your way over. There are some long, frustrating climbs, handlebar-gripping descents, and sections where you can crank up and cruise through the trees. Popular segments of the trail include the parts in Custer State Park, just to the north of there in the Iron Creek area (see Ride 76), the Pactola Reservoir area, and the Dalton Lake area. Whether you are planning just a short jaunt on the trail or are tackling a serious chunk of it, be sure to check on the most up-to-date trail conditions from area park officials or bike shops.

General location: The trail runs through the eastern Black Hills from Bear Butte State Park at the north end to Wind Cave National Park in the south.

Elevation change: There is over 2,000′ of variation as the trail climbs from the prairies into the high country of the Black Hills and back down again.

Season: Varies with elevation. From late spring to midautumn, the trail should generally be dry and passable during good weather. Lower elevations will generally be snow-free most of the year, and higher elevations in the northern and central sections of the trail will get enough snow to keep sheltered trail areas muddy and stream crossings full of water into May.

Services: Campgrounds and picnic areas are located at various points along the trail. Water is available at many of the trailheads and campgrounds. Check the brochure, *Centennial Trail User's Guide,* for details on each trailhead. All commercial services can be found in Custer, Hill City, Rapid City, and Sturgis.

Hazards: You'll find steep descents and road crossings periodically along the trail. Hunting is allowed in the national forest, in season. In remote country, don't push yourself beyond your navigational and wilderness skill levels; be prepared to turn back if necessary.

Rescue index: Portions of the trail traverse some remote country, and other trail users may be seen only occasionally, so be prepared with plenty of water, rain gear, first-aid supplies, repair tools, and navigational aids.

Land status: At least 6 public agencies have jurisdiction over the Centennial Trail corridor, including Wind Cave National Park, Custer State Park, Mount Rushmore National Memorial, Black Hills National Forest, Fort Meade Recreation Area, and Bear Butte State Park.

Maps: An informative pamphlet entitled *Centennial Trail User's Guide* is available that shows trail access points and information on adjacent recreational facilities. A pocket-size guide, *Centennial Trail Map,* is available for $5.95. A Trails Illustrated map, #238, *Black Hills South,* is a great map for use in the Custer State Park and Mount Rushmore areas of the trail. An additional map in this series, *Black Hills North,* is expected to be available in late 1996. The USGS 7.5 minute quadrangles covering the trail, south to north starting in Custer State Park are: Mount Coolidge, Iron Mountain, Mount Rushmore, Pactola Dam, Silver City, Nemo, Piedmont, Tilford, Deadman Mountain, and Fort Meade.

Finding the trail: The northern section of the trail in Bear Butte State Park and Fort Meade Recreation Area can be reached from I-90 and from Sturgis on SD 34 and SD 79. The central trail area can be reached at the Pactola Reservoir Recreation Area, west of Rapid City on SD 44 and US 385. Southern sections of the trail are accessible in Custer State Park near Legion Lake on US 16A. A number of other access points in more remote areas can also be used; check the Centennial Trail pamphlet or the Black Hills National Forest map for exact directions.

Sources of additional information:

Custer State Park
HC 83, Box 70
Custer, SD 57730
(605) 255-4515

Bear Butte State Park
Sturgis, SD 57785
(605) 347-5240

Fort Meade Recreation Area
Bureau of Land Management
310 Round Up
Belle Fourche, SD 57717
(605) 892-2526

The various district offices of the Black Hills National Forest are listed after Ride 81 below.

Notes on the trail: The Centennial Trail is marked with brown stakes with trail number 89 on them. Bear Butte is a sacred area for many Native American groups, and trail access may be restricted during ceremonial times. At the Deer Creek Trailhead north of Pactola Reservoir, the Deerfield Trail (number 40) joins the Centennial Trail, providing an additional 18-mile route alternative, and a connection to the Deerfield Lake Loop (see Ride 77). In the area around the trail on the southeast side of the Pactola Recreation Area, and in the vicinity of Dalton Lake, there are numerous dirt roads and four-wheel-drive tracks that can be utilized to form loop rides with the Centennial Trail. The Black Hills National Forest area map can be used to determine what sections are public land. Respect private property and leave all gates as you find them. The trail sections south of US 16A in Custer State Park are popular horseback riding routes, so be prepared to yield the trail. Camping is allowed in most areas of the national forest, but open fires are not. Standing and running surface water in the Black Hills cannot be assumed to be safe to drink. Construction has been scheduled to reroute part of the trail to allow mountain bikes to go around the Black Elk Wilderness; call ahead to be sure it is completed.

Creek crossings, rock outcroppings, and shady ponderosa corridors highlight the Grace Coolidge Trail in Custer State Park.

RIDE 73 *GRACE COOLIDGE TRAIL*

Officially called Grace Coolidge Walk-In Fishing Area, this trail is a three-mile (six miles total) out-and-back route closely following and repeatedly crossing Grace Coolidge Creek in Custer State Park. These stream crossings and a few rocky spots add some challenge to an otherwise relatively easy route, and the old double-track corridor is gradually being reduced to single-track by growing vegetation. The lush, forested creek valley, with occasional rocky outcroppings right down to the water provide a rich background for a leisurely ride up to Center Lake for a picnic and swim at the campground there. In hot

RIDE 73 *GRACE COOLIDGE TRAIL*

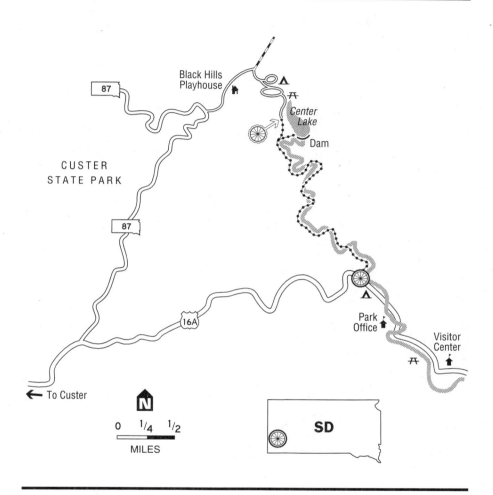

weather, the cool shade of this canyon might sound pretty good when you don't feel inclined to tackle anything too ambitious. Other mountain biking opportunities in the popular Custer State Park are described in Ride 72 and in the remarks following ride 81.

General location: In the middle of Custer State Park in the Black Hills.
Elevation change: There is a gradual rise in elevation from 4,400′ at US 16A to about 4,700′ at Center Lake Campground.

Season: Late spring to midautumn.

Services: Picnic facilities and campgrounds with water are available throughout Custer State Park. Rapid City and the town of Custer have all other services.

Hazards: Be alert for hikers and people fishing. Many of the stream crossings may be tricky or nearly impossible for biking; be prepared to dismount. Buffalo in Custer State Park can be dangerous; keep your distance.

Rescue index: Help is not far from either end of the trail during the busy summer season.

Land status: Custer State Park. A daily entrance fee or park sticker is required.

Maps: Basic location maps are available from the state park offices. These are adequate if you are only going to ride this trail. The Trails Illustrated map, *Black Hills South,* shows the trail in detail, including topographical information.

Finding the trail: The southern trailhead is a parking lot on US 16A across from the Grace Coolidge Campground. The Center Lake campgrounds and picnic area, east of SD 87, and the Black Hills Playhouse, provide access at the northern end of the trail.

Sources of additional information:

Custer State Park
HC 83 Box 70
Custer, SD 57730
(605) 255-4515 or 255-4464 (Visitor Center)

Notes on the trail: This is a trout-fishing spot, so avoid creating muddy water on stream crossings. Near the northern end of the trail is a branch trail (to the right, northbound) that goes directly to the top of the dam that forms the lake.

RIDE 74 *GEORGE S. MICKELSON TRAIL*

The 110-mile Mickelson Trail, now almost half completed, promises to become one of the nation's finest "rails-to-trails" recreational corridors. Built along a Burlington Northern rail route discontinued in 1983, the trail traverses the heart of the pine-forested Black Hills region, linking a half dozen of South Dakota's colorful "mountain" communities. The late South Dakota governor George S. Mickelson, an avid bicycle trail supporter, dedicated the first six-mile segment in 1991, and since then, local fund-raising efforts coordinated by Friends of the Mickelson Trail, matched by federal transportation grants, have produced over 47 miles of trail.

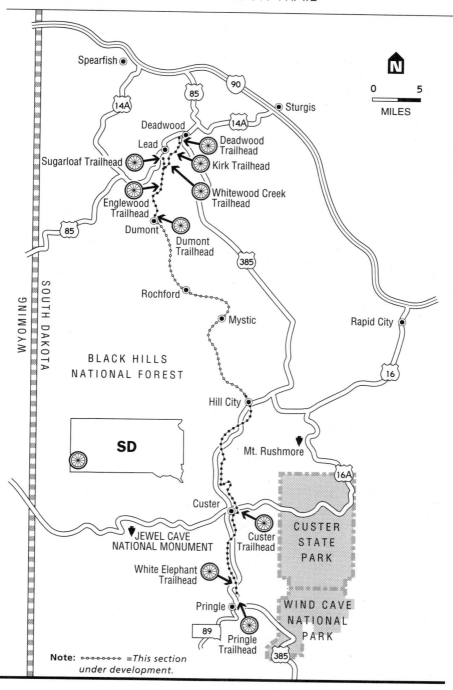

Spearfish

90

85

14A

Sturgis

14A

Deadwood

Deadwood
Trailhead

Lead

Kirk Trailhead

Sugarloaf Trailhead

Whitewood Creek
Trailhead

Englewood
Trailhead

85

Dumont

Dumont
Trailhead

385

Rochford

Mystic

Rapid City

BLACK HILLS
NATIONAL FOREST

16

SD

Hill City

Mt. Rushmore

16A

Custer

JEWEL CAVE
NATIONAL MONUMENT

Custer
Trailhead

CUSTER
STATE
PARK

White Elephant
Trailhead

Pringle

WIND CAVE
NATIONAL
PARK

89

Pringle
Trailhead

385

Note: ○○○○○○○○○ =*This section
under development.*

0   5
MILES

N

Spectacular cliffs and rock formations, sharp valleys of ponderosa pine, and small ranches at the edges of open meadowlands mark this crushed-limestone and double-track pathway. This trail offers individual riders, groups, and families an easy introduction to pedal-powered travel in the Black Hills. Finished portions of the trail include the northernmost 18-mile stretch from Deadwood, past Lead, to the Dumont Trailhead. A spur trail leads to the Sugarloaf Trailhead on US 85. From downtown Custer, a 14-mile segment continues south through a forested creek valley to Pringle. And by the time this is in print, the section from Hill City to Custer, running 15 miles through the heart of the Black Hills, should be open for use.

The city of Deadwood is actively capitalizing on its notorious past, with its restored downtown area, limited-stakes gambling operations, and the Days of '76 Celebration in August. Nearby Lead is the home of Homestake Mine, one of the ten largest gold producers in the world. Custer, another town dating back to the gold rush days, offers a variety of attractions including the National Museum of Woodcarving, the Crazy Horse Memorial, and the 1881 Courthouse Museum, with displays of the mining era and Custer's 1874 Black Hills Expedition.

General location: The trail corridor traverses most of the Black Hills from Deadwood in the north to Edgemont in the south.

Elevation change: With a maximum grade of 3 percent, elevations on the finished parts of the trail vary from about 4,500′ at Deadwood to around 5,900′ north of Custer.

Season: Midspring to midautumn.

Services: Most services are available in Deadwood, Hill City, and Custer. There is a bike shop in Deadwood.

Hazards: Watch for traffic at street and highway crossings. Afternoon storms can develop quickly over the hills in the summer months.

Rescue index: Help is readily available in the trailside towns. Most of the rest of the trail is close to regularly traveled roads.

Land status: Division of Parks and Recreation, South Dakota Game, Fish, and Parks Department.

Maps: A Mickelson Trail pamphlet with a diagram map of completed sections is available from many local sources. That, in conjunction with the Forest Service Black Hills visitors map ($3), is adequate for most trail navigation.

Finding the trail: There are 6 official trailheads on the Deadwood/Dumont section and 3 on the Custer/Pringle section. (See map.) Most are marked from the local highways. The Kirk Trailhead, on a local road several miles southwest of US 385 (turnoff is one-quarter mile south of the junction with US 85 near Lead), is a good starting point for the rural portions of the northern section. To begin right in the city of Deadwood, the trail departs from a parking lot on Sherman Avenue near the First Western Bank building and a railroad caboose.

The Mickelson Trail, one of the longest and most spectacular rail trails in the Midwest, is taking shape in the center of the Black Hills.

In Custer, the trail runs east-west through town, 1 block south of US 16, the main street of town. There is parking near the city hall.

Sources of additional information:

Division of Parks and Recreation
523 East Capitol Avenue
Pierre, SD 57501-3182
(605) 773-3391

Friends of the Mickelson Trail
447 Crook Street
Custer, SD 57730
(605) 673-5552

Notes on the trail: The northernmost portion of the trail winds its way out of historic Deadwood, through a valley below the mining town of Lead where the train tracks are still embedded in the trail surface, and south from the Kirk Trailhead into the steep, pine-forested valleys of the northern Black Hills. The grade maintains a steady climb up the Whitewood Creek valley to a divide at almost 5,900′. From there it descends to the Dumont Trailhead. South of Hill City, the new section of the trail passes the site of the Crazy Horse Memorial, an emerging counterpart to Mount Rushmore depicting

Chief Crazy Horse of the Lakota Sioux on the back of a steed. The trail from Custer to Pringle follows south through more open terrain, past more rock formations, pine stands, small ranches, and meadowlands.

Work on the section of the trail south from Dumont to Rochford was scheduled for the 1995 season, and from Hill City north to the Mystic Trailhead, for the fall of 1995; call ahead for current trail conditions. Near Mystic, the trail will cross the Deerfield Trail, allowing trail access west to Deerfield Lake or east to the Centennial Trail. Some finishing work is continuing in most completed sections, but the corridor is all mountain bikeable. A $2 trail user fee is required for bicycles, unless you are within the city limits of the various towns. Information regarding volunteer work, the Bridge Builder program, and memberships is available through Friends of the Mickelson Trail, at the above address.

RIDE 75   *CUSTER-AREA TOUR*

There are hundreds of miles of forest back roads and four-wheel-drive tracks throughout the Black Hills. Anyone willing to explore with a mountain bike and who can get a hold of appropriate maps is almost guaranteed to find some challenging terrain and see some spectacular scenery. One of the tours I did while exploring the Custer area is typical of the variety that the Black Hills back roads have to offer. This 24-mile (round-trip) tour encompasses part of the Mickelson rail trail, a number of gravel Forest Service routes, and several four-wheel-drive tracks. It offers some good climbs and descents through the ponderosa forest and past an old mining district, a few isolated ranches, and the town of Custer.

This is generally an easy to moderate course that can be done in about three or four hours including stops, or quicker, if you like to ride hard. There are few technical obstacles, but you can lengthen your ride by exploring some of the side trails if you wish. This route, or variations of it, can give newcomers to the area a taste of what to expect on the roads in the "Hills," and provide a perspective for making further plans. Be sure to carry plenty of water.

General location: South and southeast of the town of Custer in the southern Black Hills National Forest.
Elevation change: There is almost 1,000′ of variation on this route, ranging from about 5,000′ to over 6,000′ at the top of Cicero Peak.
Season: Late spring through autumn.
Services: All services can be found in Custer.
Hazards: Be alert for vehicle traffic on the main roads. Hunting is allowed in the national forest, in season.

RIDE 75   *CUSTER-AREA TOUR*

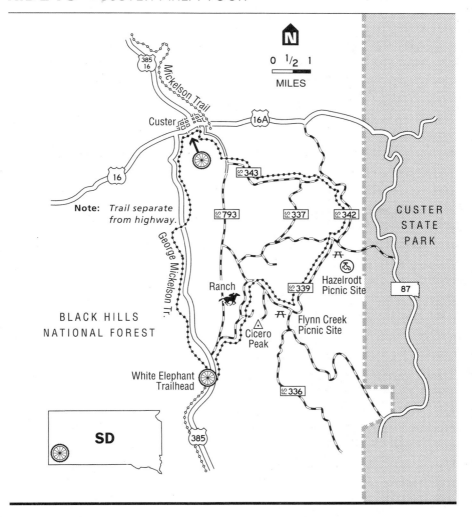

Rescue index: Help is always available in Custer. There is periodic traffic in most of the rest of the area.

Land status: Black Hills National Forest. Respect the private property that is scattered throughout the area.

Maps: The $3 Black Hills National Forest–area map shows the layout of the roads in the area and should be adequate for most needs. The USGS 7.5 minute topographical maps of the route are included on the Cicero Peak quad, with a minor portion on the Custer quad.

Finding the trail: The easiest starting point is in the town of Custer. Park in town and begin the ride on the Mickelson Trail, which runs through the center of town, south of the main commercial district.

Sources of additional information:

> Custer Ranger District
> 330 Mount Rushmore Road
> Custer, SD 57730
> (605) 673-4853 or 4852

Notes on the trail: The first 8 miles south on the Mickelson Trail are an easy slight downgrade to the White Elephant Trailhead on US 385. Ride north a short distance on the highway, and veer right, uphill, on FS 793. In about one-half mile, turn right again, onto a dirt forest road, and continue uphill. Take the next left, through a gate, and ride this double-track through the woods. When you reach an unmarked junction, keep left; the track to the right might look inviting, but it goes uphill to nowhere. The route you should stay on will descend a ways and eventually pass a ranch in a small valley. The track will continue through the pines and come out on FS 336, a much more regularly used gravel road. Turn right and head southeast.

At the top of the hill is the junction with FS 338, which is an optional side trip uphill to the top of Cicero Peak and the site of an old fire tower foundation, where there are great views of the surrounding area. FS 336 continues downhill to the Flynn Creek Picnic Ground, a nice stop, but there is no water. Follow FS 339 northeast over a divide and make the fun descent down into the French Creek valley. The road to the north becomes FS 342, and the second right turnoff of 342, near the creek, is FS 408, which leads to Hazelrodt Picnic Ground, another nice stop where there is water. To return to Custer, continue north on FS 342 along French Creek to a small group of houses, then make a sharp left and take FS 343 west over another divide to FS 793, and then it's 1 mile north back to town.

RIDE 76 *IRON MOUNTAIN TRAIL*

The Iron Mountain Trail loop forms the core of a 15-mile system on the southeast corner of the Norbeck Wilderness Preserve. This trail system is a combination of wide single-track trails and old forest access roads of generally moderate difficulty. Steady climbs and descents, rocky spots, dozens of cliff and rock formations, and a continuous forest cover of pine and aspen make this area about as close to mountain bike heaven as you can get. From a ridge on the start of the loop, you can get a great view across to the carvings on Mount Rushmore, two miles north. A portion of this seven-mile loop

RIDE 76 *IRON MOUNTAIN TRAIL*

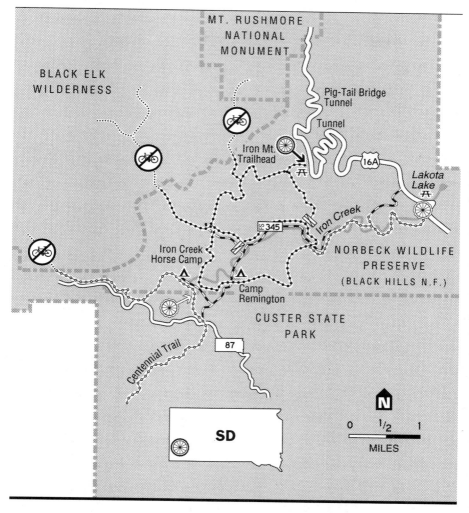

described below joins the Centennial Trail (Ride 72) for a few miles, and several other trails branch off in other directions.

Just getting to the Iron Mountain trailhead on US 16A is an interesting experience. The highway climbs over two "pig-tail" bridges, where the road doubles back over itself, and through two tunnels, one of which is aligned to give a clear view of Mount Rushmore (northbound).

The Norbeck Wildlife Preserve dates back to 1920, when Congress set the area aside to protect its animal population. In its center is located the Black Elk Wilderness Area, which was established in 1980 and is closed to all

In the heart of the granitic core of the Black Hills near Mount Rushmore, the Iron Mountain trail system provides some of the most "mountainous" biking terrain in the Great Plains.

mechanized travel, including mountain bikes. In 1995 trail construction is scheduled to reroute part of the Centennial Trail to allow mountain bikes to go around the Black Elk Wilderness.

General location: In the Norbeck Wildlife Preserve, just south of Mount Rushmore National Monument in the Black Hills.

Elevation change: This area contains mountainous terrain, with a variation on the trail from about 4,800′ to 5,300′.

Season: Late spring to midautumn.

Services: There are picnic facilities and rest rooms at the trailhead. Tourist services can be found in Keystone, 4 miles north. All services, including bike shops, are available in Rapid City.

Hazards: Portions of the dirt road are periodically open to vehicle traffic. Keep an eye out for thunderstorm weather during the hot summer months.

Rescue index: This is a popular area. There is regular traffic on US 16A and frequent use of the trails by other visitors.

Land status: Norbeck Wildlife Preserve, Black Hills National Forest.

Maps: The Trails Illustrated map #238, *Black Hills South,* covers the trails in the Norbeck preserve and the adjacent Custer State Park and includes topographic and trail information. The USGS 7.5 minute quadrangle for Iron Mountain covers this area.

Finding the trail: The Iron Mountain trailhead is located 3 miles south of Mount Rushmore Monument on US 16A. Alternate trailheads are available at Lakota Lake, farther south on US 16A, and Iron Creek Horse Camp, 1 mile off the Needles Highway, SD 87.

Sources of additional information:

> Custer Ranger District
> 330 Mount Rushmore Road
> Custer, SD 57730
> (605) 673-4853 or 4852

Notes on the trail: The trail branches off from the paved walking path that runs uphill from the parking lot of the trailhead. In one-quarter mile, an unmarked side trail veers right (north) a short distance to the top of the ridge and a rock outcropping, where you can get a view of Mount Rushmore to the north. Continuing west on the main trail, it is about 1.5 miles to the junction with the Centennial Trail, where northbound travel is restricted to hikers and horseback riders. Heading south, there are some nice ups and downs leading into an area of rock outcroppings and two more trail junctions. Keeping left will provide a quick downhill run and shortcut back to the trailhead via a Forest Service road at the trail gate below. This road, FS 345, meanders pleasantly over numerous stream crossings and past more cliffs and then meets the Iron Mountain Trail again at the next gate on the left. Continuing south along the Centennial Trail on the original route, you will pass more rocky areas and come out near the Iron Creek Horse Camp. The Iron Mountain Trail heads east to FS 345 and Camp Remington, then climbs a ridge and descends again to FS 345. Ride northwest (to the left) on the road a short distance to the gate on the right and continue on the Iron Mountain Trail uphill back to the trailhead. This last stretch of the trail is in a mountain goat–calving area, and it is closed for two months in the early summer.

The various trails are marked with numbered signposts and blazes, and many of the junctions are marked and have maps posted as well. Watch for and respect the signs indicating no biking beyond certain points (into the Black Elk and Rushmore areas). As you will see from the maps, there are a variety of alternative loops and additional directions to explore.

RIDE 77 *DEERFIELD LAKE LOOP*

The Deerfield Lake Loop Trail (40L) provides a ten-mile loop route of generally moderate difficulty through a classic Black Hills area of pine and aspen forest, grassy meadows, and some challenging hillsides on a mixture of single- and double-track trails. Rocks, sharp turns, occasional logs, and eroded spots

RIDE 77 *DEERFIELD LAKE LOOP*

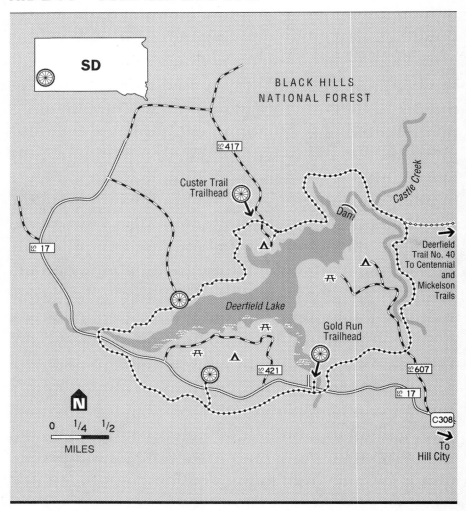

add to the technical nature of the route. At Deerfield Lake you will be in the center of the Black Hills Forest, away from the main flow of the tourist circuit farther east. Anywhere from several hours to the better part of a day can be spent in this area, and combined with the 18-mile Deerfield Trail (40) that connects this loop with the Centennial Trail to the east, the riding possibilities become limitless.

General Custer's 1874 expedition to the Black Hills camped on the creek in this area. Deerfield Lake is a reservoir that was created in the 1940s to store water for the Rapid City and Black Hills area. The original townsite of

Deerfield was established here during the gold rush period and was moved to make way for the reservoir. The lake makes a nice focal point for the trail ride, and it may become very inviting for a swim on a hot day.

General location: Deerfield Lake is 14 miles northwest of Hill City in the center of the Black Hills National Forest.

Elevation change: There are numerous ups and downs on the loop within a range of about 5,900′ to 6,200′.

Season: Late spring to midautumn.

Services: Water, campgrounds, and picnic areas are located at several sites around the lake. Other services can be found in Hill City.

Hazards: Occasional steep descents, possible downed branches, rocky spots, and water bars are present on the trail. The trail parallels FS 17 at the west end of the lake; watch for traffic when you're crossing the road there and at other points on the loop. Hunting is allowed in the national forest, in season.

Rescue index: There is generally regular visitor traffic at the various facilities and access points around the lake.

Land status: Black Hills National Forest.

Maps: A Deerfield Trail/Deerfield Lake Loop Trail brochure is available from Forest Service offices and some area businesses. It is an adequate map if you stay on the trails. The USGS 7.5 minute quadrangle for the lake area is Deerfield.

Finding the trail: Take FS 17, also marked as CR C-308, from Hill City to Deerfield Lake Recreation Area. The Gold Run Trailhead on the south end of the lake is the most convenient access from FS 17. The Custer Trail Trailhead on the north side of the lake is reachable on FS 417 from Rochford.

Sources of additional information:

Harney Ranger District
HCR Box 51
Hill City, SD 57745
(605) 574-2534

Notes on the trail: From the Gold Run Trailhead, starting out to the west (clockwise) is the easier direction to begin the ride. The trail immediately crosses to the south side of FS 17 and climbs through hills of pleasant aspen and pine forests before descending to the west end of the lake and the recrossing of FS 17. The route is marked with diamonds on the trees or brown stakes with the trail symbol, and in some spots, orange cross-country ski markers may be seen. Along the northern side of the lake, the trail again climbs into forested hills but more closely follows the shoreline, allowing periodic views of the lake. On warm, sunny days, breezes off the sparkling blue water will be most welcome. Regular climbs and descents through stands of timber and small meadowlands will bring you to the Custer Trail Trailhead and campground, a good place for a break and to fill up on water.

Cool breezes from the lake are usually present on the
Deerfield Loop.

The Custer Trail Trailhead is also considered to be the western end of the
Deerfield Trail (40), which runs east to the Pactola Reservoir area, where it
connects with the Centennial Trail (see Ride 72). The two trails become one
as they continue around to the east end of the lake and the dam. This section
ventures into more open prairie pastureland, with some steep drops and
climbs across small ravines and hillsides. There will be some fences to pass
through. Near the dam, a stretch of double-track trail will gradually climb to
the south, away from the junction with Deerfield Trail (40), eventually crossing a campground access road. From there, the trail will climb to the highest
point on the loop through a nice pine forest area, then make a long rocky
descent to the lake, returning you to the Gold Run Trailhead.

The Deerfield Trail (40) connects the Deerfield Loop with the trail system to
the east. From the east end of the Deerfield Loop, the eastbound trail passes the
Kinney Canyon Trailhead, climbs gradually for a mile to a high point of 6,200′,

then makes a steady descent for another 4 miles or so to the junction with a future section of the George S. Mickelson Trail (see Ride 74) and FS 231 in the Mystic area. After a good climb to the southeast, away from the Mickelson Trail, the Deerfield Trail follows the course of Slate Creek Canyon over 34 bridges and then follows Rapid Creek downstream to Silver City and the Silver City Trailhead. From there, a 3-mile segment with 1 more long climb and descent brings you to the Centennial Trail and US 385.

RIDE 78   *EAGLE CLIFF TRAILS*

This network of 20 interconnected trails was developed as a cross-country ski trail system by local skiers and now is maintained by the Forest Service. A variety of single-track and double-track trails in varying lengths mesh into a spaghetti-bowl of possibilities that can provide as many climbs and descents as you want and loops that can be easy to moderately difficult. You will encounter a full range of trail surfaces here, including packed soil, rocks, roots, ruts, branches, and soft and muddy spots after wet weather. Most of the area is forested with pine and aspen, but there are some open meadow areas and wider corridors worn by previous vehicle use throughout the area. Whether you intend to spend an hour or a day here, you will find it enjoyable and challenging.

General location: About 15 miles southwest of the town of Lead in the Black Hills National Forest.
Elevation change: The trail network is designed with many ups and downs within a 700′ range. The trailheads start in the middle of this range at about 6,100′.
Season: Late spring to midautumn.
Services: There are no facilities at the trailheads. Cheyenne Crossing has a store. All other services can be found in Lead, Deadwood, or Spearfish.
Hazards: There is a wide variety of trail conditions here. Watch for rocks, roots, slippery and muddy spots in sheltered areas, steep descents, and trail junctions that may not be obvious in the summertime. Hunting is allowed in the national forest, in season.
Rescue index: Nearby US 85 is a well-traveled, paved highway.
Land status: Black Hills National Forest.
Maps: An Eagle Cliff Trail pamphlet and map showing the layout and the names of the individual trail segments on a topographical background is available from Forest Service offices and some area businesses.
Finding the trail: There are two official trailheads 1 mile apart on US 85, 7 miles from Cheyenne Crossing.

A multitude of interconnected trails in the Eagle Cliff system can keep you busy all day.

Sources of additional information:

Spearfish Ranger District
2014 North Main
Spearfish, SD 57783
(605) 642-4622

Notes on the trail: There are so many loop options here that it is impossible to recommend any one way to go. The easiest strategy is to use a spur-of-the-moment method and ride into the most interesting direction at the various intersections. The western trailhead on US 85 requires steep climbs in either direction to get to the other trails. The signs with trail names at many of the junctions should help you keep track of your location. The ski difficulty ratings on the trail map should give you some relative indication of what to expect on a given run. The contour lines on the map will give an indication of

RIDE 78 *EAGLE CLIFF TRAILS*

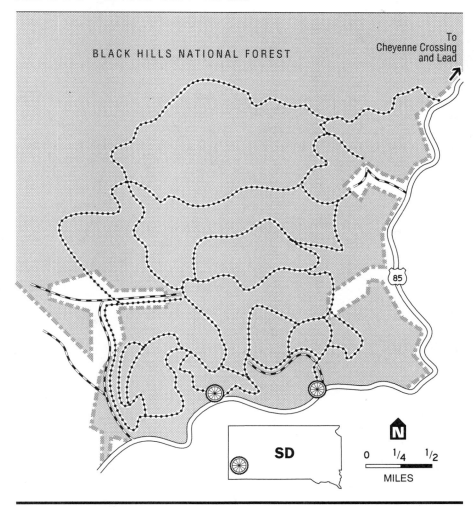

the direction and steepness of the climbs and descents, so if you like gradual climbs and fast descents, you can pick the appropriate direction to go accordingly, and vice versa.

Remember to keep track of the time and your level of energy. With over 20 miles of trails here, it may take a while to work back to your starting point. The trails are marked with either cut or painted blazes or with brown stakes. To help reduce erosion, stay on the established trails, don't cut across switchbacks, and don't ride when the trails are mostly muddy.

RIDE 79

LITTLE SPEARFISH TRAIL AND RIMROCK TRAIL

These two trails share a common trailhead and one mile of trail, forming a single 11-mile system of three interconnected loops in the rugged forested hills of the upper Spearfish Canyon area. Maintained for mountain bikers, hikers, and horseback riders, each of these mostly single-track trails offers a steady climb out of the Little Spearfish Creek valley onto the high ridges, then some fast descents back to the valley. These ups and downs, plus a trail surface varying from lush grasses to loose rocks, make for a riding experience of generally moderate difficulty, with a few difficult spots here and there to get you up out of the saddle.

This is a lush mountain environment, with tall stands of pine and aspen on the ridges and hillsides and thick greenery along the canyon floor. The filming of the winter mountain scenes for the movie "Dances with Wolves" was done in this area.

General location: About 17 miles south of Spearfish in the northern Black Hills National Forest.
Elevation change: Each of the trail loops has a climb of at least 500′. The total elevation variation of the trail system is about 900′, ranging from about 5,350′ to 6,250′.
Season: Late spring to midautumn. The area is usually quite snowy in the winter.
Services: Water and rest rooms can be found at the two nearby campgrounds on FS 222. Other services, including bike shops, can be found in Spearfish.
Hazards: Control your speed on the steep descents. Watch for traffic when crossing or riding on FS 222. Hunting is allowed in the national forest, in season, and there is logging activity going on here at times, so be alert for large trucks.
Rescue index: There are usually other forest visitors in the vicinity of the trailhead and campgrounds, but you may be alone on the trails.
Land status: Black Hills National Forest.
Maps: A Little Spearfish Trail–Rimrock Trail pamphlet and map showing the layout of the individual trails on a topographical background is available from Forest Service offices and from some area businesses.
Finding the trail: Follow US 14A south from Spearfish to Savoy and FS 222 4 miles to the trailhead. Both trails depart from the trailhead on FS 222 just west of Timon Campground. Another access point is possible at the Rod and Gun Campground 2 miles east.

An 800-foot descent is the reward for reaching the high point on the Little Spearfish Trail.

Sources of additional information:

Spearfish Ranger District
2014 North Main
Spearfish, SD 57783
(605) 642-4622

Notes on the trail: The Little Spearfish Trail loop is perhaps best ridden counter-clockwise (southwest up the creek from the trailhead) so that you can ride the east side of the ridge as an 800′ descent, the longest downhill on these trails. The first mile up Little Spearfish Creek is a pleasant ride through a lush, forested canyon. After a gate the trail will climb steadily through aspen and pine forest to the top of the ridge, where you start the long fun ride down to Ranger Draw and FS 222. To add the Rimrock Trail to your loop, cross the road and proceed east down the canyon on the trail as it parallels the road and passes some cliffs. Either the upper or lower loop route away from the road will involve a steep one-half-mile workout, but eventually you will be back up on another quiet ridge. Just past the high point on the upper loop, there is a spur trail over to the Old Baldy Trail, described in Ride 80, below. A quick descent back to FS 222 and the trailhead gives you a great 10.5-mile tour (if you did the lower loop, too) that is well deserving of a relaxing break.

The trails are marked with either cut or painted blazes or with brown stakes.

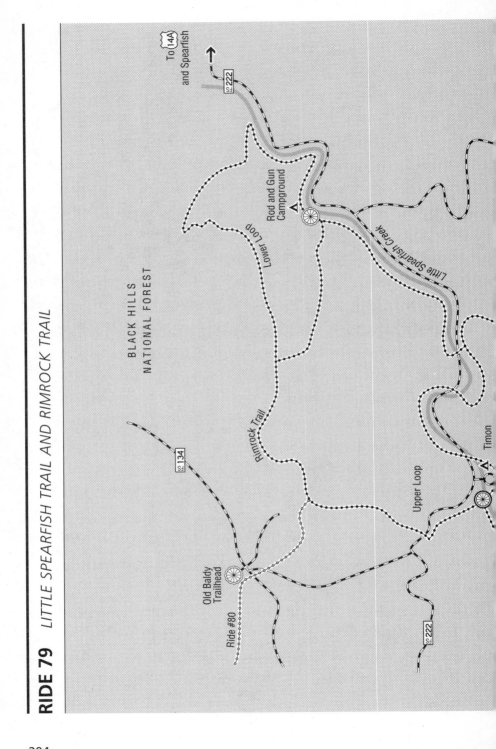

BLACK HILLS
NATIONAL FOREST

To 14A
and Spearfish

SD 222

Rod and Gun
Campground

Lower Loop

Little Spearfish Creek

SD 134

Rimrock Trail

Upper Loop

Timon

Old Baldy
Trailhead

Ride #80

SD 222

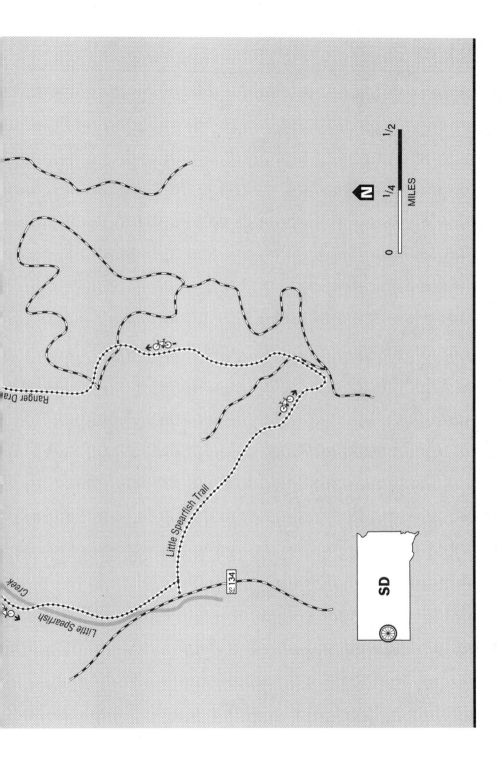

Little Spearfish Trail

Ranger Dra...

Little Spearfish Creek

FS 134

SD

N

0   1/4   1/2
MILES

RIDE 80   *OLD BALDY TRAIL*

This six-mile loop trail meanders around on a high, forested ridge in the Black Hills, allowing occasional glimpses of mountain ranch and pasture country. A three-quarter-mile spur trail leads to the summit of Old Baldy Mountain, providing a wide panorama of the surrounding northern Black Hills; you can see well into Wyoming just two miles to the west. Many areas along the ridge are mainly covered with aspen and some birch, making this a colorful, airy setting on a sunny fall day. Deer, elk, coyotes, and other wildlife are abundant in the area. Most of the trail is narrow, with trees close at hand, and with plenty of rocks and short pitches up and down, this is a moderately challenging ride.

General location: About 13 miles south of Spearfish in the northern Black Hills National Forest.
Elevation change: The elevation range on the trail is about 5,800′ to 6,120′, with the trailhead being at 6,000′ and the summit of Old Baldy at 6,096′.
Season: Late spring to midautumn.
Services: There is a toilet at the trailhead. All other services, including bike shops, can be found in Spearfish.
Hazards: Some steep, rocky descents will require some caution. Keep an eye out for thunderstorm weather while you're on the ridges and summits. Hunting is allowed in the national forest, in season.
Rescue index: There is usually periodic traffic on FS 134, but the trail traverses some remote areas, so be prepared.
Land status: Black Hills National Forest.
Maps: An Old Baldy Trail pamphlet and map showing the layout of the trail on a topographical background is available from the various Black Hills Forest Service offices and from some area businesses. The two USGS 7.5 minute quadrangles that cover this area are Old Baldy Mountain and Savoy.
Finding the trail: The trailhead is well marked on FS 134. Finding FS 134 in Spearfish, however, is not as easy. From Main Street, take a left on Utah Street, then go out past a large sawmill and left again. The road improves when it enters the national forest.

Sources of additional information:

Spearfish Ranger District
2014 North Main
Spearfish, SD 57783
(605) 642-4622

RIDE 80 *OLD BALDY TRAIL*

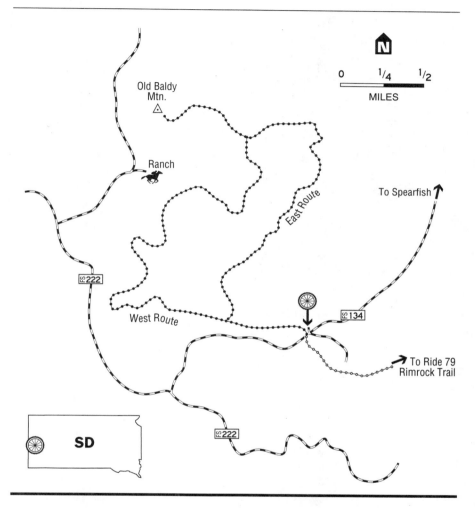

Notes on the trail: Going either direction on the loop will provide plenty of variety, but the East Route to the Old Baldy junction is a bit shorter and less hilly. This ride can be done in combination with the Rimrock and/or Little Spearfish Trails (Ride 79) for some possible 12- to 18-mile tours. A connecting trail to the Rimrock Trail departs from across the road from the Old Baldy Trailhead. The trails are marked with either cut or painted blazes or with brown stakes. Please leave fences and gates as you find them. Future Forest Service recreation plans call for expanded trails in this area.

The 6,096′ Old Baldy summit rewards riders with views into Wyoming.

RIDE 81   *BIG HILL TRAILS*

This series of interconnected loop trails totals about 15 miles in heavily wooded ridge country above the steep Spearfish Canyon. Offering a combination of ski trails and four-wheel-drive tracks, this area provides an easy to moderate biking challenge in a quiet part of the Black Hills. The generally good trail surface is well suited for those riders wishing either a pleasant forest tour or a fast, hard workout. A tour through this trail system will take you from aspen woodlands and open meadow areas to the pine-forested upper gulches of the Spearfish Canyon and back to the uplands again. Long descents and climbs above the canyon are generally moderate but steady and will provide you with an appreciation for this rugged land that resisted the influences of "civilization" for so long.

General location: About 7 miles south of Spearfish in the northern Black Hills National Forest.
Elevation change: This area has about a 500′ variation, fluctuating between 5,000′ and 5,500′.
Season: Late spring to midautumn. This area gets considerable snowfall during the winter months.

RIDE 81   *BIG HILL TRAILS*

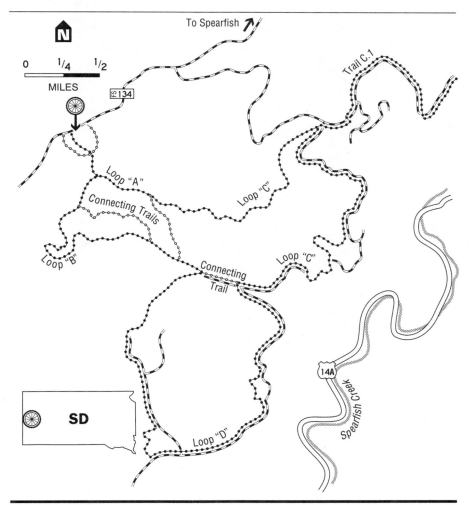

Services: There are rest rooms at the trailhead. Other services, including bike shops, can be found in Spearfish.

Hazards: Watch for downed branches, rocks, and other obstructions on long fast downgrades. Hunting is allowed in the national forest, in season.

Rescue index: There is generally traffic on FS 134, but the trails traverse some remote areas, so be prepared.

Land status: Black Hills National Forest.

Maps: A Big Hill Trails pamphlet and map showing the layout of the individual trails on a topographical background is available from Forest Service

Meadows lined with aspen and ponderosa pine are linked by some good cruising trails in the Big Hill system.

offices and some area businesses. This map is adequate as long as you stay on the trails. The USGS 7.5 minute quadrangle for the area is Maurice.

Finding the trail: The trailhead is located on FS 134. To find FS 134 in Spearfish, take Utah Street left (west) from Main Street, then out past a large sawmill and left again. The road improves when it enters the national forest. The trail begins on the other side of FS 134 from the trailhead parking lot.

Sources of additional information:

Spearfish Ranger District
2014 North Main
Spearfish, SD 57783
(605) 642-4622

Notes on the trail: The upper A and B loops traverse a predominately aspen forest with several open meadow areas. Trail loops C and D both skirt the edges of the steep Spearfish Canyon through thick pine forest, giving occasional glimpses into the canyon. The 12-mile grand tour shown on the map starts by following loop A and then C through the aspen forest and meadowlands along the crest of a relatively easy ridge for about 3 miles. At the junction with trail C.l, you have the option for an out-and-back side trip to another point above the Spearfish Canyon. From the C.1 junction, the trail meanders south along the canyon "rim" area, descending several hundred feet, then gradually climbing back to meet with trail D.

By now you are about halfway around the loop, and if it is time for a break, there are plenty of shady slopes among the pines for hot days (or little meadows that may be sunny on cool days). Trail D drops several hundred feet before climbing back as it circles around a big hill. Several old tracks head off in various directions from the marked trail; watch for the trail markers to stay on course. Loops B and A do some more gradual climbing in gentle terrain before returning you to the trailhead.

There are both tree blazes with the loop letter designation and brown signposts marking the trails. Future Forest Service recreation plans call for expanded trails in this area.

ADDITIONAL MOUNTAIN BIKING OPPORTUNITIES IN WESTERN SOUTH DAKOTA

Custer State Park has a small network of unimproved interior roads south of French Creek Natural Area where a loop trip with several side spurs are possible, providing good wildlife viewing in early morning or evening. The roads are accessible from the Blue Bell Horse Camp area and from the paved Wildlife Loop Road.

Northwest of Custer is the *Bear Mountain Ski Trail System.* This 15-mile set of loops provides generally easy to moderate mountain biking terrain deep in the interior of the Black Hills forest. The area is reached by taking FS 297 from US 16 north of Custer northwest to FS 299 and a Boy Scout camp.

There is some good back-road biking in Rochford, which is a small whistlestop about 20 miles south of Deadwood and Lead. To the west on FS 124 and FS 190 double-track routes wind over to Whitetail Peak, one of the highest points in the Black Hills. To the south double-track routes on FS 231, FS 184 up Bloody Gulch, and FS 238 can be combined to make a loop tour up to Castle Peak and back to Rochford. Check with the Forest Service district office or area bike shops for more information on this area.

The Crow Peak Trails, seven miles southwest of Spearfish, is a four-mile out-and-back trail system climbing 1,500′ to the summit of Crow Peak. The trail was not designed with mountain bikers in mind, but it will offer a challenging climb and descent for those riders willing to tackle it. There are great views to the east and west from the 5,760′ summit. Contact the Spearfish Ranger District listed below for more details.

Rapid City has a 13-mile biking/walking trail along Rapid Creek, which flows out of the Black Hills through the center of town.

Exploring Away from the Black Hills

Custer National Forest, headquartered in Billings, Montana, has several remote units in northwestern South Dakota. The unit in southeastern Harding County near the town of Reva consists of a forested ridge with a few roads and motorcycle trails that head north and south from SD 20. There are some nice views of the surrounding buttes and prairie hills. A wayside and campground is located off the highway. For more information: Custer National Forest, 2602 First Avenue North, P.O. Box 2556, Billings, MT 59103, (406) 657-6361.

Shadehill Recreation Area and *Grand River National Grassland* are adjacent to each other in Perkins County near the North Dakota border. Here you can travel various back roads to explore the wide-open, rolling prairie. Shadehill has water and camping facilities at a dam-created lake. Deer, antelope, coyotes, foxes, prairie dogs, waterfowl, and much other wildlife is found here. Jim Bridger and General Custer once passed through the area, and in 1823 explorer Hugh Glass was attacked by a grizzly bear near the Grand River and left for dead by his companions; he then managed to crawl 200 miles to safety at a fort on the Missouri River. Next time you get banged up in a bike crash and feel sorry for yourself, think of that poor character. For information on this area, contact Shadehill Recreation Area, Box 63, Shadehill, SD 57653, (605) 374-5114, or Grand River Ranger District, P.O. Box 390, Lemmon, SD 57638, (605) 374-3592.

For More Information

Black Hills, Badlands and Lakes Association
900 Jackson Boulevard
Rapid City, SD 57702
(605) 341-1462 or 341-4614 fax

Custer State Park
HC 83, Box 70
Custer, SD 57730
(605) 255-4515 or 255-4464 (Visitor Center)

Black Hills National Forest

Custer Ranger District
330 Mount Rushmore Road
Custer, SD 57730
(605) 673-4853 or 4852

Harney Ranger District
HCR Box 51
Hill City, SD 57745
(605) 574-2534

Nemo Ranger District
Box 407, US 14A East
Deadwood, SD 57732
(605) 578-2744

Pactola Ranger District
803 Soo San Drive
Rapid City, SD 57702
(605) 343-1567

Spearfish Ranger District
2014 North Main
Spearfish, SD 57783
(605) 642-4622

Custer County Chamber of Commerce
447 Crook Street
Custer, SD 57730
(605) 673-2244 or (800) 992-9818

Deadwood–Lead Chamber of Commerce
460 Historic Main Street
Deadwood, SD 57732
(605) 578-1876

Hill City Chamber of Commerce
Box 253
Hill City, SD 57745
(800) 888-1798

Clubs and Other Resources

Black Hills Mountain Bike Association
(605) 347-6476

Custer Bicycle Club
Route 2, Box 201 G
Custer, SD 57730
Weekly club rides when weather permits. The Custer Bicycle Club is a co-sponsor of the Buffalo Roundup Bicycle Rally in Custer in October, which includes mountain bike events. The festivities coincide with Custer State Park's annual buffalo roundup.

Southern Hills Adventures, Inc.
Route 2, Box 201 G
Custer, SD 57730
(605) 673-4764 or (800) 531-5923
Provides mountain bike tours and bike rentals in the Custer area.

Adventure Sport
1705 West Main Street
Rapid City, SD 57702
(605) 341-6707
Topographical maps of the southern Black Hills.

Buckstop
611 East Jackson
Spearfish, SD 57783
(605) 642-4945
Topographical maps of the northern Black Hills.

Granite Sports
Main Street
Hill City, SD 57745
(605) 574-2425
Some topographical and other maps.

Maps

Custer Area Mountain Bike Trail System, Southern Black Hills, a map produced by the Custer Bicycle Club, Custer, SD. A good resource for trails and biking information in the Custer area.

Black Hills South, map 238, by Trails Illustrated Topo Maps, Evergreen, CO, 1993.

Badlands National Park, map 239, by Trails Illustrated Topo Maps, Evergreen, CO, 1995.

Trails Illustrated maps contain topographical data, trail locations, and background information printed on water-resistant paper. Available at many outdoor stores and bike shops. An additional map edition, *Black Hills North,* is expected to be released in the near future.

Bibliography

Rogers, Hiram. *Exploring the Black Hills & Badlands: A Guide for Hikers, XC Skiers, & Mountain Bikers,* Cordillera Press Guidebook, Johnson Books, Boulder, CO, 1993.

Bike Shops

Dakota Bicycle Co.
175 Sherman Street
Deadwood, SD 57732
(605) 578-1002

Mountain Mania
4242 Canyon Lake Drive
Rapid City, SD 57702
(605) 343-6596; 348-5197 fax; or (800) 428-6596
Mountain Mania provides rentals in Custer State Park.

also located at

1940 North Avenue #8
Spearfish, SD 57783
(605) 642-1970

Rapid City Scheels
220 North Maple
480 Rushmore Mall
Rapid City, SD 57701
(605) 342-9033 or 342-9021 fax

Two Wheeler Dealer
100 East Boulevard North
Rapid City, SD 57701
(605) 343-0524

also located at

1707 A West Main
Rapid City, SD 57702
(605) 342-3705

and

310 West Jackson
Spearfish, SD 57783
(605) 642-7545

NORTH DAKOTA

North Dakota, the northernmost of the Great Plains states, is situated in the geographical center of North America. With an area of about 70,700 square miles, it is the nineteenth largest of the states, but ranks only forty-seventh in population, with 638,000 people. A quick glance at a map implies that North Dakota is a continuous flat plain, for Interstate 94 from Minnesota to Montana is about the longest straight stretch of freeway in the United States. A closer look, however, shows a series of distinct regions, each with its own unique topography and vegetation.

The eastern slice of the state, along the Red River valley, is the most level area in the Great Plains, having been at the bottom of glacial Lake Aggasiz, once the largest fresh-water lake in the world. There is a distinct difference in terrain as you enter the rolling hills of central North Dakota, a glaciated region of shallow lakes and thousands of "pothole" ponds that is a rich breeding ground for migratory bird life. Indeed, with its key position on the central migratory flyway, North Dakota claims to have more wildlife refuges than any other state. Much of the eastern half of the state was once a rich tall-grass prairie, and now is largely cropland.

Another terrain transition zone is in the northeast corner of the state where areas of extensive forest cover the Turtle Mountains and the Pembina Hills. This area is similar in terrain to the vast northern forest regions of Minnesota and Manitoba. The southwestern third of the state, which is on the other side of the Missouri River, is the region of the high plains, a more arid area largely unaffected by Ice Age glaciation. Here you will find larger hills, buttes, and North Dakota's version of heavily eroded badlands. These western plains are predominantly short-grass prairies, now used mainly for ranching. Wooded areas are confined mostly to river corridors and sheltered valleys.

North Dakota weather varies from humid to semiarid in the summer as you travel east to west across the state. Precipitation falls mostly in the summer months, often in the form of thunderstorms, and North Dakota's cold continental winters at times can produce some of the most brutal weather in the country, when snowfall and high winds combine with open spaces to produce blizzard conditions. For most travelers, however, the state's moderate summers and pleasant spring and autumn seasons provide a break from hotter weather elsewhere.

There has been human habitation in what is now North Dakota since the end of the glacial period, over 10,000 years ago. In recent Native American history, the Mandan and Hidatsa people moved into the Missouri valley and established an agricultural way of life. The Dakota (Sioux) tribes were forced west across the region, from the north by the Ojibwa (Chippewa) and from the east by the advancing European Americans. In 1738 La Vérendrye, a French explorer, visited the Missouri valley and the Mandan villages. The Lewis and

Clark Expedition wintered with the Mandan people in 1804–5 as they traveled up the Missouri River toward the west.

Permanent settlements began in the Red River Valley in the 1850s, after an earlier settlement at Pembina by Canadian colonists failed. Settlers came down the Red River valley in ox carts from Minnesota territory to the southeast. After a period of warfare resulting in the defeat of the Dakota Indians, the interior of Dakota Territory opened up for white settlement. The coming of the railroads precipitated a land boom, turning what is now North Dakota into an agricultural state, which joined the Union along with South Dakota in 1889. The railroad network spurred the growth of the major cities of Fargo, Grand Forks, and Bismarck and ushered in a period of populist politics as well.

The current economy is still driven by agricultural products, although some areas have oil and lignite coal production. Public works projects, such as the large Missouri River reservoirs, Air Force bases, and ballistic missile sites have added to the state economy. Tourism has grown in importance as more people have discovered the uncrowded, wide-open spaces and the roughrider history of the western Dakota plains.

Mountain Biking in North Dakota

Mountain biking is a relative newcomer to the outdoor recreation scene in North Dakota. Trails in the state park system have been limited to the traditional user groups such as hikers and horseback riders, but park officials at both the state and local levels have taken note of the growth of interest in off-road bicycling and seem to be interested in learning more. The state parks department is working on a plan for future biking opportunities and bike maps. Local parks are beginning to open up to trail bike use, and increases in available trails in the future are likely.

The development of trails for mountain bikers presents the mountain biking community with both an opportunity and a responsibility. We have the opportunity to provide direction and encouragement to agency officials who are still learning what mountain biking is all about and how it differs from road bicycling. But we have the responsibility, as always, to use these resources wisely, to follow the local rules, and to present a positive image to other trail user groups.

Compared to the other plains states, North Dakota may have fewer trail systems available, but the places I have found are pretty good ones. The state forests in the northeastern hill regions of the Turtle Mountains and the Pembina Hills offer some great scenery and challenging forest riding. The Sheyenne National Grassland in the southeast provides a prairie environment of tall-grass prairie and quiet oak woodlands. Scattered here and there around the state are some small parks and trails where local riders or visitors can get a good workout. And in the west, the Little Missouri National Grassland—the North Dakota Badlands—surrounds two units of Theodore Roosevelt

National Park, and can offer well over 100 miles of back roads and tracks that are the equal to those found in most mountain biking areas anywhere.

So, whether you are a resident or a visitor just passing through, don't leave your bike behind, and don't underestimate the variety that North Dakota trails can offer. You can be climbing a steep ridge surrounded by open windswept canyons where the buffalo once thundered, or you can be flying down a narrow tunnel of dense white aspen on a cool, foggy morning a mile or two from Canada. Enjoy yourselves as I did.

For Further Information

North Dakota Tourism Department
604 East Boulevard Avenue
Bismarck, ND 58505
(701) 328-2525 or (800) HELLO ND

North Dakota state forests:
North Dakota Forest Service
First and Brander
Bottineau, ND 58318
(701) 228-5422

North Dakota Parks and Recreation Department
1835 Bismarck Expressway
Bismarck, ND 58504
(701) 328-5357

Bibliography

Knue, Joseph. *North Dakota Wildlife Viewing Guide,* Falcon Press, Helena, MT, 1992.

Eastern North Dakota

The vast, flat Red River valley, some of the richest farmland in North America, is about as far from mountain bike country as one would expect to get. The valley was formed at the end of the last ice age by a vast lake, Lake Aggasiz, the remnants of which are now Lakes Winnipeg and Manitoba in Canada. It is some of the flattest land in the United States, and the former lake bed provides rich soil for intensive crop agriculture, where wheat, sunflowers, potatoes, and sugar beets are among the staple harvests.

To the west of the valley, a line of hills—the coteau region—stretches from South Dakota to the Pembina Escarpment near the Canadian border, marking the transition into the rolling hills and prairie potholes of central North Dakota.

Fargo and Grand Forks both became transportation centers in the early 1800s as the Red River and the ox-cart trails formed a transportation route between the Mississippi, at St. Paul, and the Canadian north, at Winnipeg. Both cities have continued in that role as first the railroads, then interstate highways, replaced the riverboats and wagons. Almost 20 miles of recreational bike paths and bike routes exist in each city.

In this section, I will describe trail systems in a national grassland, in a state park, and in a state forest.

RIDE 82 NORTH COUNTRY TRAIL SEGMENT/ SHEYENNE NATIONAL GRASSLAND

Sheyenne National Grassland is one of the easternmost units of the widely scattered national grasslands system. (See the discussion of the national grasslands in the Buffalo Gap chapter, Ride 71). Here you'll find segments of the once vast tall-grass prairie and an oak savannah woodland spread out over some gently rolling sand hills deposited during the Ice Age on the shores of prehistoric Lake Agassiz. This multiple-use area offers much more than just cattle grazing, and mountain bikes are perhaps one of the most ideal way to experience it. For riders wishing to experience a bit of the natural prairie environment on some moderately challenging trails, this is the best place in eastern North Dakota.

The 25-mile trail running through this area is the only major finished segment of the North Country National Scenic Trail in North Dakota. This ambitious trail project is expected eventually to run from Lake Sakakewea in central North Dakota through the Great Lakes region to upstate New York, providing hikers and other nonmotorized users with one of the longest trail networks in North America. This national grassland segment will certainly be one of the highlights of the 435-mile North Dakota portion.

The greatest variety of scenery on this trail is on the eastern half, closest to the Sheyenne River valley. Portions (or all) of the trail can be done as out-and-back rides or combined with segments of county and Forest Service roads to create various loops. Some of these local roads, however, can be rather straight and uninteresting. Bicycling challenges on the trail include a few short, steep ups and downs, sandy areas, and open spaces where you will have to pay attention to signpost blazes to stay on course. Camping is allowed in most areas of the grassland, opening up the possibility of an overnight tour into the area.

The grassland habitat supports a wide variety of migratory and upland birds, including the rare greater prairie chicken. You may also spot deer, foxes, raccoons, or rabbits. Wildflowers in the late spring and colorful leaves in autumn add bright touches to the prairie landscape. Whether you spend just a few hours, or even a few days, the Sheyenne National Grassland can offer an enjoyable visit.

General location: About 45 miles southwest of Fargo, or 20 miles east of Lisbon in Ransom and Richland Counties.

Elevation change: Gently rolling low hills provide some elevation change in an otherwise flat region.

Season: Midspring to midautumn. Off-season use may be possible during periods of dry winter or spring weather.

Services: All commercial services can be found in Lisbon and Fargo.

Hazards: Some sections of the trail can be soft and sandy. Water found along the trail in wells or streams should not be considered safe to drink unless adequately treated. Hunting is allowed in the grassland. Check North Dakota regulations or with local officials to determine seasons.

Rescue index: Some stretches of the trail are rather remote and lightly traveled, so plan ahead.

Land status: Sheyenne National Grassland is a unit of the Custer National Forest.

Maps: A national grassland pamphlet, *North Country National Scenic Trail,* describes the area and provides a basic map. The $3 forest visitor's map covering the Sheyenne National Grassland shows land ownership patterns and many of the area's four-wheel-drive tracks. Both of these can be obtained from the USFS office in Lisbon, just south of ND 27 on ND 32. USGS 7.5 minute quads covering the trail are Power, Coburn, McLeod, and Venlo.

Finding the trail: Trailheads with parking areas are located at either end of the trail: at the west end on CR 54, 3 miles south of ND 27, or at the east end, on CR 23, 6 miles north of ND 27. CR 23 takes a 1-mile jog to the east as it heads north to the trailhead.

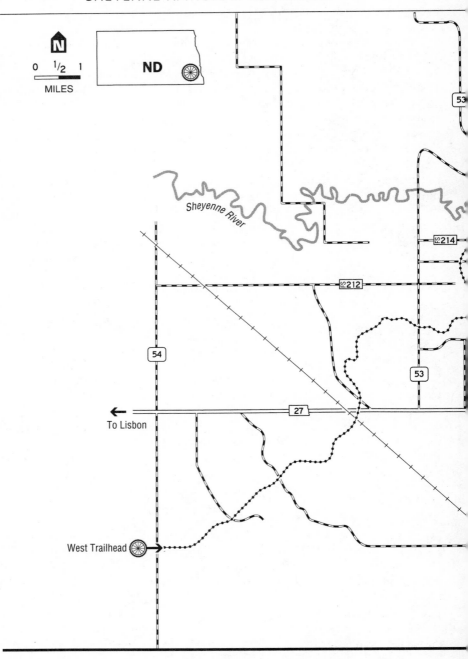

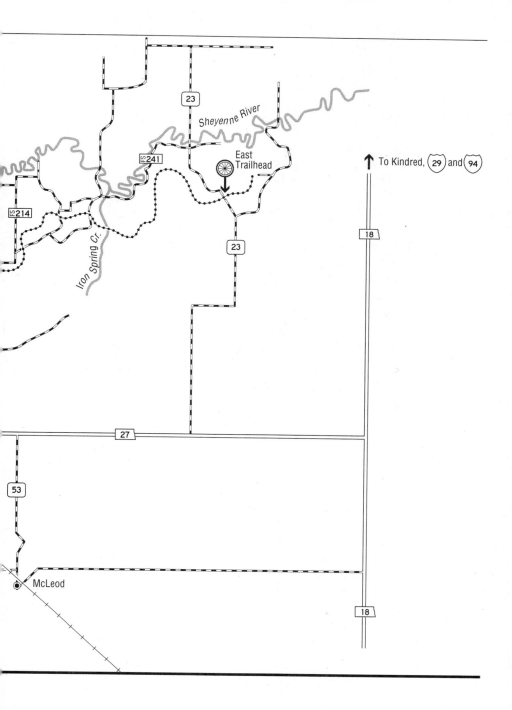

23

Sheyenne River

KS 241

East
Trailhead

KS 214

Iron Spring Cr.

↑ To Kindred, (29) and (94)

18

23

27

53

18

McLeod

The North Country Trail in Sheyenne National Grassland is great for exploring a remnant prairie and oak savannah environment.

Sources of additional information:

Sheyenne National Grassland
Sheyenne Ranger District, Custer National Forest
P.O. Box 946
Lisbon, ND 58054
(701) 683-4342

North Country Trail Association
P.O. Box 311
White Cloud, MI 49349
(616) 689-1912

Notes on the trail: The eastern trailhead on CR 23 is the best point to begin a ride. A short segment of trail heads east and north for a bit more than a mile through the typical oak savannah habitat. Riding west, you will meander through the mixed oak and prairie hills for several miles toward the Sheyenne River valley, which can be seen from the tops of some of the hills. There is a creek crossing to make at Iron Spring Creek, about 5 miles along. Private property blocks access from the trail to FS 241 near the creek, but as the trail makes its way southwest, there are several local roads that lead out to the county and state highways. The western third of the trail traverses more open country and seems to be less heavily used. If you are doing part of the trail as an out-and-back ride, be sure to allow enough time to make your return trip. Other loops are possible, using some of the local county and Forest Service roads. Check locally at the office in Lisbon for current road information.

The trail is marked with blue diamonds on posts spaced at several-hundred-foot intervals. Respect the ranching heritage of the area. Many of the gates along the trail route are designed to be self-closing, but be sure to leave them as you find them. Be sensitive to the fragile prairie environment and stay on the trails as much as possible.

RIDE 83 *TURTLE RIVER STATE PARK*

Turtle River State Park is a wooded oasis in the flat agricultural plains of the Red River valley. The meandering Turtle River provides a focal point for the park's recreational facilities, and the diverse habitat of the river corridor provides shelter for owls, hawks, deer, and even an occasional moose. Nearby, in a mixed wooded and wetland area, a short series of trails has been recently marked for mountain bike use. This two-plus-mile loop system provides a quick and generally easy ride in a pleasant setting on a wide, mowed grass and packed-dirt single-track surface. An intermediate section adds some short hills and curves, and an advanced trail is being developed, which will add some more technical alternatives in the future.

The park features a variety of other recreational attractions including Civilian Conservation Corps structures dating back to the 1930s, making this park a nice location for anyone looking for an introduction to trail riding. Experienced mountain bikers might find this area good for a few training laps in an area otherwise devoid of challenging terrain. To the east of the park, Grand Forks is North Dakota's second largest city and home to the University of North Dakota, where you might want to check out the Geology Museum.

RIDE 83 *TURTLE RIVER STATE PARK*

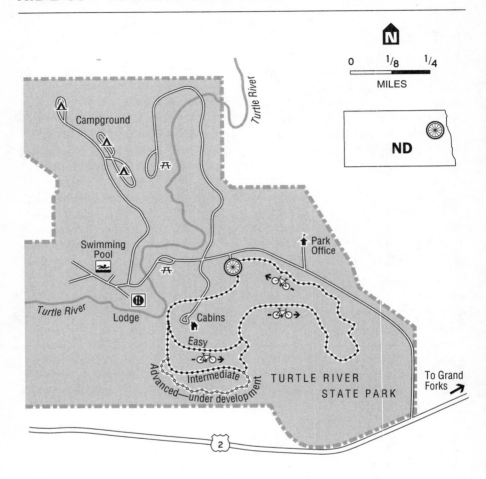

General location: About 20 miles west of Grand Forks in Grand Forks County.

Elevation change: This is a very flat region, where old river banks provide most of the short hills.

Season: Late spring to midautumn. The area is used for cross-country skiing in the winter.

Services: The state park has rest rooms, water, a swimming pool, a concession building, and picnic and camping facilities. Other services can be found in Larimore and Grand Forks.

Turtle River State Park west of Grand Forks has a short mountain bike loop good for a quick spin.

Hazards: Watch for traffic on the park roads.

Rescue index: Help is generally available in the park.

Land status: Turtle River State Park is managed by the North Dakota Parks and Recreation Department.

Maps: A basic park map showing the trails is available at the park office.

Finding the trail: The park is located just off US 2 near Arvilla. The trailhead is about one-quarter mile west of the park office, on the south side of the road.

Sources of additional information:

> Turtle River State Park
> Route 1, Box 9A
> Arvilla, ND 58214
> (701) 594-4445

Notes on the trail: The trail is well marked with yellow diamonds on posts and is intended as a one-way route. Please stay on the designated trail and follow the park rules. Park officials and the ski and bike club volunteers who assisted them are to be commended for setting up this trail system, and it is hoped that if the system gets sufficient use, it can be expanded with additional loops and cut-offs to add some more variety.

RIDE 84 *TETRAULT WOODS STATE FOREST*

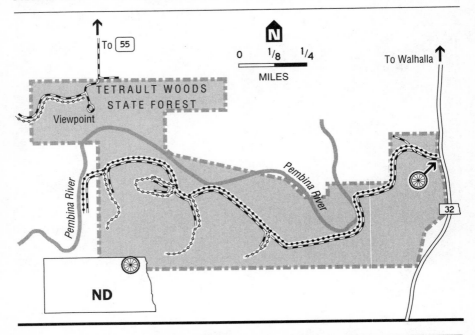

RIDE 84 *TETRAULT WOODS STATE FOREST*

The Pembina River valley is one of the most heavily forested regions of North Dakota. Only a few miles from Manitoba, Canada, this area is referred to as the "Rendezvous Region," because of its central location on the routes used by fur traders and settlers. Walhalla was originally an outpost during the fur trade era; the region was eventually settled in the 1870s by Icelandic immigrants. Today, much of the area is still forested with elm, aspen, and oak, and these woodlands are a haven for wildlife such as beaver, waterfowl, coyotes, deer, and occasional elk and moose. West of Walhalla in the Pembina Gorge is North Dakota's largest downhill ski area, and in late spring, the Pembina River is a popular canoeing route.

The Tetrault Woods State Forest is a 432-acre preserve containing a good cross section of this forest environment from the meandering Pembina River to the steep bluffs above. A four-wheel-drive road and double-track trail run the length of the forest area allowing an out-and-back ride along the river banks, through meadowlands and marshlands, and on the forested hillsides.

A series of trails in Tetrault Woods State Forest terminates at the Pembina River.

Several short spur trails and small loops add to the areas to explore, making possible a round-trip total of over six or seven miles. The riding is relatively easy to moderate in difficulty, with some short, steep climbs, and a good variety of trail surfaces ranging from grassy to rocky to muddy and sandy spots. This should be a particularly beautiful area during the autumn color season in late September and early October.

General location: Just south of Walhalla in Pembina and Cavalier Counties.
Elevation change: The bluffs rise almost 200′ above the Pembina River at 950′. Most of the trails are in the lower slopes close to the river.
Season: Late spring to midautumn. This area is usually snow covered from late November through March. Trails can be muddy or flooded in the spring and after periods of rainfall.
Services: Most commercial services are available in nearby Walhalla. Icelandic State Park, 18 miles southeast, has water, rest rooms, and camping.
Hazards: There may be occasional vehicles on the state forest road. Hunting is allowed here in season.
Rescue index: Help can be obtained in Walhalla.
Land status: North Dakota Forest Service.
Maps: A brochure with forest information and a rough map are available from the district forest office.

Finding the trail: The state forest entrance is located on ND 32, 1.5 miles south of Walhalla. Watch closely for the wooden state forest sign at a gravel turnoff, part way up the hill from the valley floor. Park anywhere on the grass, but don't block the dirt road leading down into the valley.

Sources of additional information:

> District Forester, Northeast District
> Route 1, Box 1
> Walhalla, ND 58282
> (701) 549-2441
>
> Icelandic State Park
> HCR3, Box 64A
> Cavalier, ND 58220
> (701) 265-4561

Notes on the trail: About a mile in on the state forest road is an area where sand has washed out from a ravine and covered the trail. Stick this section out, and beyond there you will begin to encounter various spur trails leading up into the forested slopes. In late summer some of these grassy trails may be somewhat overgrown. The main double-track trail crosses out of the state forest area on the west and ends along the river. Wet conditions on the trail may persist into late spring on the north-facing hillsides.

ADDITIONAL MOUNTAIN BIKING OPPORTUNITIES IN EASTERN NORTH DAKOTA

At first, the task of finding places to mountain bike in this region seemed hopeless; several bike shop people I contacted could only suggest places in Minnesota. However, further exploration revealed several scenic areas having back roads worth investigating.

The Pembina Gorge/Walhalla Area in Pembina and Cavalier Counties is one of these quietly beautiful regions with interesting back roads for mountain biking. The Pembina River valley is the most heavily forested region in North Dakota and offers habitat for much wildlife, including native moose and elk populations. Several loop rides are possible on local gravel and dirt roads that start at Icelandic State Park and head generally northwest into the hill region. Many of these roads are not well marked, and the use of county or topographical maps is advisable. Check with park officials at Icelandic State Park for further information: Icelandic State Park, HCR3, Box 64A, Cavalier, ND 58220, (701) 265-4561.

The Viking Highway is a gravel road running for 25 miles along the Sheyenne River in Ransom County from Little Yellowstone County Park on ND 46 to the town of Lisbon. The low hills of the river valley shelter a fairly continuous forest cover. Fort Ransom State Park and Sheyenne State Forest contain some small sections of the North Country Trail that are bikeable, and there are water, picnic, and camping facilities at the state park. The nearby quiet village of Fort Ransom is worth a visit. For information, contact: District Forester, Southeast District, Box 604, Lisbon, ND 58054, (701) 683-4323.

One of the bike shops in Fargo reports that several of the parks along the Red River in Fargo and Moorhead have some informal trail systems of partially groomed, often muddy loops.

Bike Shops and Clubs

Great Plains Cycling Club
P.O. Box 5085
Fargo, ND 58105

The bike shops mentioned below provided me with useful information. There are a number of other good bicycle shops in the larger towns of eastern North Dakota; check the area yellow pages for more information.

Bikes Unlimited, Inc.
2745 Main Avenue
Fargo, ND 58103
(701) 280-1119 or 280-9724 fax

Fargo South Scheels
3202 13th Avenue South
Fargo, ND 58201
(701) 298-2918 or 298-0706 fax

Grand Forks Scheels
1375A South Columbia Road (Med Park Mall)
Grand Forks, ND 58201
(701) 780-9424 or 772-1781 fax

Island Park Cycles
101 South 8th Street
Fargo, ND 58103
(701) 280-1796

Ski and Bike Shop
121 DeMers Avenue
Grand Forks, ND 58201
(701) 772-5567

Central North Dakota

The central part of North Dakota is the meeting place for three regions of the prairie landscape. As in South Dakota, the Missouri River acts as a boundary between the flat, glaciated prairie lands in the east and the more rugged hills of the arid west. The vast central prairie east of the river is made up of rolling hills, low valleys and scattered lakes and potholes providing critical habitat for migrating waterfowl. Much of the surrounding land is cultivated cropland, and the Ice Age left a variety of soil types that favor wheat and other grain production. To the west of the Missouri, farms give way to ranches and grazing land in a drier, more treeless environment.

The flat plains of the north-central part of the state show a transition toward the northern forest regions with the wooded and lake-dotted landscape of the Turtle Mountains. With terrain more typical of northern Minnesota, this hilly area is a popular recreational destination. Lake Sakakawea, a man-made reservoir on the Missouri River, appears on a map to be the dominant feature of central and western North Dakota, and this is certainly true from a recreational standpoint. As the largest man-made lake in the United States, with more miles of shoreline than California, Lake Sakakawea is a fishing and boating paradise surrounded by state parks and other recreational spots.

The major cities of the region are Minot, Bismarck, and Mandan. Each of these cities offers all modern services, including good bike shops and a bit of urban culture. North of Bismarck is the Knife River Villages, a National Historic Site commemorating some 9,000 years of Native American habitation. It is the only national park unit in the country honoring the Native Americans. In the last few hundred years before the coming of white settlers, Mandan and Hidatsa Indians lived in the area, growing squash and corn and trading with other tribes.

It was near these villages that the Lewis and Clark Expedition spent the winter of 1804–05 and made the fortunate contact with the friendly Mandan people, who taught them much about the lands to the west. Here they gained the help of a French-Canadian fur trapper and his Shoshoni wife, Sacagawea, who together acted as interpreters. Fort Abraham Lincoln just south of Mandan has been restored to look like it did in 1876, when it was the last command post of Lt. Col. George A. Custer before he left on the fateful expedition that led to the Little Bighorn River in Montana. The park also includes a replica Mandan Indian village and a museum featuring the Lewis and Clark Expedition's visit to the area.

Mountain biking is a relative newcomer to the bicycling scene in central North Dakota. The focus has been more on traditional road biking, since this area of open spaces has many lightly traveled, paved roads. The premier event of the area is the annual CANDISC (Cycling Around North Dakota In Sakakawea Country) ride in early August, a 400-mile tour around the area of Lake Sakakewea, starting at Fort Stevenson State Park near Garrison. Other parks around the reservoir have a few trails, and the surrounding countryside offers some scenic unpaved back roads, but little exists yet in the way of mountain biking routes. Several mountain bike races have been held at Lake Sakakawea State Park near Pick City. The possibility of permanent trails in that vicinity is being considered for the future. In this section, I will describe a city riverfront trail system, an off-road-vehicle area, and a more extensive state forest trail system.

RIDE 85   *BISMARCK RIVERFRONT TRAIL SYSTEM*

Along the Missouri River in the city of Bismarck there is a paved, five-mile multiple-use pathway that connects Pioneer Park with about six additional miles of recreational trails on the south side of town. At Pioneer Park an access path ascends the river bluffs to a vantage point with a great view of the Missouri River valley and the city of Mandan. Also on the bluff at that location is the Ward Earthlodge Village Historic Site, an interpretive trail among the remnants of an eighteenth-century Mandan Indian village. On the sides of the grassy bluffs to the south is a small system of unofficial hilly single-track trails providing a mile or two of some more challenging riding for mountain bikers. Additional trails on the bluffs can be found to the west of Bismarck State College on the south side of the freeway.

Two additional parks, Sertoma and Cottonwood, are also connected to the trail system. This network of trails is a great resource for the Bismarck community, and it offers visitors and through-travelers on Interstate 94 a place to do some biking. The North Dakota Heritage Center, near the state capitol building, provides insights into the history of this area and into life on the northern plains.

General location: Along the Missouri River in the city of Bismarck.
Elevation change: Mostly flat, except for the trails in the bluffs above Pioneer Park.
Season: Midspring through late autumn.
Services: Pioneer Park has parking and picnic facilities. All other services are available in Bismarck.
Hazards: Be on the lookout for pedestrians on the trails and for vehicles at the various road and driveway crossings.
Rescue index: Help is close by in this area.

RIDE 85 *BISMARCK RIVERFRONT TRAIL SYSTEM*

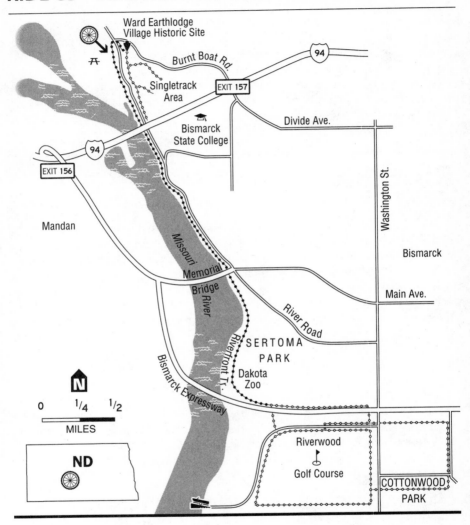

Land status: Bismarck Parks and Recreation District.

Maps: A very general trail layout map is available in the activity schedule brochure printed by the Bismarck Parks and Recreation District.

Finding the trail: There is parking at Pioneer Park on River Road, north of the I-94 overpass. I-94/exit 157 and Burnt Boat Road provide quick access to River Road and Pioneer Park.

Bismarck's urban trail system features good views of the Missouri River from the bluffs above Pioneer Park.

Sources of additional information:

Bismarck Parks and Recreation District
420 East Front
Bismarck, ND 58504
(701) 222-6455

Notes on the trail: Use courtesy and caution when passing other trail users. There are additional nonmotorized-use trails along the river on the Mandan side, north of the Memorial Highway bridge. Area bike shops can provide more information on the local biking scene. Bismarck parks are open from 6 A.M. to 11 P.M. daily.

RIDE 86   *ROUGHRIDER OFF-ROAD-VEHICLE AREA/GARRISON DAM*

This off-road-vehicle area is a heavily used, 100-acre site on an open, hilly bluff overlooking the Missouri River at the point where it flows out of the massive Garrison Dam. The area is crisscrossed with vehicle tracks, many of

RIDE 86 *ROUGHRIDER OFF-ROAD-VEHICLE AREA / GARRISON DAM*

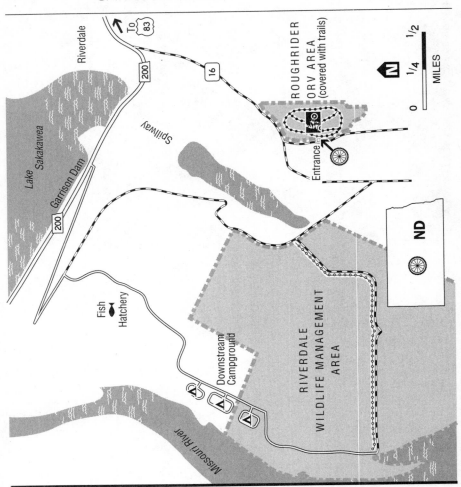

which go up and down the steepest of the hills, providing virtually impossible challenges for human-powered bikes. More moderate tracks on the fringes of the most heavily used sections usually offer more realistic riding. This area is good for riders who really want to work on their climbing and hard-riding skills, and as an alternative spot when other trails in more fragile areas may be too wet for riding. Use caution when there are fast-moving motorized vehicles in the area.

Quiet double-track trails can be found in the Downstream Campground area adjacent to the Roughrider ORV Area.

The Garrison Dam is one of the largest earth dams of its type in the world, forming the largest man-made lake in the United States. Other recreational facilities and points of interest are plentiful around the lake. The nearby Riverdale Wildlife Management Area, about one mile west along the Missouri River, offers several miles of relatively level four-wheel-drive roads through the cottonwood forest of the river bottoms, where you'll have a quieter, more secluded, easy ride. Follow the road to the Downstream Campground through to the end to a parking and access area. Bald eagles usually winter in the area. Deer and grouse are common, as are many other types of birds and small mammals.

General location: One mile south of the town of Riverdale near the site of the Garrison Dam in McLean County.
Elevation change: The area is a hilly river bluff with lots of short and steep ups and downs.
Season: Late spring through midautumn. Off-season use may be possible during periods of dry winter or spring weather.
Services: Camping facilities and water can be found at the Downstream Campground or Lake Sakakawea State Park. All other basic services can be found in Riverdale or Pick City.
Hazards: Use caution during times of motorized vehicle use.

Rescue index: Help can be found in the towns of Riverdale or Pick City.
Land status: U.S. Army Corps of Engineers.
Maps: A pamphlet titled *Roughrider Off-Road Vehicle Area* with a location map is available from the Corps of Engineers office in Riverdale.
Finding the trail: Take CR 16 south 1 mile from ND 200 near the west end of Riverdale. Enter through a fence on the side road running along the west side of the ORV area.

Sources of additional information:

U.S. Army Corps of Engineers, Garrison Dam
P.O. Box 527
Riverdale, ND 58565-0527
(701) 654-7411

Notes on the trail: The ORV area includes a dirt bike course that was designed by the local Jaycees group. There may be special events going on here, so check with the Riverdale administration office for more details. Hours of operation are sunrise to sunset.

RIDE 87　　*TURTLE MOUNTAIN STATE FOREST*

The Turtle Mountains are a group of isolated hills containing dozens of small lakes and wetlands in an oak and aspen forest more typical of the Minnesota or Manitoba northwoods than of the Dakota plains. Straddling the United States–Canadian border, this popular region has many well-developed recreational facilities, as well as a good network of back roads and trails of interest to all sorts of bicycling enthusiasts. More than ten miles of trails in the Turtle Mountain State Forest provide some moderately challenging terrain for mountain bikers.

This trail system, which forms a loop with several additional side trails, is made up of some old double-tracks, winter snowmobile, and cross-country ski trails. Some sections are being redesigned or rerouted for mountain biking so as to avoid low, wet areas and reduce erosion. At the time of this writing, trail conditions varied from dry, packed-dirt or grassy corridors through the woods and along the perimeters of old farm fields, to a brushy, potentially wet corridor through the thickest of the oak and aspen forest. Plans for improving the signage on some of the routes are also in the works for the future.

Elk and moose may be seen in this area if you are lucky. Deer are more likely to be encountered, and the drumming of ruffed grouse is often heard in the springtime. At a fast pace or a leisurely one you will get a good workout

RIDE 87 *TURTLE MOUNTAIN STATE FOREST*

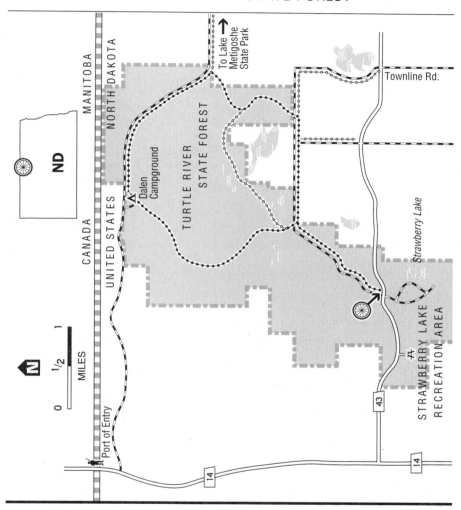

in this northern woodland setting. Be sure to stop and enjoy your surroundings on this most northern of the Great Plains rides.

Many other attractions in the Turtle Mountain region make this a worthwhile tourist trip. Lake Metigoshe State Park is a four-season attraction on popular Lake Metigoshe, which spills across the border into Manitoba. To the east of Lake Metigoshe lies the International Peace Garden, a parklike collection of formal gardens, scenic drives, and memorials to the world's longest unfortified international boundary. Belcourt is the center of the Turtle Mountain Chippewa Band and has two excellent cultural centers and a casino. The town of Rugby, 50 miles to the south, is considered to be the geographical center of the North American continent and is marked with a stone cairn.

General location: Adjacent to the Canadian border about 10 miles north of Bottineau in Bottineau County.

Elevation change: The trails consist of regular ups and downs within a range of 100′ or so.

Season: Late spring to midautumn. Periods of rainy weather can make portions of the trails pretty soggy or impassable.

Services: Camping and water are found at Strawberry Lake Recreation Area across from the trailhead. Other tourist facilities are located at many points around the Turtle Mountains. Additional commercial services are available in Bottineau.

Hazards: Low areas on the trail can be soft and muddy. Exposed roots, stumps, and rocks may be encountered on new trail sections. Deadfalls are possible anywhere. On warm summer evenings, mosquitoes can be a nuisance in low, protected areas.

Rescue index: There is regular traffic on ND 43, but some of the interior sections of the trail are somewhat remote.

Land status: Turtle Mountain State Forest is administered by the North Dakota Forest Service.

Maps: A map of the trail system is posted at the start of the trail across the highway from the Strawberry Lake Recreation Area. New trail signs and a new handout map are expected to be available by the summer of 1995.

Finding the trail: The trailhead and Strawberry Lake Recreation Area are located on ND 43, about 2 miles east of ND 14 and 8 miles west of the Lake Metigoshe State Park turnoff.

Sources of additional information:

North Dakota Forest Service
First and Brander
Bottineau, ND 58318
(701) 228-5422 or 228-5448 fax

Greater Bottineau Chamber of Commerce
Box 84
Bottineau, ND 58318
(701) 228-3849

Val's Cyclery
222 East Central Avenue
Minot, ND 58701
(701) 839-4817

Turtle Mountain State Forest contains a challenging mountain bike trail network made up of cross-country ski trails, snowmobile routes, and old double-tracks.

Notes on the trail: The mountain bike trail starts across the highway from the entrance to the recreation area, just to the east of the trail map sign and hiking trail trailhead. The trail angles northeast through thick aspen forest for about 1.5 miles until it reaches the marked junction where the 8-mile loop begins. The trail traveling east passes through several gates; please leave them as you find them. A winter cross-country ski trail crosses the area near the edge of an open field, adding another route possibility that bisects the main loop. The outer loop passes through the Dalen Recreation Area, just 1 or 2 miles south of the Canadian border, before continuing south back to the start.

ADDITIONAL MOUNTAIN BIKING OPPORTUNITIES IN CENTRAL NORTH DAKOTA

Highway 1806, from Mandan to Cross Ranch State Park, is part of the *Lewis and Clark Trail*, a scenic highway tour along the river route of the Lewis and Clark Expedition. The 18-mile Oliver County section is unpaved and offers nice vistas of a free-flowing section of the Missouri River.

Lake Metigoshe State Park, east of Turtle Mountain State Forest (see Ride 87), has a network of cross-country ski trails that are available for mountain bike use in the off-season. Some of these may have sections that are too wet most of the time for biking. Check with officials at Lake Metigoshe State Park, Bottineau, ND 58318, (701) 263-4651.

The Roughrider Trail is the only major rail trail corridor in North Dakota and is maintained primarily as a winter snowmobile route by snowmobile license revenues. Some sections of the trail corridor are leased only in the winter months, and most of the rest are not actively maintained during the summer. However, mountain bike exploration is possible in some sections. It is best to check with Fort Abraham State Park officials; they can point out areas for possible riding. There is all-terrain-vehicle use on some sections at various times of the year, and the corridor is mowed in late summer in preparation for the winter season. The Roughrider Trail follows the Missouri River valley lined with stands of cottonwood trees and stretches of open prairie. For current information: Fort Abraham Lincoln State Park, Route 2, Box 139, Mandan, ND 58554, (701) 663-9571.

The Velva Trail is a hilly single-track route beginning in the Minot area southeast to the town of Velva in McHenry County. For further information, check with Val's Cyclery in Minot, listed below.

Bike Shops

Dakota Cyclery
211 South Third Street
Bismarck, ND 58504
(701) 222-1218

The Bike Route
225 West Broadway
Bismarck, ND 58501
(701) 223-5610

Val's Cyclery
222 East Central Avenue
Minot, ND 58701
(701) 839-4817

Western North Dakota

The southwestern third of North Dakota, separated from the rest of the state by the Missouri River, is a rolling to hilly expanse of high plains that largely escaped the last period of glaciation. Among the many hills and buttes in the area is the state's highest point, White Butte, at 3,506 feet. This relatively arid area is better suited for ranching than for crop agriculture, so the region has a more Western than Midwestern aura to it. The northwest corner of the state, bordering Saskatchewan, is a continuation of the relatively flat, glaciated prairie and lake region of north-central North Dakota. This northern extension of the Great Plains stretches well into Canada before merging with the vast subarctic boreal forest region.

The rugged, eroded terrain of the southwest corner offers plenty of open grassland, but it also provides protected ridges and valleys that collect winter moisture and create shelter for trees and animal life. In this diverse habitat, you may see mule and white-tail deer, elk, pronghorn antelope, coyotes, prairie dogs, bighorn sheep, and wild horses. Bald eagles, pheasants, grouse, and wild turkeys can be seen in various areas. Rattlesnakes may also be encountered, and poison ivy may be present in wooded areas. Buffalo (bison) herds have been re-established in both the southern and northern units of Theodore Roosevelt National Park. Wild horses, possibly descendents of the stock from Chief Sitting Bull's war parties, roam the central badlands near the southern unit of Theodore Roosevelt Park.

The recreational focal point of southwestern North Dakota is a 100-plus-mile stretch of rugged, heavily eroded plateau country surrounding the Little Missouri River, known informally as the North Dakota Badlands. Administratively, much of this area makes up the Little Missouri National Grassland, the largest of the national grasslands in the Great Plains states. This area surrounding the two units of Theodore Roosevelt National Park offers many recreational opportunities in a setting rich with history and unique, spectacular scenery—and is not to be confused with South Dakota's Badlands National Park.

Human habitation of the Badlands region goes back at least 11,000 years to a culture based on the mining of Knife River flint in the vicinity of Dunn Center in Dunn County.

Some of the last herds of free-roaming buffalo in the plains made their final stands in these rugged hills. Once numbering about 60 million, by 1891 only 541 buffalo were left in the United States. With the demise of the buffalo came the end of the plains Indian culture. It was here in the Badlands that the Dakota (Sioux), too, made their last stand; Chief Sitting Bull surrendered in 1881 at Fort Buford on the Missouri River near Williston.

The later history and present-day geography of the North Dakota Badlands is intertwined with the story of Theodore Roosevelt, the soon-to-be U.S. president, who became fascinated with the open spaces of the area in the 1880s and established a series of cattle ranches. Together with the French nobleman, the Marquis de Mores, who founded the town of Medora, he helped to establish the cattle industry, which boomed with the coming of the railroads. Theodore Roosevelt came away from here with a philosophy of land and conservation that he later applied to legislation that led to the creation of the National Park Service.

The town of Medora acts as a gateway to the Roosevelt Park and Badlands areas, providing tourists with a heavy dose of wild-west lore and hospitality. Saloons, museums, theaters, and shops along a busy "western" main street stand in contrast to the open spaces and wind-blown hills of the Little Missouri River country. Dinosaur enthusiasts will find this area to be of great interest. Many important paleontological discoveries from the days of the dinosaurs and the early mammals have been made at digs in the Badlands. The Dinosaur Museum in Dickinson and the Pioneer Trails Regional Museum in Bowman, south of Belfield, both offer fossil exhibits open to the public. Southwest of Williston, almost in Montana, is the restored Fort Union Trading Post, a National Historic Site. Located at the strategic confluence of the Missouri and the Yellowstone Rivers, this fort controlled most of the fur trade in the upper Missouri basin from 1829 to 1867.

Although Theodore Roosevelt National Park has some of the most spectacular of the Badlands scenery, bicycles are not allowed off the established road system. The park has scenic drives, good campgrounds, hiking trails, and excellent interpretive centers for those interested in learning more about this area. The north unit of the park is much less heavily visited, has some of the best scenery in the Badlands, and has a new visitor center.

But it is in the Little Missouri National Grassland that you will find some of the best mountain biking in the Great Plains. Over one million acres of public land are interspersed with private and state holdings in the grassland and are connected with many miles of back roads, four-wheel-drive tracks, and old trails. (See the discussion of the national grasslands in the Buffalo Gap chapter, Ride 71.) The three rides described below are only a sampling of the possibilities in this area. While researching this book, I underestimated the extent of this area and wish I had spent more time there. This was one of my favorite areas, and I plan to be back!

Adventurous mountain bikers will want to get hold of the appropriate maps and do some more exploration. Camping is allowed in most areas of the grassland, so overnight tours are a possibility here. Check with local rangers or with bike shops in Bismarck, Dickinson, or Williston for more ideas.

RIDE 88 *CUSTER'S LAST TRAIL*

This ride, on one of many similar roads in the area, provides an opportunity to see some of the Badlands terrain and take in one of the major historical points in the area. The roads here are mostly four-wheel-drive and double-track and will be in varying condition depending upon amount of recent rainfall, erosion, and previous use. The ride along FS 740 avoids the steepest terrain in the area, but a stream crossing, some soft spots, and a few hills make this a moderate effort. Most of the surrounding scenery is open, eroded hill country, but there are a few stands of cottonwood and brush along the creek bottoms. Mule deer, pronghorn antelope, and bighorn sheep are among the animals you may see in this area.

Done as an out-and-back ride, this route can be as much as a 13-mile round-trip, depending upon how far you choose to drive in to start. Either the north or south end of FS 740 is driveable for up to a couple of miles before the terrain gets too rough.

Near the southern end of FS 740, at a point where it is possible to drive in with most vehicles, is Initial Rock. Custer's 7th Cavalry camped near here on their way west in pursuit of the Dakota (Sioux) in May 1876. Two of his men carved their initials into the rock here on the side of the valley. Aging and vandalism have taken its toll on this site, but the initials are still visible. Custer's ill-fated expedition ended up at Little Bighorn River in Montana several weeks later. Custer headed down the valley to the northwest, and it is possible to ride a ways along his route.

About 20 miles to the south is Burning Coal Vein Campground, an interesting side trip. For over a century, a nearby vein of coal burned steadily, giving off fumes that stunted the growth of the surrounding juniper trees. There is no water available at the campground.

General location: Seven miles southeast of Medora and Interstate 94 in Little Missouri National Grassland.

Elevation change: This moderately hilly area has about 200′ of variation in elevation.

Season: Midspring through late autumn. Off-season riding may be possible in times of dry winter and spring conditions.

Services: Most tourist facilities can be found in Medora. All other commercial services are available in Belfield and Dickinson.

Hazards: Keep an eye out for threatening weather during thunderstorm season.

Rescue index: There is periodic traffic on the improved gravel roads of the area, and help is always at hand in Medora.

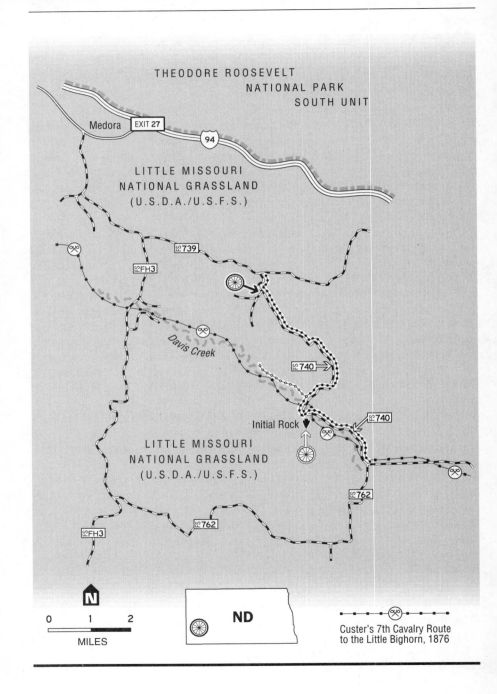

THEODORE ROOSEVELT
NATIONAL PARK
SOUTH UNIT

Medora EXIT 27 94

LITTLE MISSOURI
NATIONAL GRASSLAND
(U.S.D.A./U.S.F.S.)

FS739

FSFH3

Davis Creek

FS740

FS740

Initial Rock

FS740

LITTLE MISSOURI
NATIONAL GRASSLAND
(U.S.D.A./U.S.F.S.)

FS762

FSFH3

FS762

N

0   1   2
MILES

ND

Custer's 7th Cavalry Route
to the Little Bighorn, 1876

A ride on FS 740 in Little Missouri National Grassland reaches a rock where some of Custer's men carved their initials during their fateful expedition to the Little Bighorn.

Land status: Little Missouri National Grassland is a division of Custer National Forest.

Maps: The $3 Forest Service visitor's map, *Little Missouri National Grassland,* shows land ownership patterns, access roads, and most of the four-wheel-drive tracks in the area. Contour lines in meters provide a good representation of the topography, making this map adequate for general use. For detailed exploration, plan on obtaining the USGS 7.5 minute quad for Tracy Mountain.

Finding the trail: Head southeast about 7.5 miles from Medora on FS FH3 and FS 739 to FS 740. It is possible to drive on FS 740 almost another mile to a junction near an oil pump. Keep left and start your ride southeast on FS 740 at any point. An alternate starting point is on the south end of FS 740, accessible via FS FH3 and FS 762. Vehicles with relatively high clearance can drive into Initial Rock.

Sources of additional information:

Little Missouri National Grassland
Medora Ranger District
161 21st Street West
Dickinson, ND 58601
(701) 225-5151

Notes on the trail: A stream crossing immediately north of Initial Rock may be difficult in times of high water. FS 740 heads north from there out of the main creek valley, which was the route of Custer's expedition. The grassland is an active grazing area; be sure to leave any gates as you find them.

RIDE 89   *SHEEP CREEK RIDGE*

This is a great out-and-back ride that starts on a high plateau and follows the crest of a ridge gradually down toward the Little Missouri River with great views in either direction. The one-way distance can be up to five miles, but it is scenic all the way, and you can do as much as you like and have an enjoyable time. The road is a rough four-wheel-drive route over dirt and rock, eventually fading into a double-track that continues through the grass. Some steep spots, deep ruts, and rocky sections make this a moderately challenging ride, but you can cruise along some sections without difficulty, just enjoying the setting.

This was one of the most pleasant rides I did; it was a calm, sunny autumn morning and the changing light patterns and shadows in the canyons gave each succeeding ridge crest a whole new perspective. On the drive into the trailhead, the little village of Grassy Butte is an interesting stop. The old log cabin there, which is now a museum, was the original post office, built in 1914.

General location: About 5 miles south of the Theodore Roosevelt National Park, North Unit, in the Little Missouri National Grassland.

Elevation change: A steady elevation drop of over 300′ occurs along the ridge over the 5-mile route.

Season: Midspring through midautumn. Off-season riding may be possible in times of dry winter and spring conditions.

Services: Limited services are available in Grassy Butte. All other commercial services can be found in Watford City, Belfield, or Dickinson.

Hazards: There are occasional steep drop-offs along the route. Watch for potential stormy weather during the thunderstorm season.

Rescue index: The back roads in this area are relatively lightly used. You may have to go out to US 85 and Grassy Butte for help.

Land status: Little Missouri National Grassland is a division of Custer National Forest.

Maps: The $3 Forest Service visitor's map, *Little Missouri National Grassland,* shows land ownership patterns, access roads, and most of the four-wheel-drive tracks in the area. Contour lines in meters provide a good representation of the topography, making this map adequate for general use.

RIDE 89 *SHEEP CREEK RIDGE*

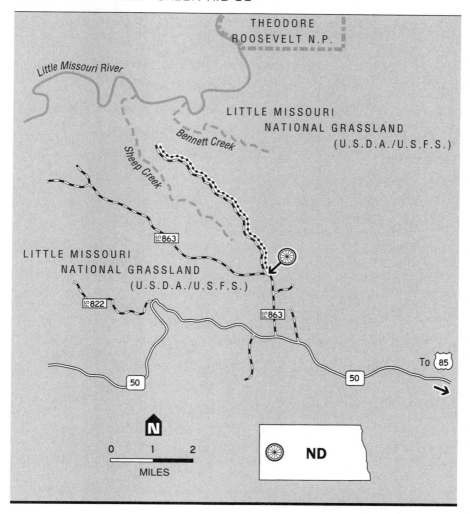

For detailed exploration, plan on obtaining the USGS 7.5 minute quads for Wolf Coulee and Sperati Point.

Finding the trail: From Grassy Butte on US 85, take CR 50 west about 8.8 miles to FS 863. Go north almost 2 miles, just past the curve to the west, and there will be a turnoff leading one-quarter mile into an excavation site surrounded by a fence. Park somewhere around there and start your ride. The small excavation site sits on top of the original route; go around the outside of the fence and pick up the trail to the north.

Unusual erosion formations accent the panorama of North Dakota Badlands scenery along the Little Missouri River.

Sources of additional information:

Little Missouri National Grassland
McKenzie Ranger District
HC 2, Box 8
Watford City, ND 58854
(701) 842-2393

Notes on the trail: After less than a mile, the route will become too rough for most vehicles, and you should have the ridge to yourself. The return trip will take more time, since you will be gaining back the elevation lost on the ride out. The Grassland map shows the symbol for a prairie dog town near the end of the double-track. But they must have moved on by the time I got there, because I didn't see any.

RIDE 90 *SUMMIT RIDGE*

This ride follows a high ridge overlooking the Little Missouri River valley and the many surrounding ridges and ravines that make up this rugged landscape. The four-wheel-drive road can be done as an out-and-back route, with

RIDE 90 *SUMMIT RIDGE*

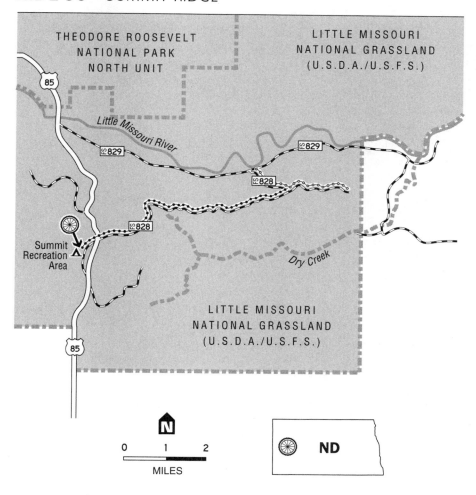

THEODORE ROOSEVELT
NATIONAL PARK
NORTH UNIT

85

Little Missouri River

🚲829

🚲829

🚲828

🚲828

Summit
Recreation
Area

LITTLE MISSOURI
NATIONAL GRASSLAND
(U.S.D.A./U.S.F.S.)

Dry Creek

LITTLE MISSOURI
NATIONAL GRASSLAND
(U.S.D.A./U.S.F.S.)

85

N

0   1   2
MILES

ND

round-trips of up to 13 miles possible. A number of steep climbs make this route moderately difficult, but the biking is generally smooth sailing, with a few rocky and soft, sandy spots to watch for.

A mile out from the start, in a draw on the north, is Christ Springs, an area fenced in since 1960 as an experiment to study a cattle-free habitat. Farther on, a small, partially wooded valley features some erosion formations along the perimeter. This open, breezy ridge will also give you a sense of the grandeur and drama of the western Dakota skies. The nearby North Unit of

The hilly terrain of the Little Missouri National Grassland has miles and miles of double-track riding.

Theodore Roosevelt National Park is a good place to see and learn about more of the Badlands area, although bicycles are restricted to the paved road system.

General location: In Little Missouri National Grassland, about 18 miles south of Watford City in McKenzie County, near the North Unit of Theodore Roosevelt National Park.

Elevation change: There is about a 250′ variation in elevation along the ridge line, and another 400′ down to the Little Missouri River valley.

Season: Midspring through midautumn. Off-season riding may be possible in times of dry winter and spring conditions.

Services: Several campsites and toilets are located at the Summit Recreation Site on US 85. Commercial services can be found in Watford City, Belfield, or Dickinson.

Hazards: Vehicles may be encountered along the road. Watch for potential stormy weather during the thunderstorm season.

Rescue index: Help can be found at the ranger station in the nearby Theodore Roosevelt National Park unit.

Land status: Little Missouri National Grassland is a division of Custer National Forest.

Maps: The $3 Forest Service visitor's map, *Little Missouri National Grassland,* shows land ownership patterns, access roads, and most of the four-wheel-drive tracks in the area. Contour lines in meters provide a good representation of the topography, making this map adequate for general use. For detailed exploration, plan on obtaining the USGS 7.5 minute quad for Lone Butte.

Finding the trail: Park somewhere in the Summit Recreation Site off US 85, and start up FS 828, across the highway from the north exit of the recreation site.

Sources of additional information:

> Little Missouri National Grassland
> McKenzie Ranger District
> HC 2, Box 8
> Watford City, ND 58854
> (701) 842-2393

Notes on the trail: The road starts out along the top of the ridge, then after 2 miles drops into a little valley with a pond and a variety of erosion formations. After ascending back to the crest of the ridge, FS 828 will pass through a fence and continue east for a couple more miles before dropping sharply down into the river valley and to FS 829. Another dirt track continues east along the ridge.

It is possible to make this ride a loop of about 15 miles by continuing on FS 828 as it drops down to FS 829, then west along the Little Missouri to US 85 and then making a 3-mile climb back to the Summit Recreation area. Watch for fast-moving traffic on US 85. Carry plenty of water, and leave gates as you find them.

ADDITIONAL MOUNTAIN BIKING OPPORTUNITIES IN WESTERN NORTH DAKOTA

The Killdeer Mountain Area northwest of the town of Killdeer is a privately owned plateau region that is rich in wildlife. To the west is Killdeer Mountain Wildlife Management Area, a unit of North Dakota Game and Fish Department. This area is covered by a number of unpaved county and local roads that may offer some interesting mountain bike riding. County maps (Dunn County) and/or topographical maps will be necessary to navigate in this area. Respect private property by staying on the roads. And carry plenty of water.

Logging Camp Ranch in the southern part of the Little Missouri National Grassland near the town of Amidon is a working ranch that rents cabins and allows mountain biking on designated trails. Parts of this area include the only major stand of ponderosa pines in North Dakota. Amidon (population: 43) is no doubt one of the smallest county seats in the United States. Nearby is

White Butte, the highest point in North Dakota (3,506 feet). For further information, contact Logging Camp Ranch, HC1, Box 27, Bowman, ND 58623, (701) 279-5501.

Theodore Roosevelt National Park, South Unit, has a 36-mile paved loop road through some of the rugged Badlands scenery and past the local buffalo herds. Mountain bikes are not allowed off the paved park roads. Future plans for trails in this region include a multi-use corridor running between the two units of the national park, about 50 miles apart. The nature of this trail has not yet been determined, but it most likely will include some form of bicycle travel.

In *Medora,* in the heart of the North Dakota Badlands area, Rough Rider Adventures, a cooperative promotional effort between the Theodore Roosevelt Foundation and Dakota Cyclery of Bismarck, has set up a system of three mountain bike trails. Each of these four- to seven-mile loops starts from Medora and run through some of the surrounding hills. Further information on these trails is available in Medora. The group runs twice-daily guided tours, in season, along these routes. Rough Rider Adventures can also provide assistance with the full range of other activities happening in the Medora area. For further information, contact them at the listing below.

The Badlands Area is full of hundreds of possible mountain bike rides. Using the National Grassland visitor's map, you can determine which sections are public land and then do some exploration on your own. I recommend a short tour in a typically interesting landscape on the Moody Plateau, which is about 14 miles south of Medora. To get there take FS FH3 south to FS 762, and go east about two miles. As the road descends a hill and begins a curve to the left, there is a double-track on the right heading south into the buttes. Go a few miles out and back on this trail and you'll see some unique terrain. In fact, I even had a close encounter with a mountain sheep on a ridge along this trail.

For More Information

Little Missouri National Grassland is administered by Custer National Forest.

Medora Ranger District
161 21st Street West
Dickinson, ND 58601
(701) 225-5151

McKenzie Ranger District
HC 2, Box 8
Watford City, ND 58854
(701) 842-2393

Forest Supervisor
Custer National Forest
2602 First Avenue North
P.O. Box 2556
Billings, MT 59103
(406) 657-6361

Theodore Roosevelt National Park
Medora, ND 58645
(701) 623-4466

Bike Shops

Badlands Bike Service
401 35th Street West
Williston, ND 58801
(701) 572-7038

Dakota Cyclery/Rough Rider Adventures
Box 198
Medora, ND 58645
(701) 623-4808

Steffan's Saw & Bike
121 3rd Avenue East
Dickinson, ND 58601
(701) 225-5075

Afterword

LAND-USE CONTROVERSY

A few years ago I wrote a long piece on this issue for *Sierra* magazine that entailed calling literally dozens of government land managers, game wardens, mountain bikers, and local officials to get a feeling for how riders were being welcomed on the trails. All that I've seen personally since, and heard from my authors, indicates there hasn't been much change. We're still considered the new kid on the block. We have less of a right to the trails than equestrians and hikers, and we're excluded from many areas, including:

a) wilderness areas
b) national parks (except on roads, and those paths specifically marked "bike path")
c) national monuments (except on roads open to the public)
d) most state parks and monuments (except on roads, and those paths specifically marked "bike path")
e) an increasing number of urban and county parks, especially in California (except on roads, and those paths specifically marked "bike path")

Frankly, I have little difficulty with these exclusions and would, in fact, restrict our presence from some trails I've ridden (one time) due to the environmental damage and chance of blindsiding the many walkers and hikers I met up with along the way. But these are my personal views. The author of this volume and mountain bikers as a group may hold different opinions.

You can do your part in keeping us from being excluded from even more trails by riding responsibly. Many local and national off-road bicycle organizations have been formed with exactly this in mind, and one of the largest—the National Off-Road Bicycle Association (NORBA)—offers the following code of behavior for mountain bikers:

1. I will yield the right of way to other non-motorized recreationists. I realize that people judge all cyclists by my actions.
2. I will slow down and use caution when approaching or overtaking another cyclist and will make my presence known well in advance.
3. I will maintain control of my speed at all times and will approach turns in anticipation of someone around the bend.
4. I will stay on designated trails to avoid trampling native vegetation and minimize potential erosion to trails by not using muddy trails or short-cutting switchbacks.

5. I will not disturb wildlife or livestock.
6. I will not litter. I will pack out what I pack in, and pack out more than my share whenever possible.
7. I will respect public and private property, including trail use signs and no trespassing signs, and I will leave gates as I have found them.
8. I will always be self-sufficient and my destination and travel speed will be determined by my ability, my equipment, the terrain, the present and potential weather conditions.
9. I will not travel solo when bikepacking in remote areas. I will leave word of my destination and when I plan to return.
10. I will observe the practice of minimum impact bicycling by "taking only pictures and memories and leaving only waffle prints."
11. I will always wear a helmet whenever I ride.

Now, I have a problem with some of these—number nine, for instance. The most enjoyable mountain biking I've ever done has been solo. And as for leaving word of destination and time of return, I've enjoyed living in such a way as to say, "I'm off to pedal Colorado. See you in the fall." Of course it's senseless to take needless risks, and I plan a ride and pack my gear with this in mind. But for me number nine smacks too much of the "never-out-of-touch" mentality. And getting away from civilization, deep into the wild, is, for many people, what mountain biking's all about.

All in all, however, NORBA's is a good list, and surely we mountain bikers would be liked more, and excluded less, if we followed the suggestions. But let me offer a "code of ethics" I much prefer, one given to cyclists by Utah's Wasatch-Cache National Forest office.

Study a Forest Map before You Ride
Currently, bicycles are permitted on roads and developed trails within the Wasatch-Cache National Forest except in designated Wilderness. If your route crosses private land, it is your responsibility to obtain right of way permission from the landowner.

Keep Groups Small
Riding in large groups degrades the outdoor experience for others, can disturb wildlife, and usually leads to greater resource damage.

Avoid Riding on Wet Trails
Bicycle tires leave ruts in wet trails. These ruts concentrate runoff and accelerate erosion. Postponing a ride when the trails are wet will preserve the trails for future use.

Stay on Roads and Trails
Riding cross-country destroys vegetation and damages the soil.

Always Yield to Others
Trails are shared by hikers, horses, and bicycles. Move off the trail to allow horses to pass and stop to allow hikers adequate room to share the trail. Simply yelling "Bicycle!" is not acceptable.

Control Your Speed
Excessive speed endangers yourself and other forest users.

Avoid Wheel Lock-up and Spin-out
Steep terrain is especially vulnerable to trail wear. Locking brakes on steep descents or when stopping needlessly damages trails. If a slope is steep enough to require locking wheels and skidding, dismount and walk your bicycle. Likewise, if an ascent is so steep your rear wheel slips and spins, dismount and walk your bicycle.

Protect Waterbars and Switchbacks
Waterbars, the rock and log drains built to direct water off trails, protect trails from erosion. When you encounter a waterbar, ride directly over the top or dismount and walk your bicycle. Riding around the ends of waterbars destroys them and speeds erosion. Skidding around switchback corners shortens trail life. Slow down for switchback corners and keep your wheels rolling.

If You Abuse It, You Lose It
Mountain bikers are relative newcomers to the forest and must prove themselves responsible trail users. By following the guidelines above, and by participating in trail maintenance service projects, bicyclists can help avoid closures which would prevent them from using trails.

I've never seen a better trail-etiquette list for mountain bikers. So have fun. Be careful. And don't screw things up for the next rider.

Dennis Coello
Series Editor

Glossary

This short list of terms does not contain all the words used by mountain bike enthusiasts when discussing their sport. But it should serve as an introduction to the lingo you'll hear on the trails.

ATB
: all-terrain bike; this, like "fat-tire bike," is another name for a mountain bike

ATV
: all-terrain vehicle; this usually refers to the loud, fume-spewing three- or four-wheeled motorized vehicles you will not enjoy meeting on the trail—except, of course, if you crash and have to hitch a ride out on one

bladed
: refers to a dirt road which has been smoothed out by the use of a wide blade on earth-moving equipment; "blading" gets rid of the teeth-chattering, much-cursed washboards found on so many dirt roads after heavy vehicle use

blaze
: a mark on a tree made by chipping away a piece of the bark, usually done to designate a trail; such trails are sometimes described as "blazed"

blind corner
: a curve in the road or trail that conceals bikers, hikers, equestrians, and other traffic

BLM
: Bureau of Land Management, an agency of the federal government

buffed
: used to describe a very smooth trail

catching air
: taking a jump in such a way that both wheels of the bike are off the ground at the same time

clean
: while this may describe what you and your bike *won't* be after following many trails, the term is most often used as a verb to denote the action of pedaling a tough section of trail successfully

combination
: this type of route may combine two or more configurations; for example, a point-to-point route may integrate a scenic loop or out-and-back spur midway through the ride; likewise, an out-and-back may have a loop at its farthest point (this configuration looks like a cherry with a stem attached; the stem is the out-and-back, the fruit is the terminus loop); or a loop route may have multiple

out-and-back spurs and/or loops to the side; mileage for a combination route is for the total distance to complete the ride

dab   touching the ground with a foot or hand

deadfall   a tangled mass of fallen trees or branches

diversion ditch   a usually narrow, shallow ditch dug across or around a trail; funneling the water in this manner keeps it from destroying the trail

double-track   the dual tracks made by a jeep or other vehicle, with grass or weeds or rocks between; mountain bikers can ride in either of the tracks, but you will of course find that whichever one you choose, and no matter how many times you change back and forth, the other track will appear to offer smoother travel

dugway   a steep, unpaved, switchbacked descent

endo   flipping end over end

feathering   using a light touch on the brake lever, hitting it lightly many times rather than very hard or locking the brake

four-wheel-drive   this refers to any vehicle with drive-wheel capability on all four wheels (a jeep, for instance, has four-wheel drive as compared with a two-wheel-drive passenger car), or to a rough road or trail that requires four-wheel-drive capability (or a *one*-wheel-drive mountain bike!) to negotiate it

game trail   the usually narrow trail made by deer, elk, or other game

gated   everyone knows what a gate is, and how many variations exist upon this theme; well, if a trail is described as "gated" it simply has a gate across it; don't forget that the rule is if you find a gate closed, close it behind you; if you find one open, leave it that way

Giardia   shorthand for *Giardia lamblia,* and known as the "backpacker's bane" until we mountain bikers expropriated it; this is a waterborne parasite that begins its life cycle when swallowed, and one to four weeks later has its host (you) bloated, vomiting, shivering with chills and living in the bathroom; the disease can be avoided by "treating" (purifying) the water you acquire along the trail (see "Hitting the Trail" in the Introduction)

gnarly	a term thankfully used less and less these days, it refers to tough trails
hammer	to ride very hard
hardpack	used to describe a trail in which the dirt surface is packed down hard; such trails make for good and fast riding, and very painful landings; bikers most often use "hardpack" as both a noun and adjective, and "hard-packed" as an adjective only (the grammar lesson will help when diagramming sentences in camp)
hike-a-bike	what you do when the road or trail becomes too steep or rough to remain in the saddle
jeep road, jeep trail	a rough road or trail passable only with four-wheel-drive capability (or a horse or mountain bike)
kamikaze	while this once referred primarily to those Japanese fliers who quaffed a glass of sake, then flew off as human bombs in suicide missions against U.S. naval vessels, it has more recently been applied to the idiot mountain bikers who, far less honorably, scream down hiking trails, endangering the physical and mental safety of the walking, biking, and equestrian traffic they meet; deck guns were necessary to stop the Japanese kamikaze pilots, but a bike pump or walking staff in the spokes is sufficient for the current-day kamikazes who threaten to get us all kicked off the trails
loop	this route configuration is characterized by riding from the designated trailhead to a distant point, then returning to the trailhead via a different route (or simply continuing on the same in a circle route) without doubling back; you always move forward across new terrain, but return to the starting point when finished; mileage is for the entire loop from the trailhead back to trailhead
multi-purpose	a BLM designation of land which is open to many uses; mountain biking is allowed
ORV	a motorized off-road vehicle
out-and-back	a ride where you will return on the same trail you pedaled out; while this might sound far more boring than a loop route, many trails look very different when pedaled in the opposite direction; unless otherwise noted, mileage figures are the *total* distance out *and* back

pack stock   horses, mules, llamas, et cetera, carrying provisions along the trails . . . and unfortunately leaving a trail of their own behind

point-to-point   a vehicle shuttle (or similar assistance) is required for this type of route, which is ridden from the designated trailhead to a distant location, or endpoint, where the route ends; total mileage is for the one-way trip from the trailhead to endpoint

portage   to carry your bike on your person

pummy   volcanic activity in the Pacific Northwest and elsewhere produces soil with a high content of pumice; trails through such soil often become thick with dust, but this is light in consistency and can usually be pedaled; remember, however, to pedal carefully, for this dust obscures whatever might lurk below

quads   bikers use this term to refer both to the extensor muscle in the front of the thigh (which is separated into four parts) and to USGS maps; the expression "Nice quads!" refers always to the former, however, except in those instances when the speaker is an engineer

runoff   rainwater or snowmelt

scree   an accumulation of loose stones or rocky debris lying on a slope or at the base of a hill or cliff

signed   a "signed" trail has signs in place of blazes

single-track   a single, narrow path through grass or brush or over rocky terrain, often created by deer, elk, or backpackers; single-track riding is some of the best fun around

slickrock   the rock-hard, compacted sandstone that is *great* to ride and even prettier to look at; you'll appreciate it even more if you think of it as a petrified sand dune or seabed (which it is), and if the rider before you hasn't left tire marks (from unnecessary skidding) or granola bar wrappers behind

snowmelt   runoff produced by the melting of snow

snowpack   unmelted snow accumulated over weeks or months of winter—or over years in high-mountain terrain

spur   a road or trail that intersects the main trail you're following

switchback   a zigzagging road or trail designed to assist in traversing steep terrain: mountain bikers should *not* skid through switchbacks

technical	terrain that is difficult to ride due not to its grade (steepness) but to its obstacles—rocks, logs, ledges, loose soil . . .
topo	short for topographical map, the kind that shows both linear distance *and* elevation gain and loss; "topo" is pronounced with both vowels long
trashed	a trail that has been destroyed (same term used no matter what has destroyed it . . . cattle, horses, or even mountain bikers riding when the ground was too wet)
two-wheel-drive	this refers to any vehicle with drive-wheel capability on only two wheels (a passenger car, for instance, has two-wheel-drive); a two-wheel-drive road is a road or trail easily traveled by an ordinary car
water bar	an earth, rock, or wooden structure that funnels water off trails to reduce erosion
washboarded	a road that is surfaced with many ridges spaced closely together, like the ripples on a washboard; these make for very rough riding, and even worse driving in a car or jeep
whoop-de-doo	closely spaced dips or undulations in a trail; these are often encountered in areas traveled heavily by ORVs
wilderness area	land that is officially set aside by the federal government to remain *natural*—pure, pristine, and untrammeled by any vehicle, including mountain bikes; though mountain bikes had not been born in 1964 (when the United States Congress passed the Wilderness Act, establishing the National Wilderness Preservation system), they are considered a "form of mechanical transport" and are thereby excluded; in short, stay out
wind-chill	a reference to the wind's cooling effect upon exposed flesh; for example, if the temperature is 10 degrees Fahrenheit and the wind is blowing at 20 miles per hour, the wind-chill (that is, the actual temperature to which your skin reacts) is *minus 32 degrees*; if you are riding in wet conditions things are even worse, for the wind-chill would then be *minus 74 degrees!*
windfall	anything (trees, limbs, brush, fellow bikers) blown down by the wind

ANDY KNAPP has been an outdoor adventurer for almost thirty years and has pursued interests in bicycle touring, wilderness backpacking, mountaineering, canoeing, and sea kayaking. After a 7,460-mile bike trip to Alaska and back as a teenager, Andy has since gone on to bike through 33 states, all 12 Canadian provinces and territories, and 11 foreign countries. The immense growth of mountain biking as a sport has added a new dimension to his enthusiasm for cycling, and the work on this book has provided him with a new source of adventure closer to his native Minnesota.

As a pioneer of sea kayaking on Lake Superior, Andy has recently been active in the effort to develop a paddler's "water trail" around the lake.

He has also found the time to combine these exciting avocations with a profession; Andy has worked for twenty years in the outdoor equipment industry as a retail buyer and has participated in a number of trade groups, conferences, and symposiums that promote the "human-powered" outdoor sports.

At home, Andy looks forward to teaching his four-year-old daughter to ride a bike and enjoy the benefits of an active life.

Dennis Coello's America By Mountain Bike Series

Happy Trails

Hop on your mountain bike and let our guidebooks take you on America's classic trails and rides. These "where-to" books are published jointly by Falcon Press and Menasha Ridge Press and written by local biking experts. Twenty regional books will blanket the country when the series is complete.

Choose from an assortment of rides—easy rambles to all-day treks. Guides contain helpful trail and route descriptions, mountain bike shop listings, and interesting facts on area history. Each trail is described in terms of difficulty, scenery, condition, length, and elevation change. The guides also explain trail hazards, nearby services and ranger stations, how much water to bring, and what kind of gear to pack.

So before you hit the trail, grab one of our guidebooks to help make your outdoor adventures safe and memorable.

Call or write
Falcon Press or Menasha Ridge Press
Falcon Press
P.O. Box 1718, Helena, MT 59624

1-800-582-2665

FALCON™

Menasha Ridge Press

Menasha Ridge Press
3169 Cahaba Heights Road, Birmingham, AL 35243
1-800-247-9437